IMAGES
of America

FOSTER

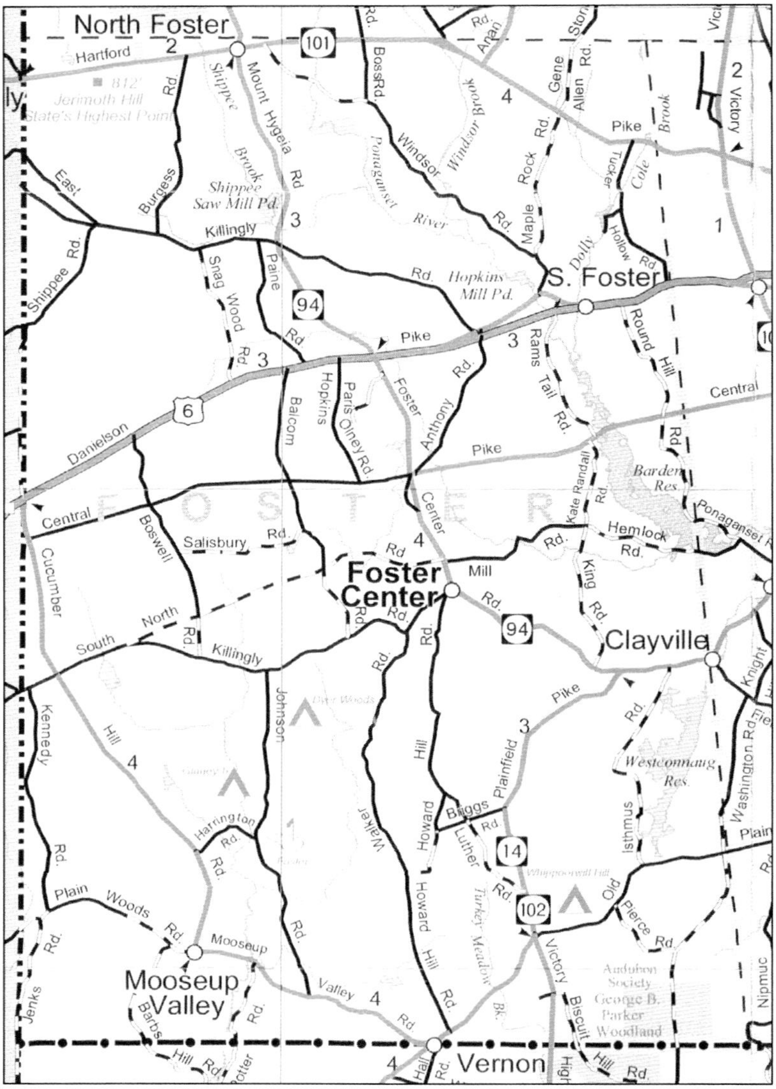

This is a very interesting 2011 map. First, Moosup is spelled with an *E*, which is wrong. Second, Vernon is actually Mount Vernon. Also, South Foster is located in the northern part of Foster; however, it is south of North Foster. Last but not least, the very distinct area of Hopkins Mills is not identified. Otherwise, it will be very helpful as one reads this new book on the history of Foster. (Author's collection.)

ON THE COVER: This photograph was probably taken in the late 1800s or early 1900s. Neighbors helping other neighbors are shown cutting the field of hay by hand to prepare for the coming winter. Those pictured are unidentified. (Courtesy of Cathy Walls.)

IMAGES
of America

FOSTER

Raymond A. Wolf

ARCADIA
PUBLISHING

ISBN 978-0-7385-7690-9

Published by Arcadia Publishing
Charleston, South Carolina

Printed in the United States of America

Library of Congress Control Number: 2011937251

For all general information, please contact Arcadia Publishing:
Telephone 843-853-2070
Fax 843-853-0044
E-mail sales@arcadiapublishing.com
For customer service and orders:
Toll-Free 1-888-313-2665

Visit us on the Internet at www.arcadiapublishing.com

To my mom, Helen O. Larson, whose great-great-grandmother Melissa Ann Hopkins-Burchard was born in Foster

Contents

ACKNOWLEDGMENTS

The force that keeps driving me to write these books is the memory of my mom. Her ancestors originated in Foster, and she would visit relatives there whenever possible. Many of the readers and attendees at my presentations have commented that her poetry brings life to the books. Therefore, I have included all-new verses of her poetry for your reading pleasure.

The townspeople of Foster are a unique group of individuals. I am proud to have met and worked with each of the following people who have made contributions and supplied photographs, documents, and information making it possible for you to hold this book in your hands: Sandra Ball, Glennis Hopkins-Beltram, Rus Benson, Susan Boucher, Dorothy Pierce-Brayton, George Brayton, Janet Brayton, Arline Bucci, Heidi Colwell, Mildred Arline Corey, Maurice Dunbar, Frances Grass, Michele Harris, John Hess III, John Lewis, Johnston Historical Society president Louis McGowan, Brenda Moffat, George Newman, Ed Robinson, Ernest Ross, Carol Lyons Sholly, Richard Siembab, Mary Thoman, Viola Ulm, and Cathy Walls.

Again, thanks go to Richard Blodgett of Providence Water for allowing me to utilize its archives. I also wish to give special recognition to Viola Ulm, the Foster historian. She not only gave me access to her huge collection of photographs but also shared valued information on each one.

I would like to extend a great big thank-you to Ed Robinson of the Foster Preservation Society for requesting I do a book on Foster. He spent many hours with me sorting through numerous files of photographs, slides, and documents. He also shared the vast knowledge he has on the subject of Foster.

I wish to acknowledge my deepest appreciation to my resident proofreader, Jenn Carnevale. In the past, she has proofread *The Lost Villages of Scituate*, *The Scituate Reservoir*, and *West Warwick*. Yet again, she has taken time out of her busy schedule to include *Foster* on her list. Thank you so much, Jenn.

I would be amiss if I left out a special thank-you to Heidi Colwell and George Newman. Together, they proofread the entire book for historical correctness.

Finally, I want to thank the extraordinary team I work with at Arcadia Publishing: Lissie Cain, acquisitions editor; Gervase Kolmos, publicity manager; Beth McKenna, senior regional sales and marketing manager; Jennifer Pratt, regional sales and marketing manager; and all the people behind the scenes who make the Images of America series possible.

Unless otherwise noted, all images appear courtesy of the Foster Preservation Society archives.

INTRODUCTION

The area we now know as Foster was originally part of the Scituate Township when Scituate broke away from Providence in 1731 and was known as the Outlands. The population was estimated at 600, living on almost 66,000 acres. The first town meeting was held at Thomas Angell's tavern in South Scituate on March 18, 1731. Stephen Hopkins was chosen moderator, with Ezekiel Hopkins as councilman, Joseph Brown as town clerk and town packer, and Joseph Hopkins as overseer of the poor. Later, Stephen Hopkins was a four-time colonial governor of Rhode Island and went on to be a signer of the Declaration of Independence.

John Harrington relocated from Smithfield in 1704 and settled in the southwestern corner of Scituate, on the east bank of the Moosup River. The earliest deed reference for John Harrington is dated 1714, for land on the west bank of the Moosup River. By 1730, he had acquired 670 acres; erected a house, barn, and fences; planted an orchard; and improved his holdings.

John and William Tyler from Connecticut bought their first piece of property in 1728 and also settled in the southwestern corner of Scituate. Ten years later, in 1738, Thomas Foster bought 150 acres on the Moosup River, located south and east of John Tyler's land.

Isaac Howard moved from Coventry to this same area in 1750 and acquired 150 acres in 1752. His son Daniel remained in the area, as did Daniel's seven sons. The vicinity became and is still known as Howard Hill Road. The Howards owned land on both sides of the road.

In north central Scituate, settlement began in the 1720s along the Ponagansett River. Joseph, Ezekiel, and William Hopkins took up residence on land partly purchased and inherited from their father, Thomas Hopkins. By 1723, Ezekiel and William had built the town's first water-powered gristmill and sawmill on the Ponagansett River. This area became and is still called Hopkins Mills.

All of the locations listed above were destined to become the new township of Foster. There was a town meeting at James Brown's tavern on Danielson Pike in Scituate near Hopkins Mills on December 25, 1780. The constituent members voted that "the town be divided into two distinct and separate towns." On August 24, 1781, the Rhode Island General Assembly divided the town into eastern and western portions. The western portion was named Foster in honor of Theodore Foster, coauthor of the bill of incorporation of Foster. In response, Theodore Foster gave the town a bookcase and 30 books, including eight blank volumes for keeping town records. They still exist today. Fifty years after Scituate had broken away from Providence, Foster had finally broken away from Scituate. The first town meeting was held in Thomas Hammond's tavern in Foster Center on November 19, 1781. John Williams was named town moderator, with John Westcott as town clerk.

From 1781 through 1820, there was tremendous growth in constructing buildings, and the population rose to 2,900. One of two religious structures still in existence is the elder John Hammond's meetinghouse on Howard Hill Road in Foster Center. It was built in 1796–1797, and the first town meeting was held there was in 1801. In 1822, the town acquired the building, and it has been known since as the Foster Town House.

Between 1820 and 1830, the town's population went into a tailspin that continued well past the turn of the century. It was not until 1975, when the population reached a little over 3,000, that Foster would surpass the 1820 statistics.

The building of the Scituate Reservoir from 1915 to 1925 was devastating to Foster. Although little land was taken from Foster, construction of the reservoir had a ripple effect. The Clayville Mill was closed along with the mills in Rockland, Ashland, Richmond, South Scituate, and Kent. Many Foster residents worked in these mills. Besides that, the Providence & Danielson Railroad decided it was not worth the cost of relocating its tracks, considering five of the villages were being destroyed and flooded. Therefore, the decision to abandon the service cut off the transportation system of getting goods to and from Providence and workers to their jobs in the mills, which would no longer exist. This only added to the decline in the population of Foster.

Today, Foster exemplifies the real definition of country living. The townspeople have elbow room and plenty of open space along with clean air and clean streams. They have the only covered bridge on a public road in Rhode Island along with the only nudist campground in the state. Foster also holds title to the highest elevation in Rhode Island, with Jerimoth Hill at 812 feet above sea level. The town has maintained the tradition of passing the Boston Post Cane to the oldest resident for over 100 years. It is a paradise for anyone interested in buildings from 1700s and 1800s in excellent condition. You can attend one of the barn tours or purchase the video and enjoy it in the comfort of your home. Enjoy the journey you are about to take through time and the history of Foster.

The author's mother, Helen O. Larson, was born in 1910 in Rockland, one of the above villages. She wrote poetry from the age of 12 until she was 94 years old and composed over 1,700 verses. The author would like to share with his readers the poem she wrote on August 2, 1991, at the age of 80.

"The Old White Church"

When evening shades are falling
I walk down a country lane
I sit in the shade by the church
And live old memories again

The old white church in the village
It was so dear to me
Where I used to go as a child
And I was happy as could be

The bell would ring Sunday morning
It would toll so loud and clear
And we knew we must attend
The church we loved so dear

You could see the people walking
Going humbly on their way
Hustling off to the old white church
To sing, to kneel and pray

When the summer weather was fair
And the windows were open wide
You could hear the congregation
Singing the old hymns inside

Oh! That beautiful old church
Painted a gleaming white
It looks just like a vision
When the moon is shining bright

That beautiful old church
Forget it I can not
For it will forever be
Embedded in my heart

So I stand up again
And slowly walk away
But I know I'll go back again
To that beautiful church some day

—Helen O. Larson

One

Clayville and the Scituate Reservoir

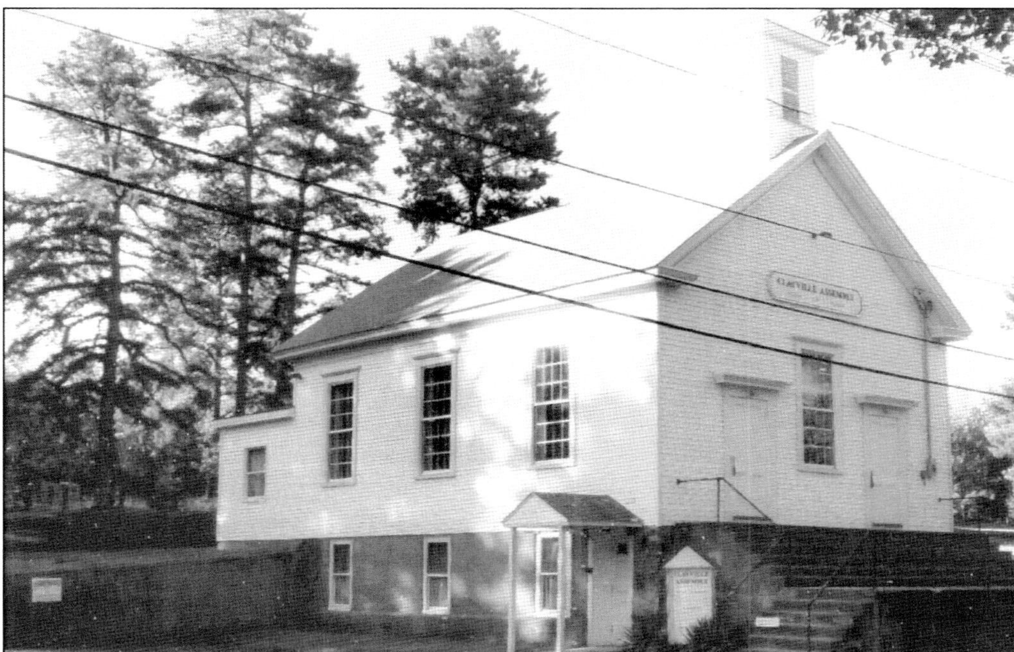

The Clayville Christian Society Union was incorporated in 1851, and by 1871, the congregation had constructed its Clayville Christian Union Church, pictured here. Even though it was built in the style of most churches and schools of that era, it was unique for two reasons. It had a walk-out basement and massive stairs across the entire front, which climbed to the dual entrance doors. The cemetery behind the church has headstones dating back to the mid-1800s. The congregation still assembles on Sundays. (Author's collection.)

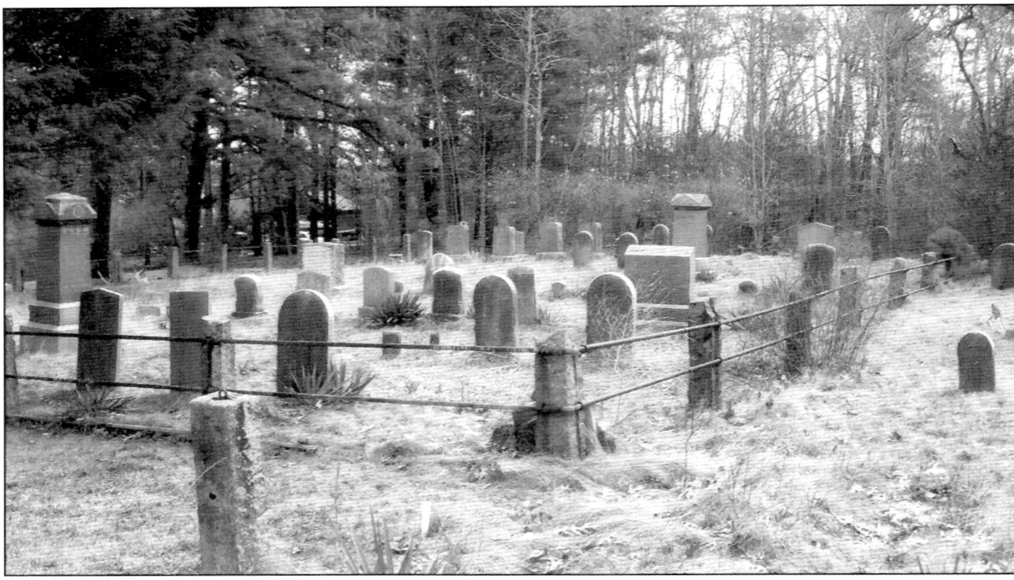

Rhode Island Historical Cemetery No. 68 is located on the hill directly behind the Clayville Church. This photograph, taken in 2011, shows only a portion of the existing cemetery as it has flowed beyond the boundaries that were set by the elders in the mid-1800s. Shown in the photograph below, the headstone on the right reads, "George B. Lawton, / Died April 11, 1852, / Interred in San Juan, / Central America. / Aged 26 years." Below this inscription, it reads, "George Wheaton, / son of / George B. & Lucinda P. / Lawton. / Died August 6, 1854, / aged 2 years & 10 months." The tall headstone in the rear records that Joseph M. Wells died on April 4, 1886, in his 89th year. It also states that his wife, Diana Wells, died on April 24, 1886, in her 85th year, only 20 days later. (Both, author's collection.)

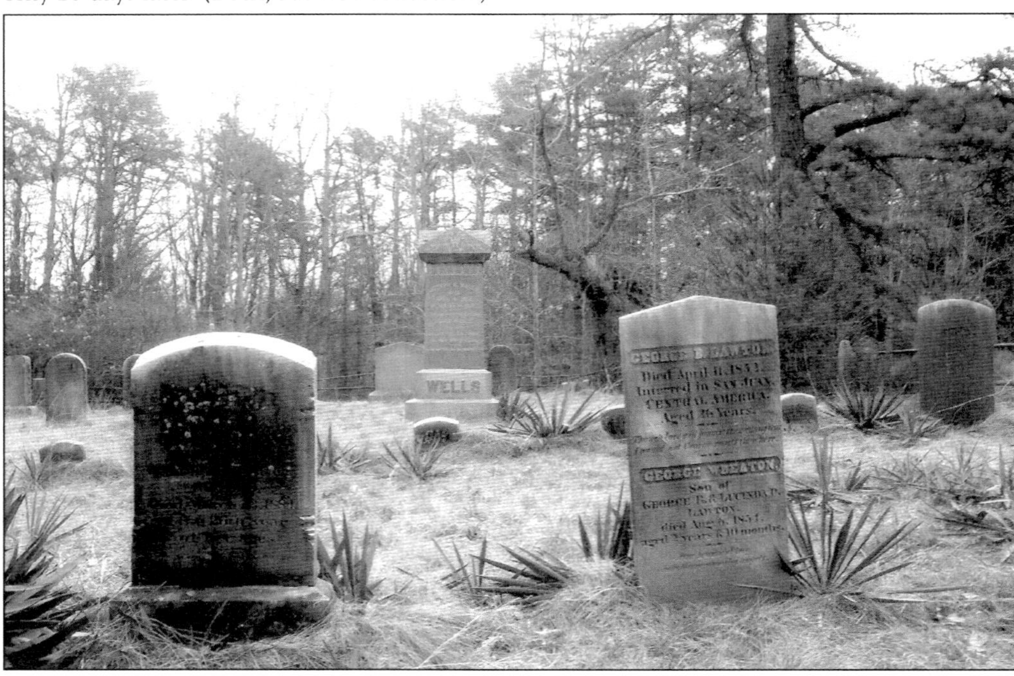

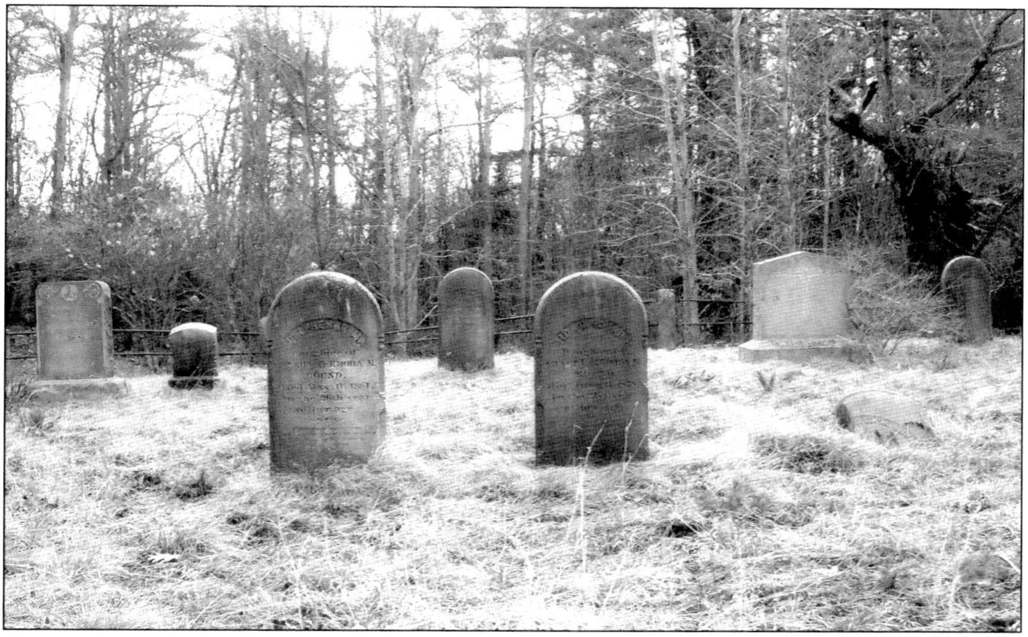

Shown above, the headstone in the front on the right reads, "Ida C. Round / Daughter of Caleb L. and Rhoda M. Round / died June 11, 1878 / in the 21st year of her age." The headstone beside it to the left reads, "Delphenor M. / Daughter of Caleb L. and Rhoda M. Round / died May 11, 1881 / in her 26th year of her age." Caleb and Rhoda had lost two daughters in their 20s within three years of each other. Shown below and partially buried, the small stone reads, "David E. / son of Horace E. and Sarah C. Burchard / died February 16, 1866." He was only four years, five months, and 16 days old when he died. (Both, author's collection.)

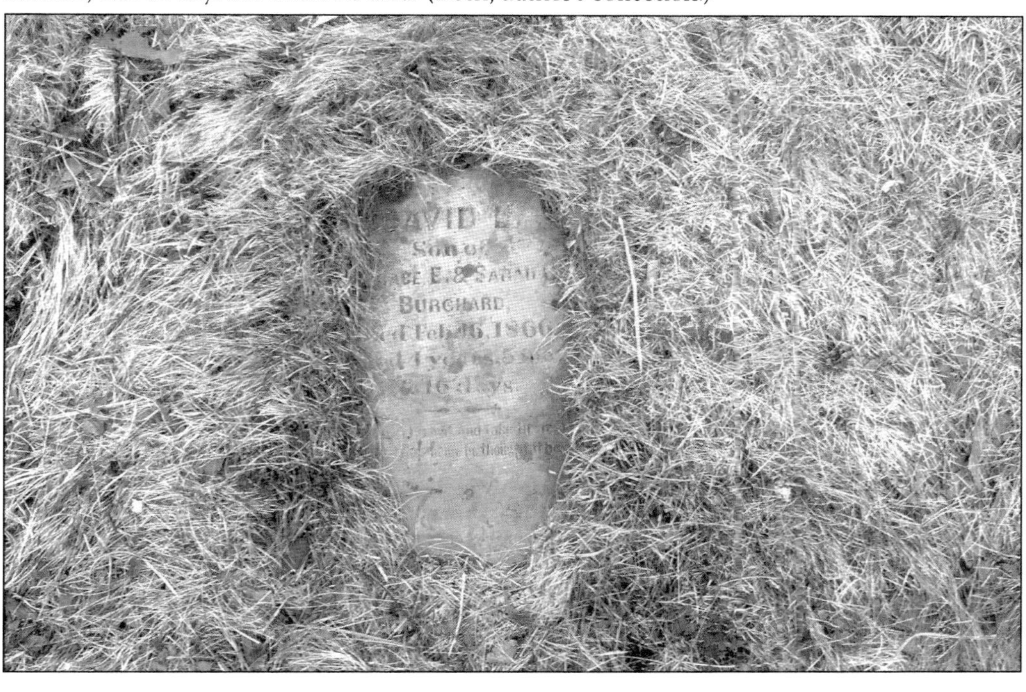

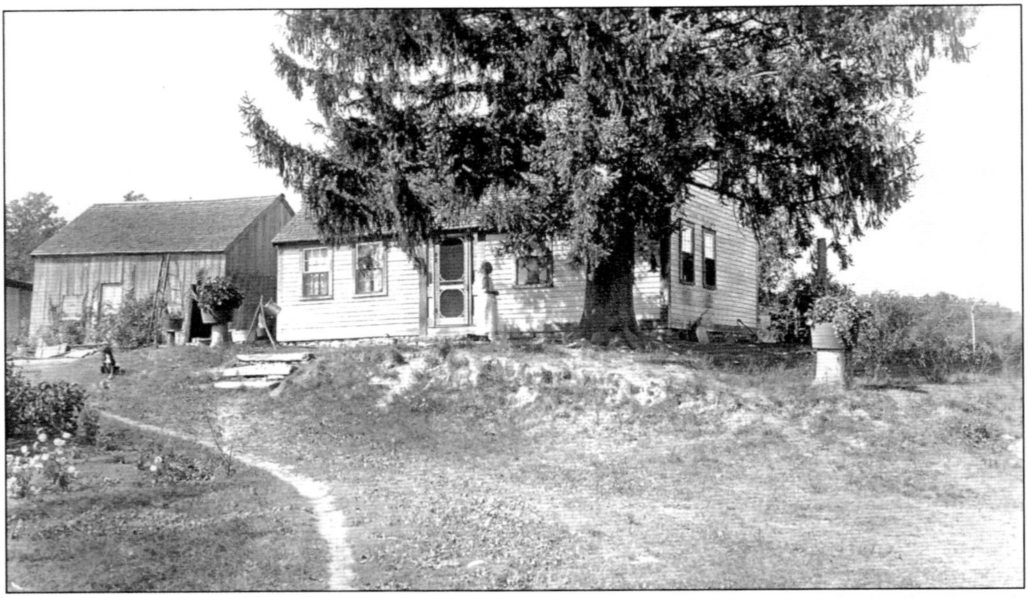

Both of these photographs were taken on September 20, 1916. They are of Charles Rixon's property, Parcel 677, on the east side of Isthmus Road. He and his wife (above to the right of the door) lived on this 27-acre farm along with the family dog, seen sitting on the lawn to the left. They also owned the abutting half-acre lot, Parcel 686, on the Westconnaug Reservoir, which was where the well-maintained house pictured below was located. Note the barrel at the corner of the shed. It was used to collect rainwater from the roof as it drained from the gutter. It could be used to water the animals or the plants in the barrels on top of the stumps. (Both, courtesy of Providence Water.)

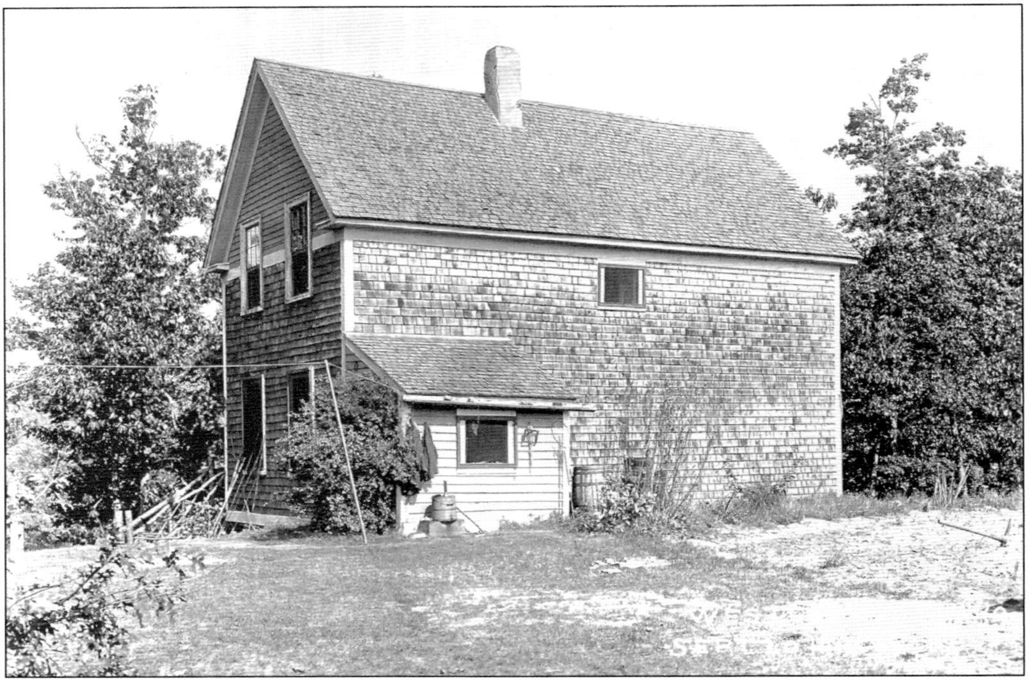

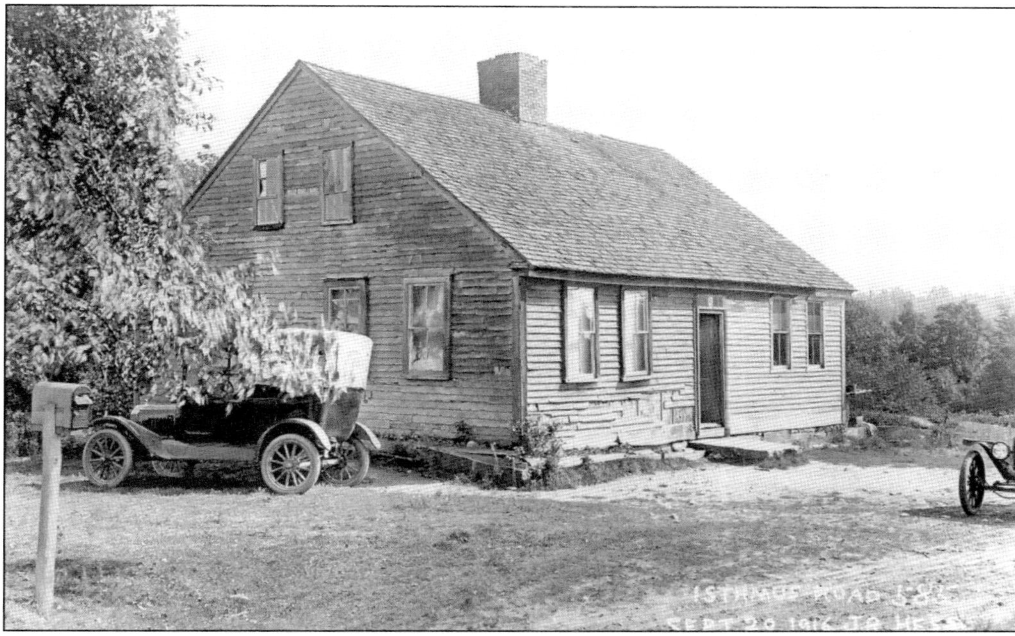

Herbert F. Card owned this home with 16.72 acres on Parcel 680 on the east side of Isthmus Road. He also owned the house pictured below on 31 acres. It appears this structure on Parcel 678 has already been abandoned. Both photographs were taken on September 20, 1916, which was at the beginning of the reservoir project. Each property abutted the Westconnaug Reservoir; therefore, they were taken by the city. It is not clear if Card and his family lived in these houses (including the one on the next page) or if he rented them. The following verse is from "You Have a Right to Dream" by Helen O. Larson: "Even though you may live, in a humble little shack / You have a right to dream, don't let it hold you back." (Both, courtesy of Providence Water.)

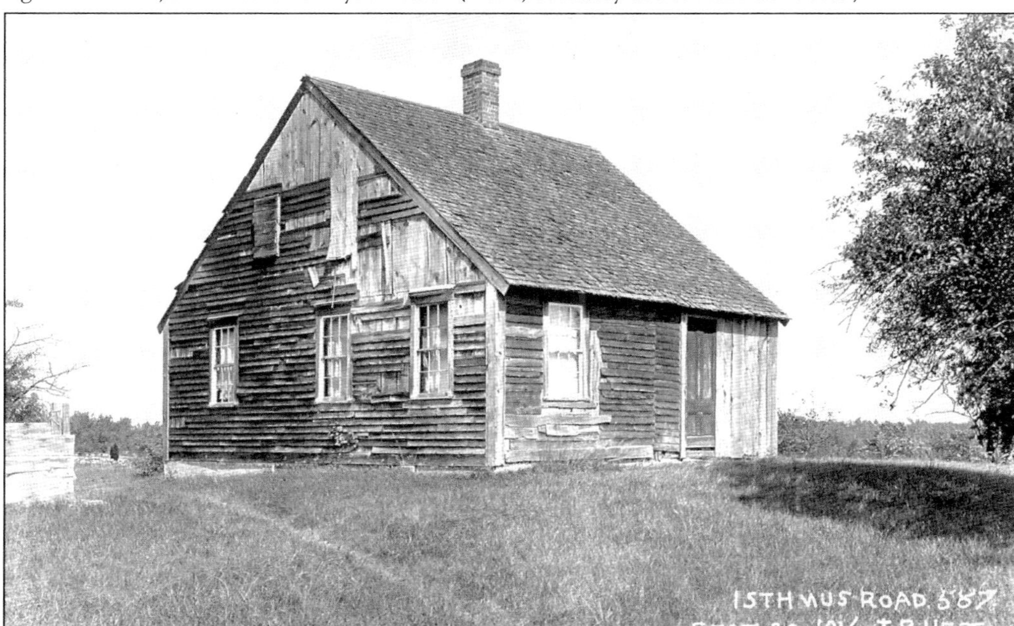

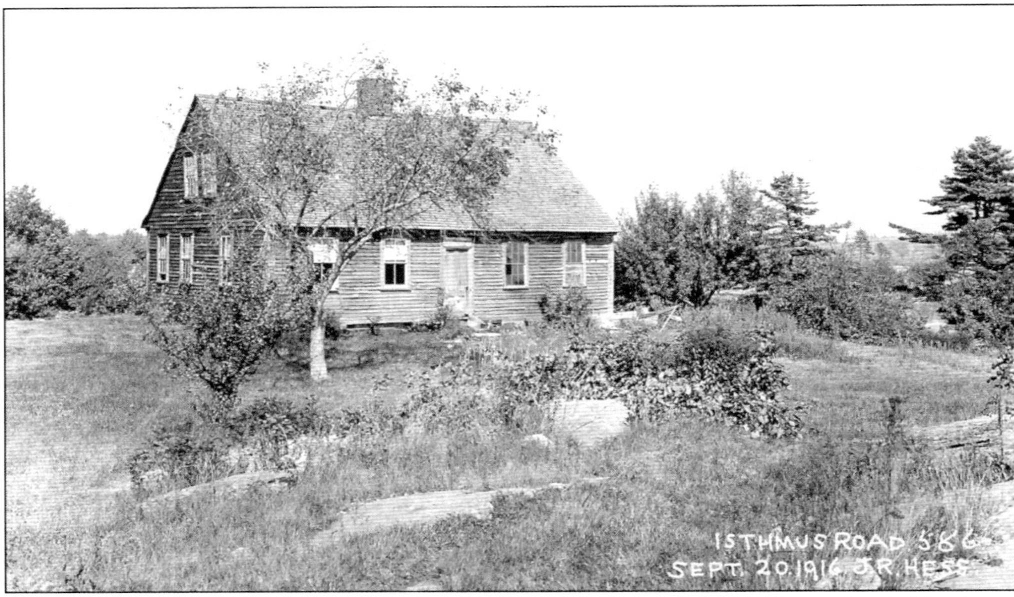

This is a third property that Herbert F. Card owned on the east side of Isthmus Road. This house and the barn below were located on Parcel 679, which included 50.9 acres of land that also abutted the Westconnaug Reservoir. Once more, being in the watershed, they had to go. The barn appears to have not been utilized in quite some time and has really gone into disrepair for lack of attention. The photograph of the house was taken on September 20, 1916; however, John R. Hess did not come back until July 11, 1917, to photograph the barn. The following verse is from "Little Gray House" by Helen O. Larson: "There was a little gray house, down a country lane / Where we children used to play, every day it would rain." (Both, courtesy of Providence Water.)

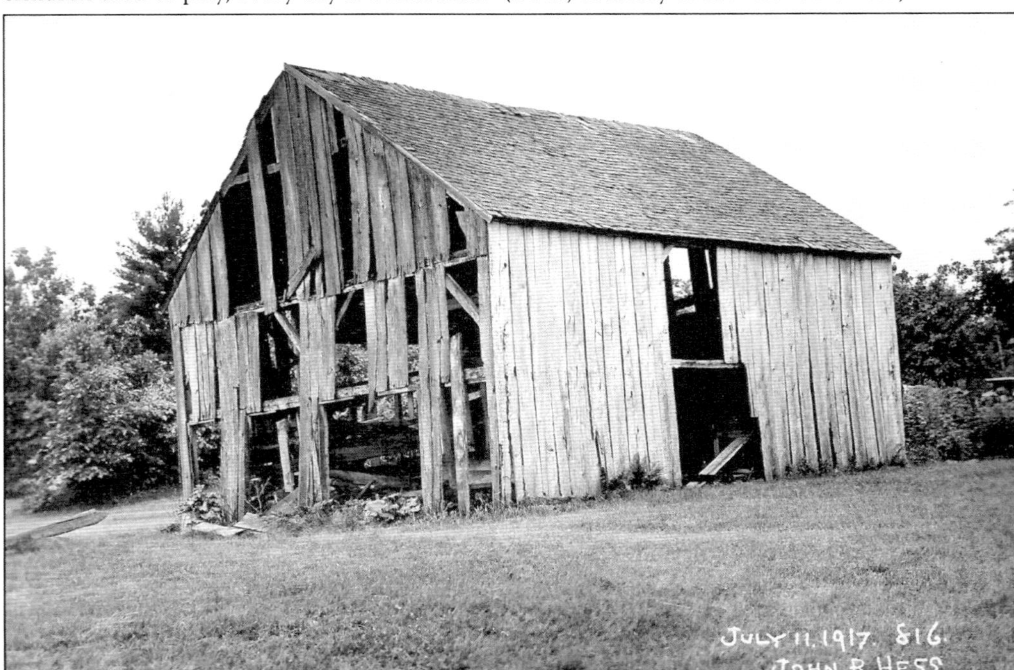

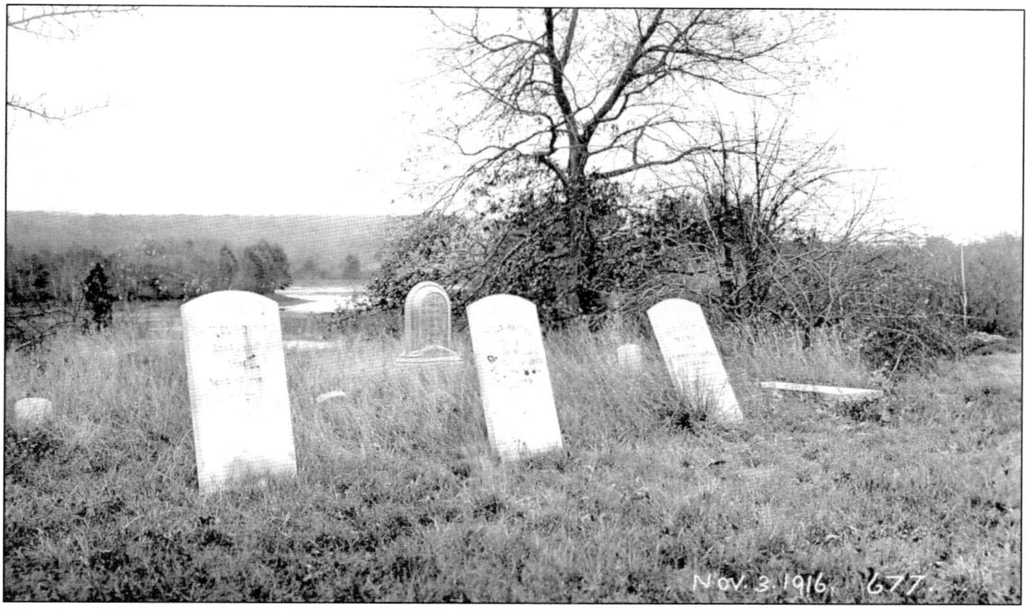

The four headstones in the front, from left to right, read, "Samuel Howard died 1889," "Dilla his wife," "Joseph L. Hill died 1877," and, lastly, "Sarah / Wife of Joseph L. Hill / died January 19, 1885." The last marker, on the ground, is currently in an upright position (as seen in the image below). The Westconnaug Reservoir can be seen in the distance. (Courtesy of Providence Water.)

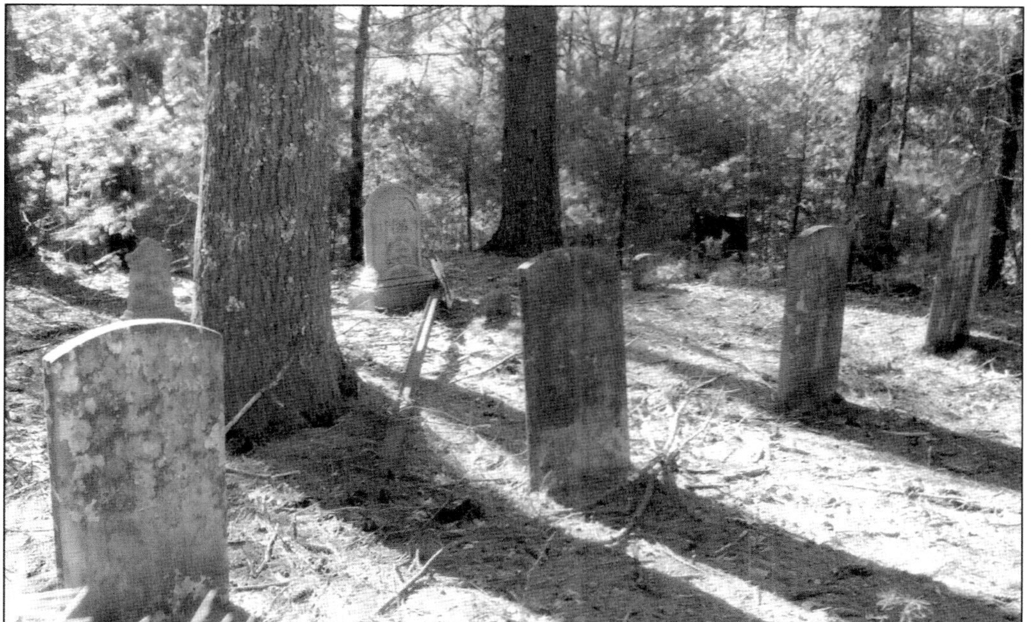

This photograph taken in 2011 reveals a small headstone located in the left background. It reads, "Phebe A. / Wife of George W. Wood / died January 23, 1873 / 44 yrs. 3 mos. 27 days." The stone to the right of the tree reads, "Martha F. Wood / Wife of George W. Wood / 1853–1898." It is known from these two headstones that George Wood was married twice, both of his wives died in their 44th year, and he gave his second wife a much larger gravestone. (Author's collection.)

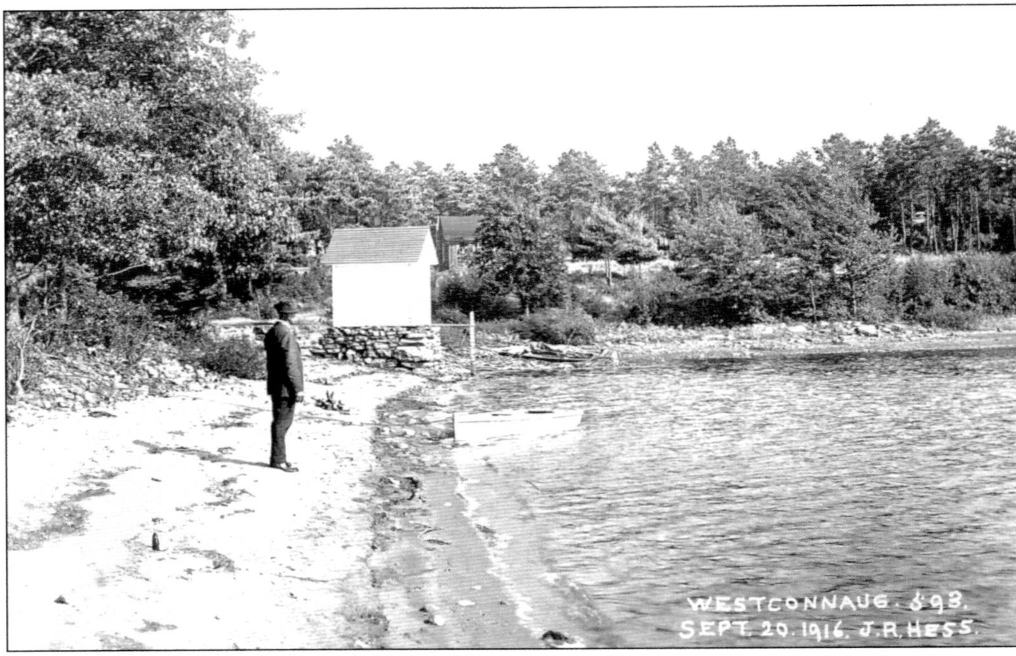

This city official is overlooking the future Westconnaug Reservoir project as John R. Hess snaps his picture on September 20, 1916. Below, these men are already busy working on reconstructing the dam on December 12, 1916. It was located on Parcel 984 at the north end of the reservoir. At this time, manpower, not machines, got the job done. The finished Westconnaug Reservoir project would become an integral part of the Scituate Reservoir System. (Both, courtesy of Providence Water.)

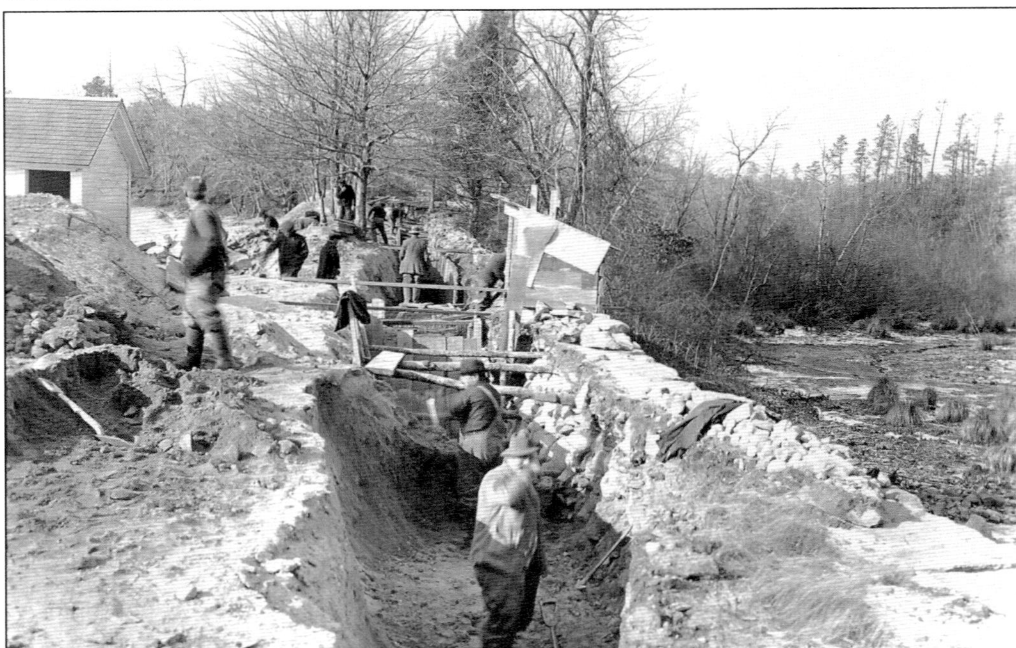

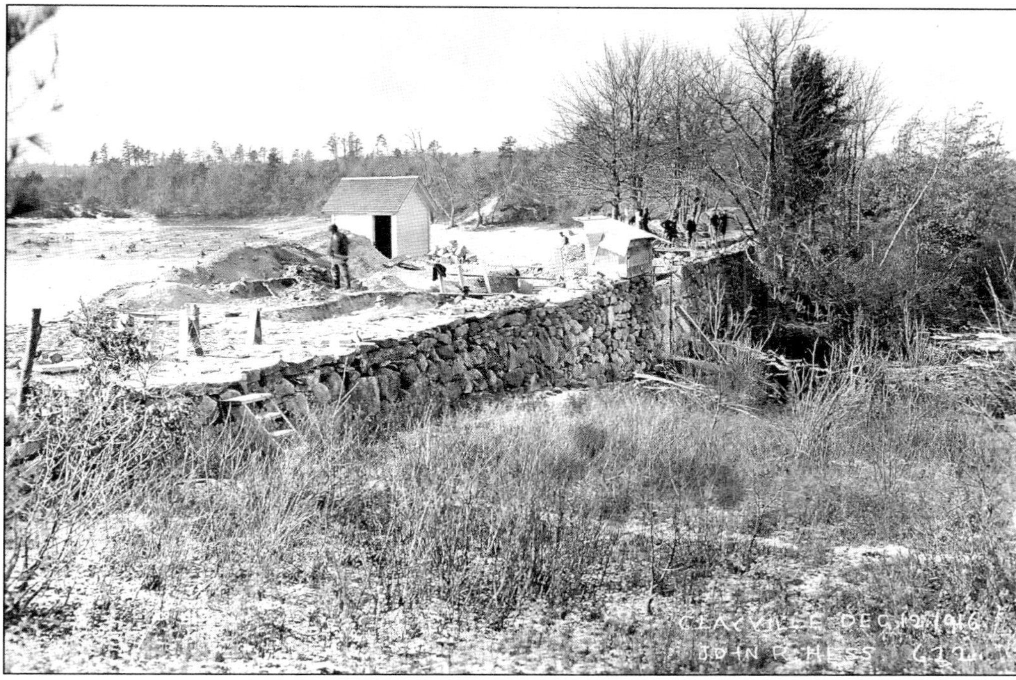

Both of these photographs were taken on December 12, 1916. The one above gives an excellent view of the face of the dam. The photograph below shows work has come to a standstill. It appears the reservoir has been drained while work is being done on the dam. The dam would eventually be completed, and the reservoir filled. Today, the Westconnaug Reservoir supplies water to the main Scituate Reservoir. (Both, courtesy of Providence Water.)

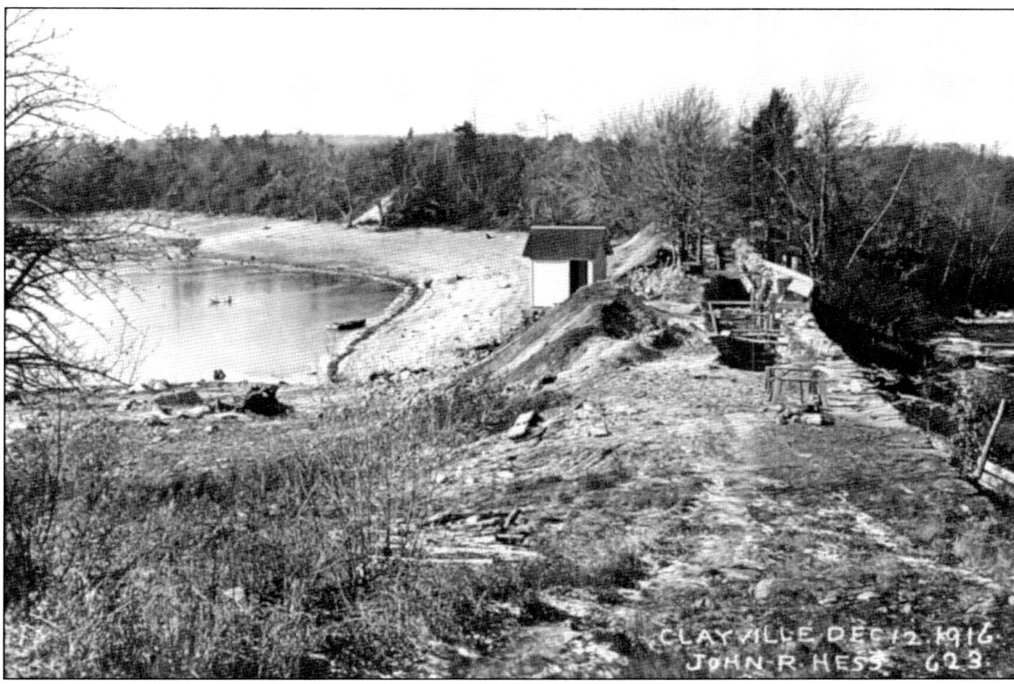

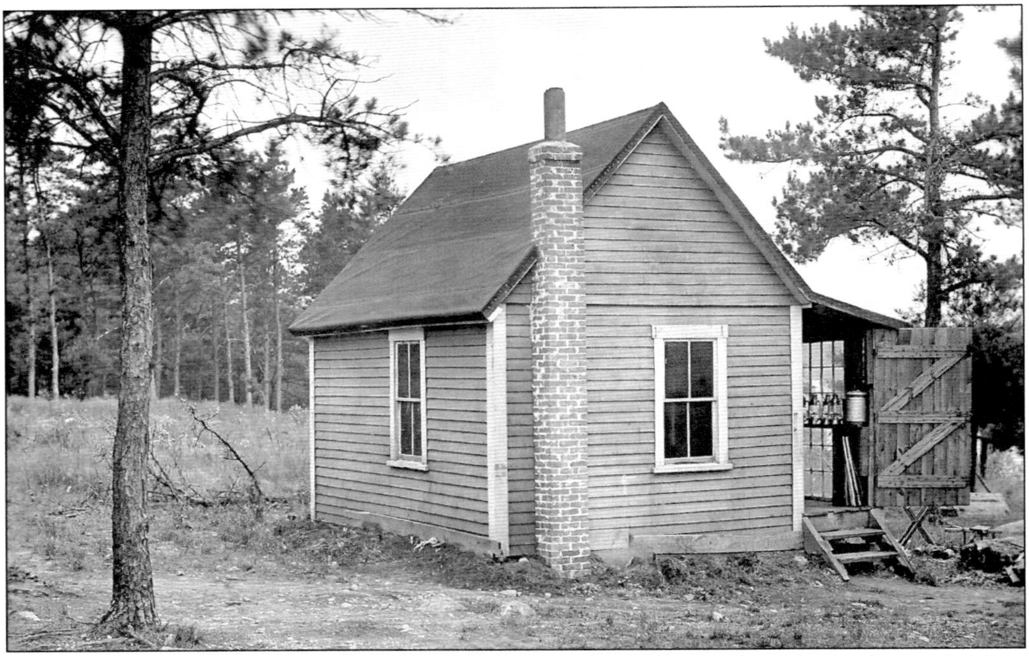

This cabin was owned by the Westconnaug Reservoir Company and was located near the dam on Parcel 984. The City of Providence Water took this four-acre lot because it was within the watershed area. John R. Hess photographed this on July 12, 1917. Delphine Ducharme owned the camp below. It sat on a 13.69-acre lot, Parcel 986, and was near the north end of the reservoir. The photograph below shows Hess busy recording history on September 20, 1916. The following verse is from "Little Gray House" by Helen O. Larson: "This little house was driftwood gray / I can still see it, in my memory today." (Both, courtesy of Providence Water.)

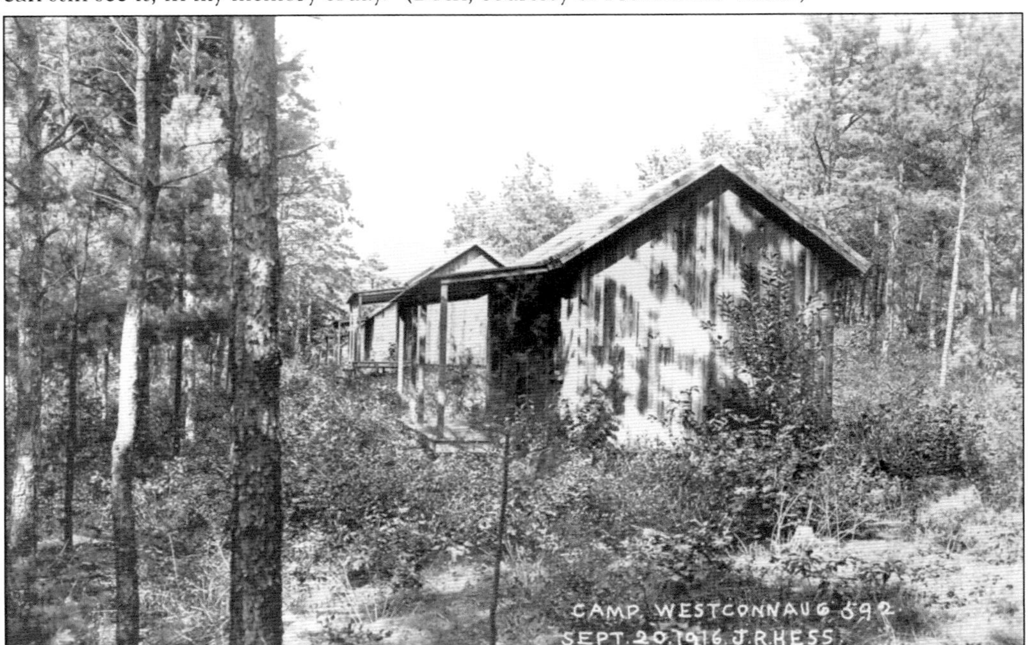

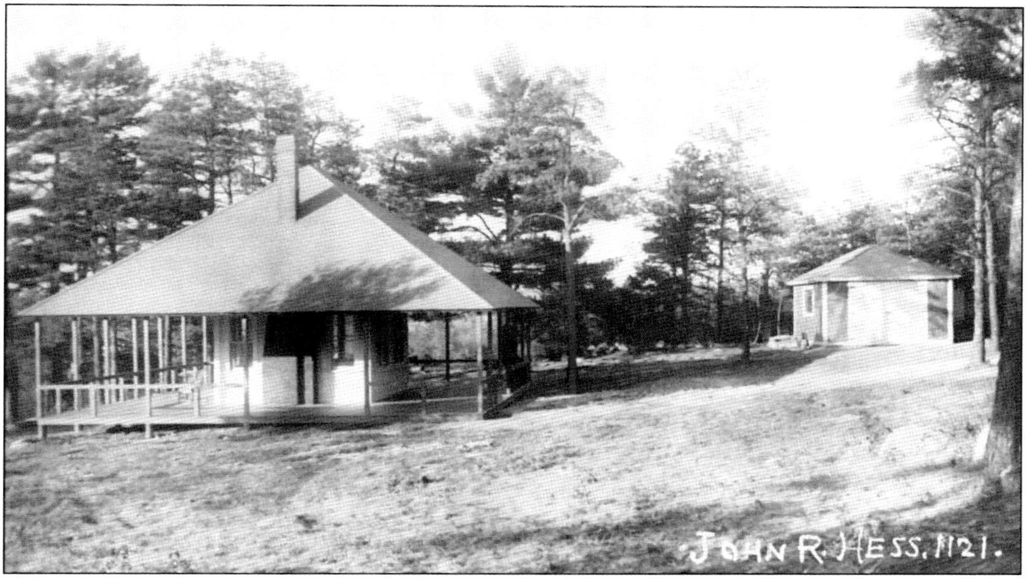

Joslin Manufacturing Company remodeled a house that was on this site. Knowing that in less than three years the City of Providence Water would tear them down, the company built this bungalow and the garage to the right in August 1922. Hess returned here on November 1, 1922, to record its existence. Joseph P. Burlingame owned Parcel 707 below. It was a .34-acre island in the middle of the northern end of the reservoir complete with this clubhouse. It must have been a serene setting. The photograph was taken September 20, 1916. The following verse is from "Little Gray House" by Helen O. Larson: "The house was empty, the family had moved away / For it was condemned, to build a reservoir one day." (Both, courtesy of Providence Water.)

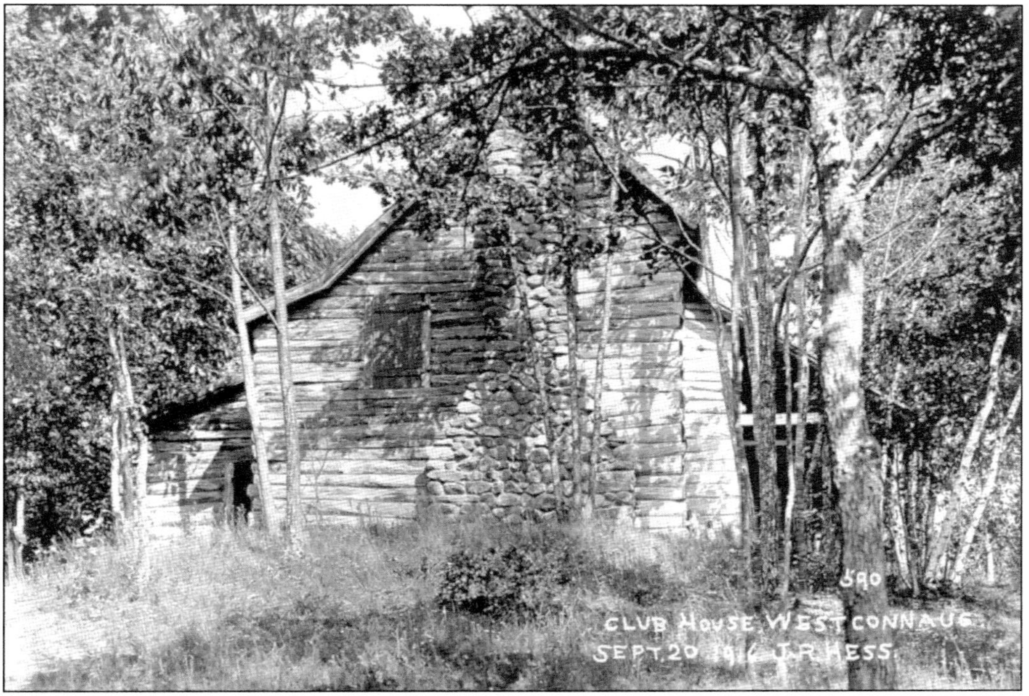

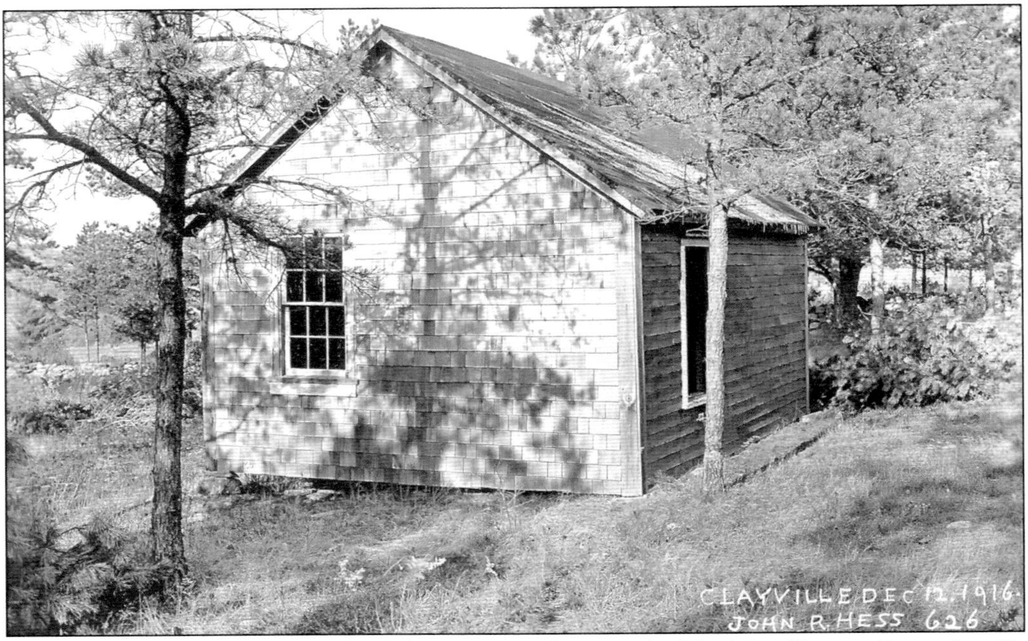

Delphine Ducharme owned both of these camps, photographed by John Hess on December 12, 1916. They were located on the same 13.69-acre Parcel 986 as the camp seen at the bottom of page 18. Considering she owned these three camps, Ducharme may have rented them in the summer months to vacationers. It looks like it would have been an enjoyable, inexpensive, and relaxed vacation for a family. Both cabins were taken. The following verse is from "Little Gray House" by Helen O. Larson: "A man from the city told us, folks needed clean water to drink / I stared in amazement at him, my childish mind couldn't take it." (Both, courtesy of Providence Water.)

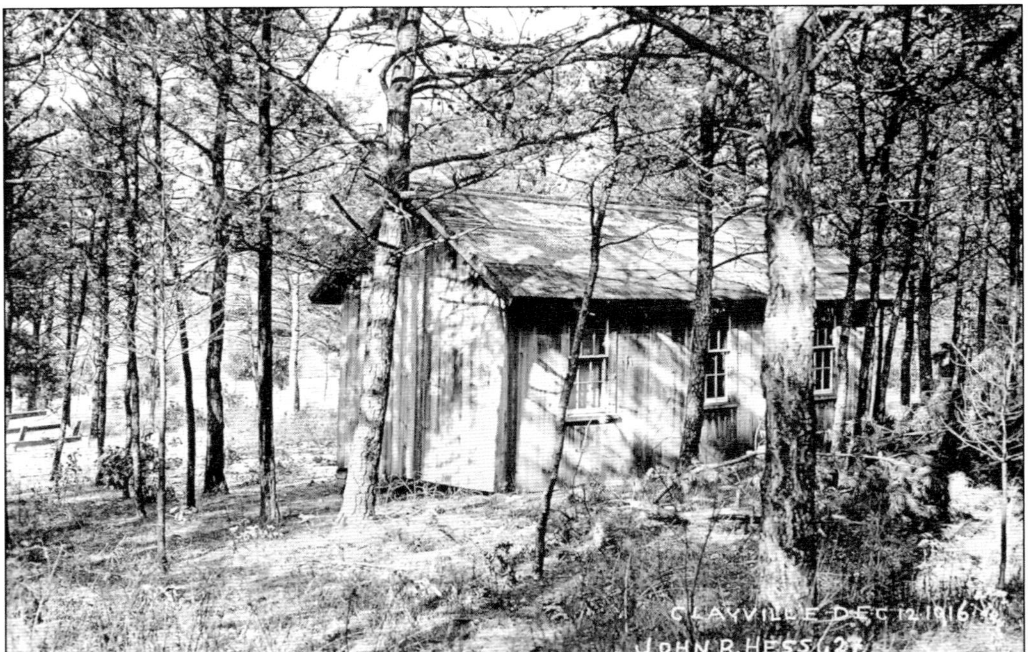

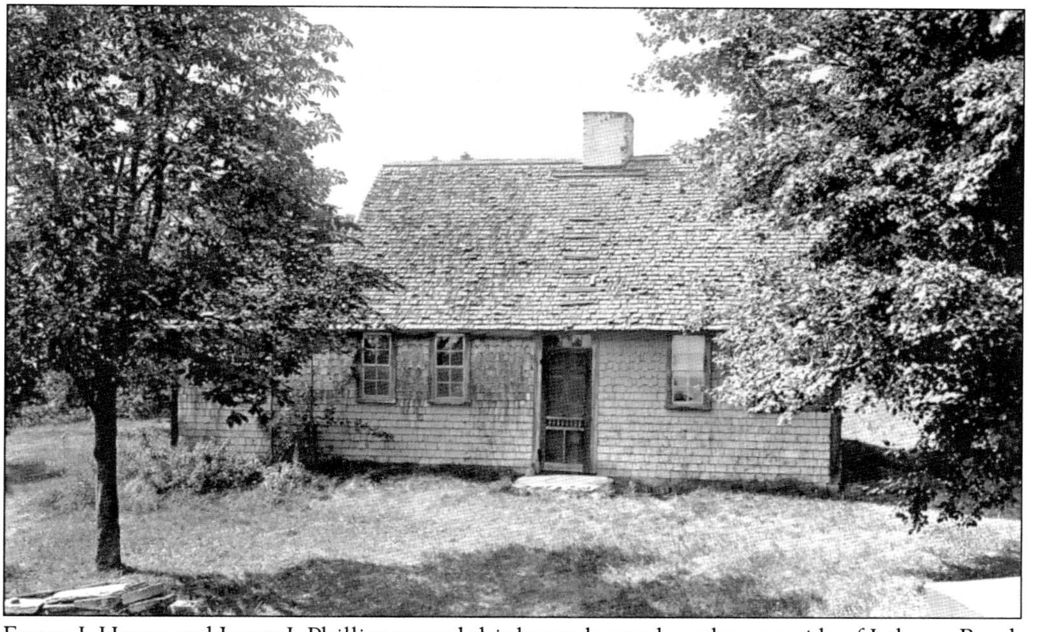

Emma I. Henry and James I. Phillips owned this house located on the west side of Isthmus Road; Hess photographed it on September 20, 1916. Luckily, it was out of the watershed area of the Westconnaug Reservoir; therefore, it was not taken. However, their barn across the road on Parcel 681, totaling 13.68 acres, was taken. Hess traveled back on July 11, 1917, to record it. The following verse is from "Little Gray House" by Helen O. Larson, written in December 1986 at the age of 76: "Then one night I looked up, I saw flames in the skies / They were burning the little gray house, and tears filled my eyes." (Both, courtesy of Providence Water.)

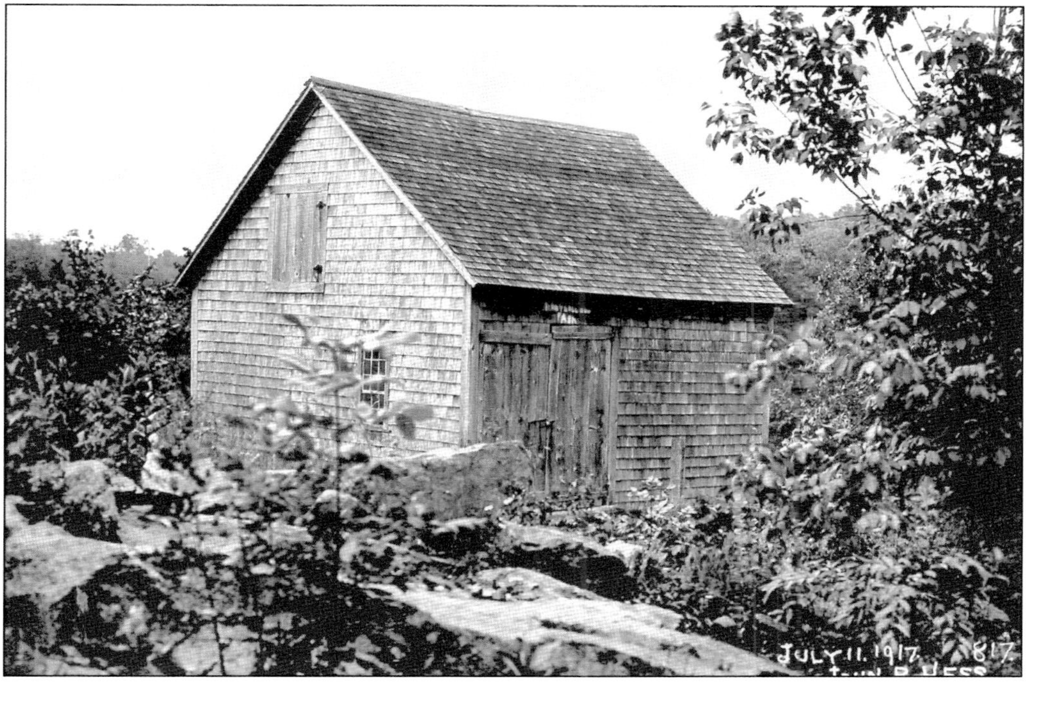

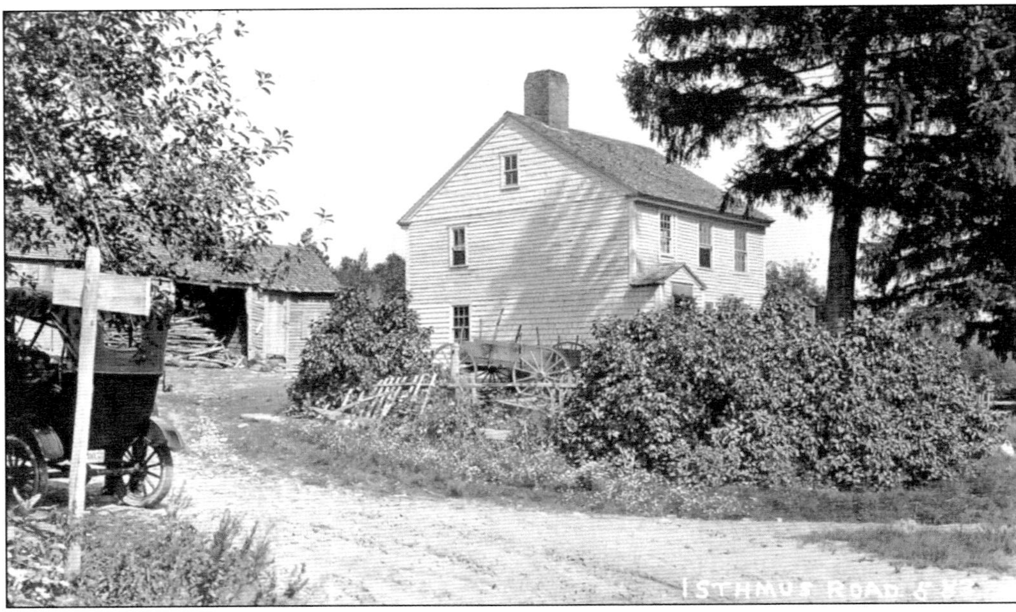

Byron E. Lewis was not one of the lucky ones. His farm, Parcel 682, was located on the north side of Plainfield Pike (now listed as Old Plainfield Pike) and east of Isthmus Road. He had a nice 20-acre corner spread that abutted the Westconnaug Reservoir, and therefore, Providence Water took it. He also lost 23 acres of his Parcel 684 on the east side of the Westconnaug Reservoir and north of Plainfield Pike. John R. Hess took the photograph of the farmhouse on September 20, 1916, but returned on July 11, 1917, to record the barn shown below. (Both, courtesy of Providence Water.)

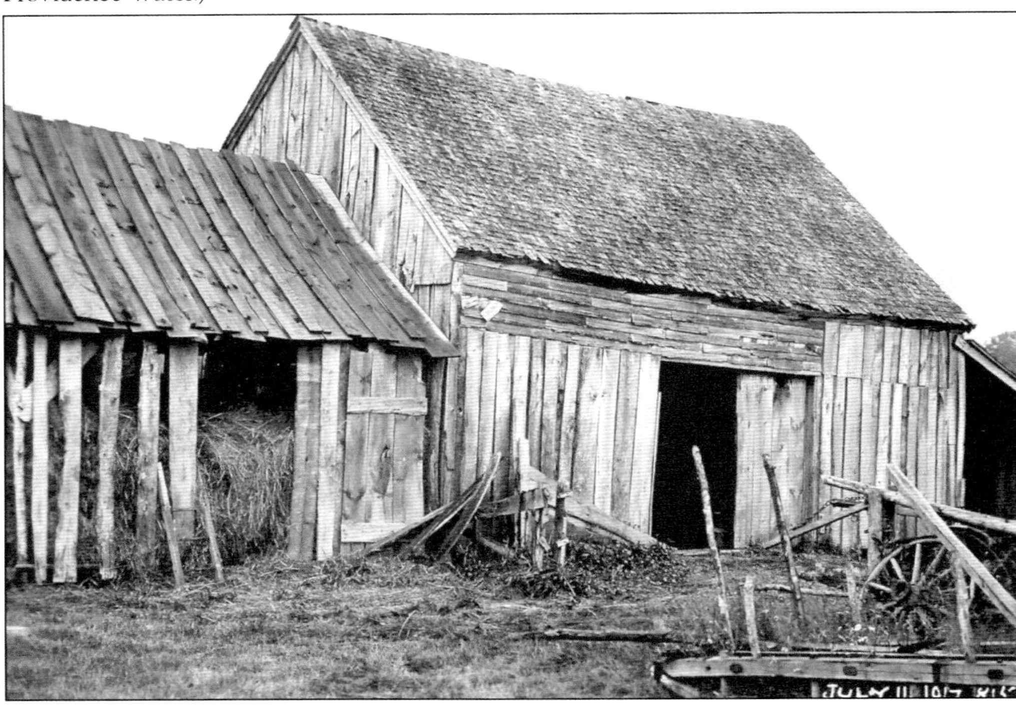

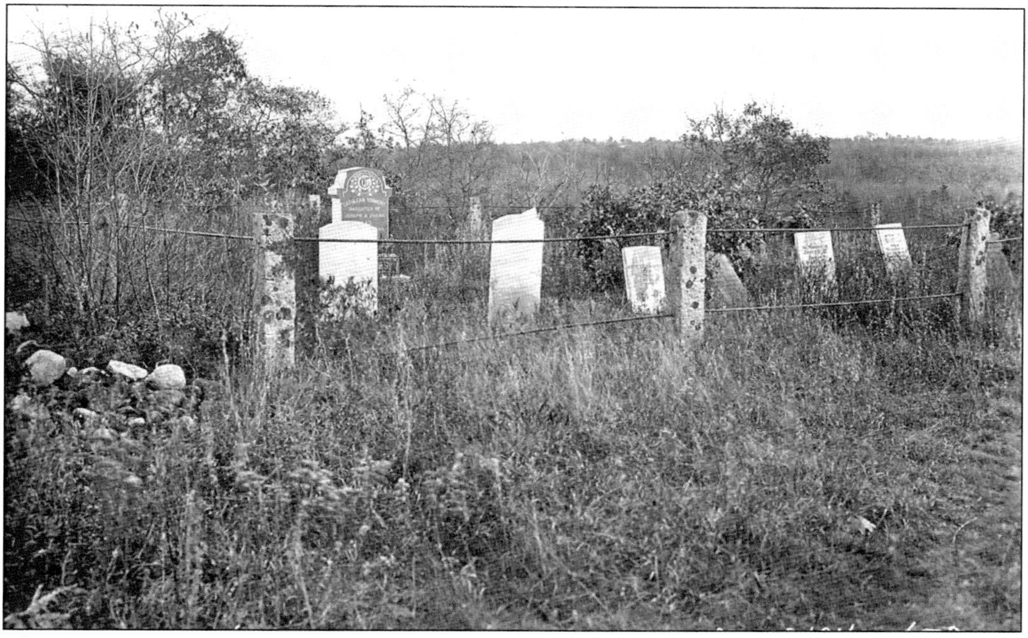

The cemetery pictured above was also located on Byron E. Lewis's Parcel 682. However, these graves were to remain resting in peace. The large marker in the back reads, "Cathlean Simmons / daughter of Joseph and Pheba Card / aged 37 years." Even though it does not state it, history has recorded she died March 2, 1905. Below is the home of Brayton A. Round, another lucky one, kind of. He lost 16.91 acres of his 19.62-acre farm, Parcel 985, but was able to keep his house located on the corner of Isthmus Road and the Clayville to Foster Center Road, now Plainfield Pike. The tracks of the Providence & Danielson Railway can be seen in the roadbed heading to Foster Center and beyond. The house and barn no longer exist, and Providence Water has since acquired the property. (Both, courtesy of Providence Water.)

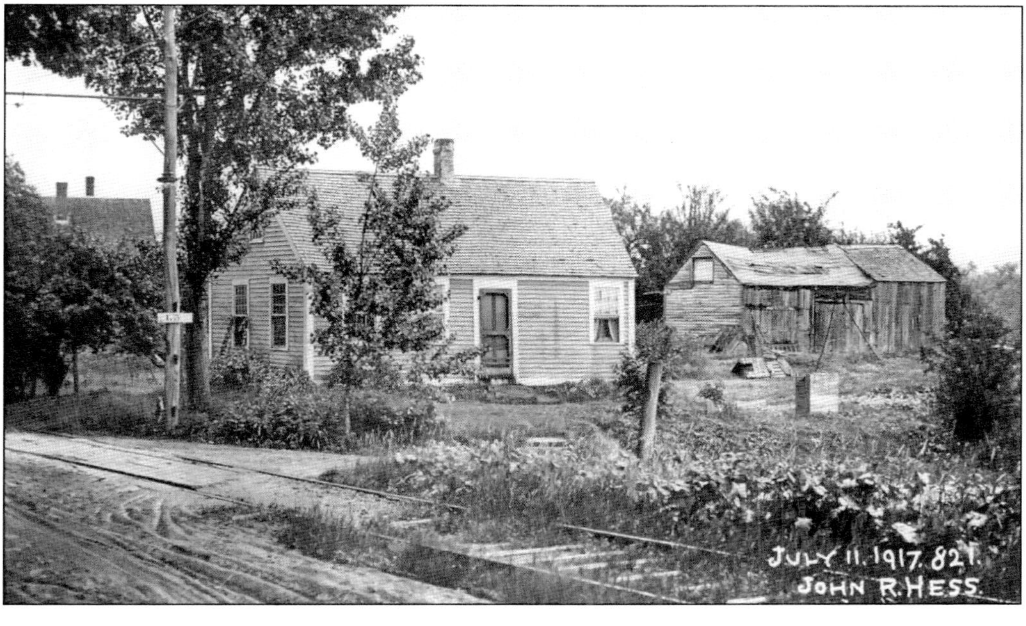

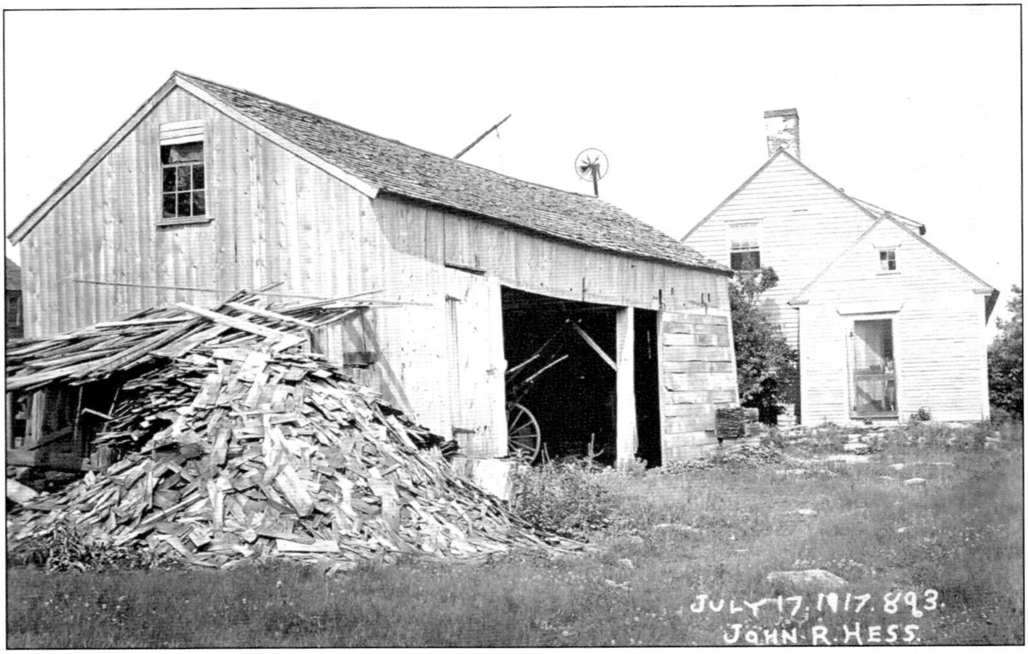

Both photographs of Rhoda E. Briggs 41-acre farm were taken on July 17, 1917. It was located on Hopkins Mills Road on Parcel 894. She was another lucky one, as the city only took 10.4 acres of her land located along the Barden Reservoir. The image of the huge barn below shows the back side and how it was designed to be open underneath. When the stalls were cleaned above, a row of planks in the floor would be opened for the manure to fall through. Then it was accessible to load and spread on the fields in the spring. The following verse is from "Little Gray House" by Helen O. Larson: "One by one the houses, were torn down and taken away / And now it's gone forever, the little house of driftwood gray." (Both, courtesy of Providence Water.)

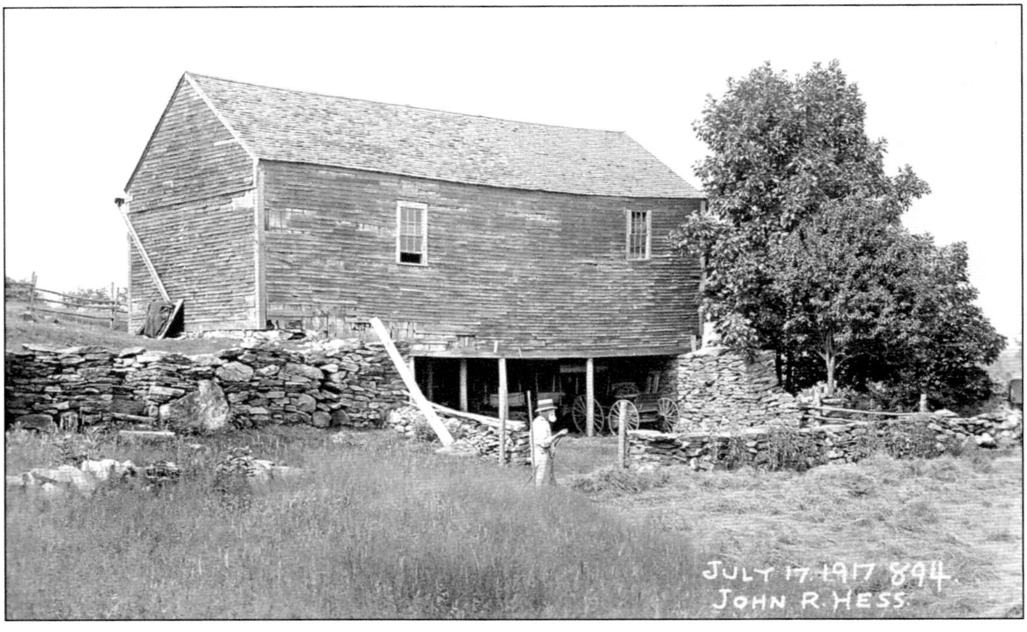

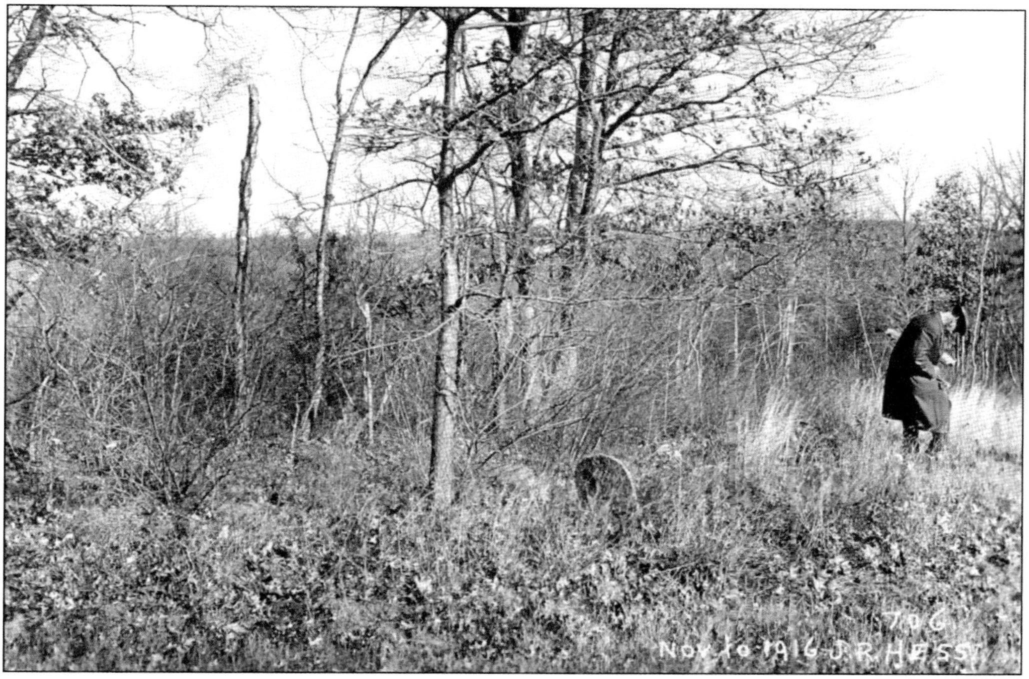

Hess located both of these burial grounds on November 10, 1916. The lone headstone above was on George A. Wetherbee's Parcel 954. It was a 30.44-acre parcel running between the Clayville to Hopkins Mills Road and the Barden Reservoir. The cemetery below was located on the south side of Saundersville Pike near Clayville to Hopkins Mills Road. It was Parcel 906, owned by the Barden Reservoir Company. (Both, courtesy of Providence Water.)

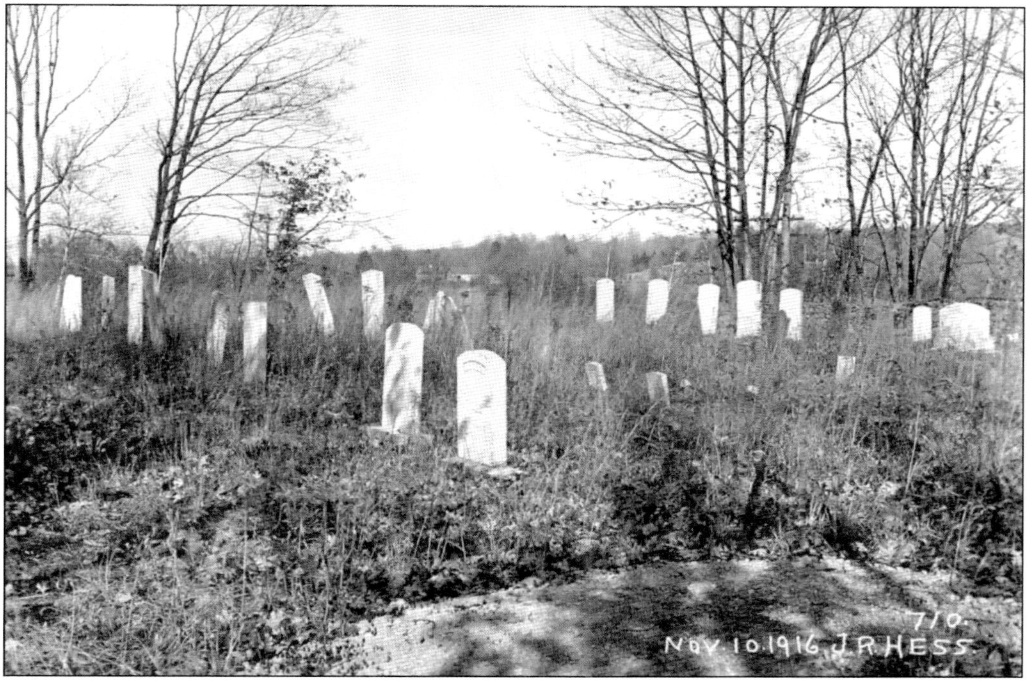

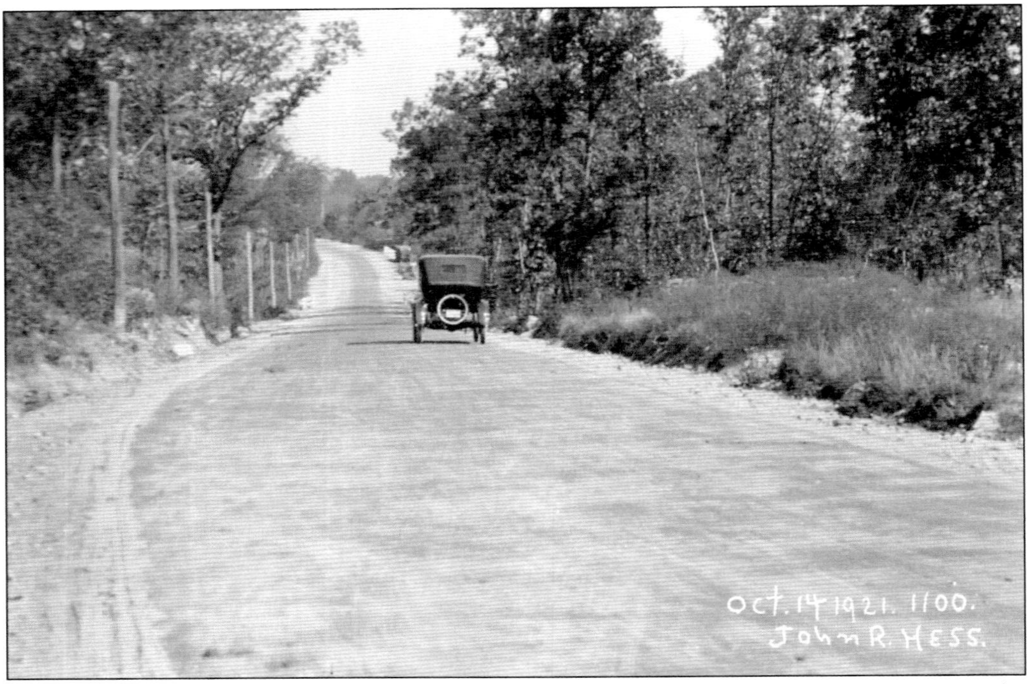

This is a view of the relocated Plainfield Pike, northward from the junction of Briggs Road. At this point, it is traversing Walter Dunham's property on its way to Route 94. The city had to build 26 miles of new roads to replace the 36 miles that were taken by the project. (Courtesy of Providence Water.)

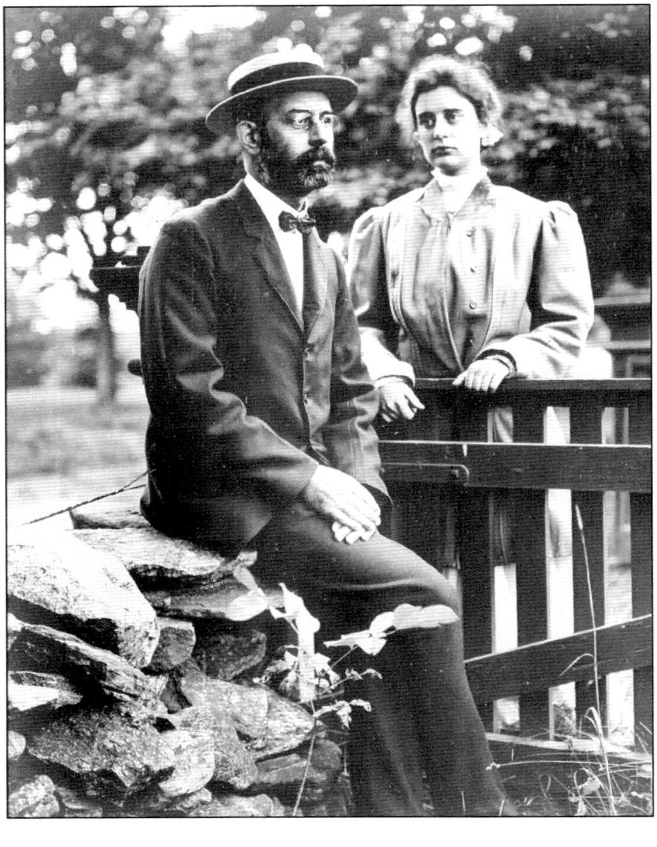

John R. Hess and his only daughter, Clara, pose for the camera in 1906. The City of Providence Water Supply Board commissioned him to photograph all the buildings in the five villages and surrounding area before they were destroyed; this included all burial grounds. He also recorded the entire construction of the reservoir. His work can be seen in *The Scituate Reservoir* and *The Lost Villages of Scituate,* both by Arcadia Publishing. (Courtesy of John R. Hess III.)

Two

Foster Center Area

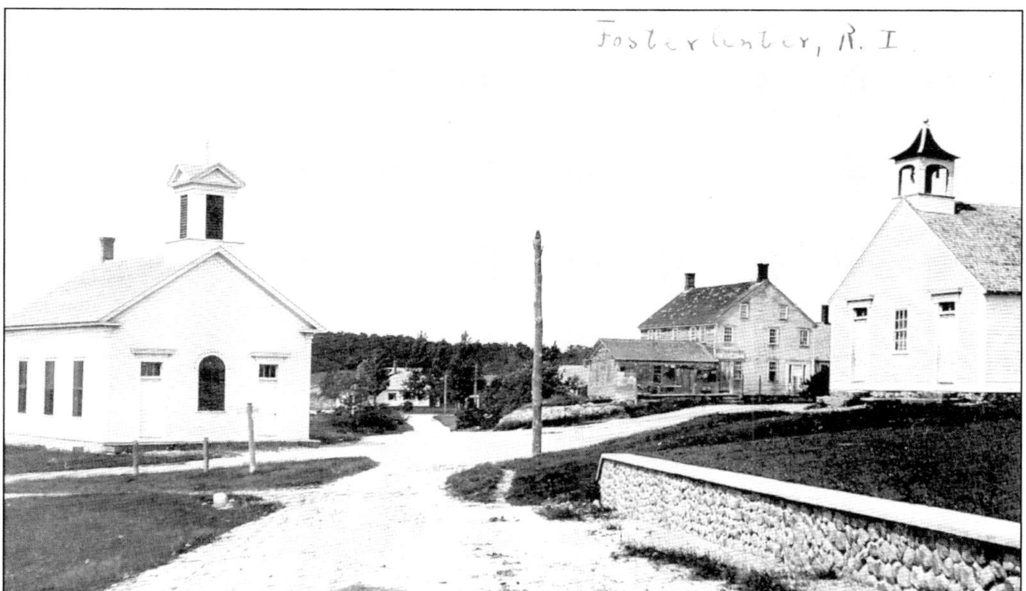

This is a late-1800s view of Foster Center. The Foster Center Christian Church (on the left) is pictured before it was turned to face the school (on the right). The Welcome Rood Tavern is pictured between them. This was a time before the arrival of trolleys in 1901. All roads were dirt, and the mode of travel was either horse and carriage or walking. Howard Hill Road is shown in the foreground. Today, the former school building is the Foster Center Library.

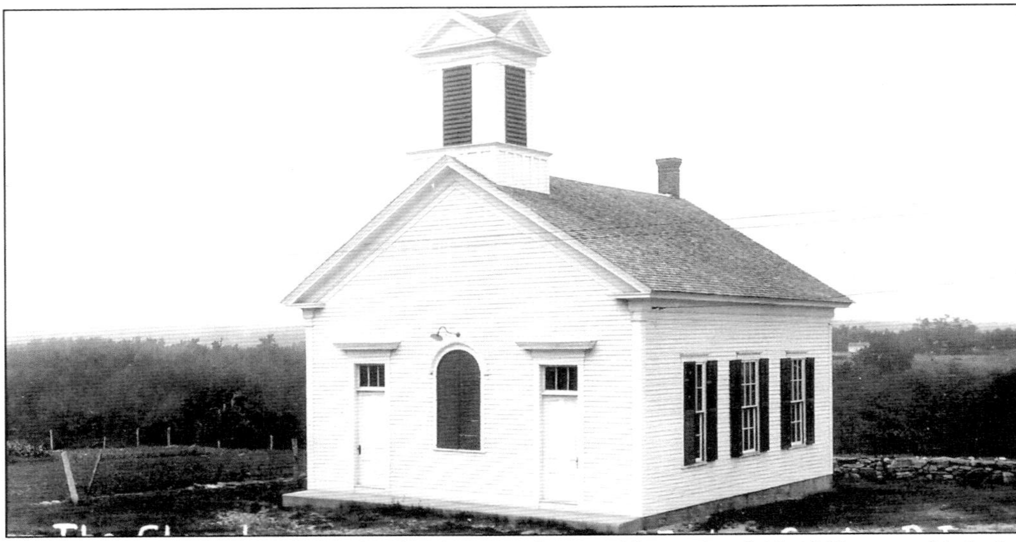

A charter was given by the Rhode Island General Assembly on April 27, 1881, to establish the Foster Center Christian Church. Members of the congregation formed the Foster Center Ladies Home Mission Society, shown below, on September 26, 1882. Its mission was to help people in need. On this day, May 27, 1916, members met at the Foster Town House to prepare dinner for the Masons. From left to right are (first row) Lena Howard Simmons, John W. Bowen (Mason), Adelia Howard Bowen, Susan Howard Nichols, and Maria Phillips Clapp; (second row) Junie Pierce Gorton, Annie Card Knight, Eva Sutcliffe Hopkins, Alice Cole Bennett, Teresa Howard Brayton, Phebe Pierce Gorton, and Frank Brayton (helper); (third row) Jennie Hopkins, Caroline Arnold, Clarissa Sweet Howard, Phebe Waterman Howard, and Louisa Stone Howard; (fourth row) Sarah Simmons, Lura Howard Cole, Allie Howard Luther, Agatha Cole Howard, Edith Weatherbee, and Susan Phillips Birtwell. The woman standing to the left is unidentified.

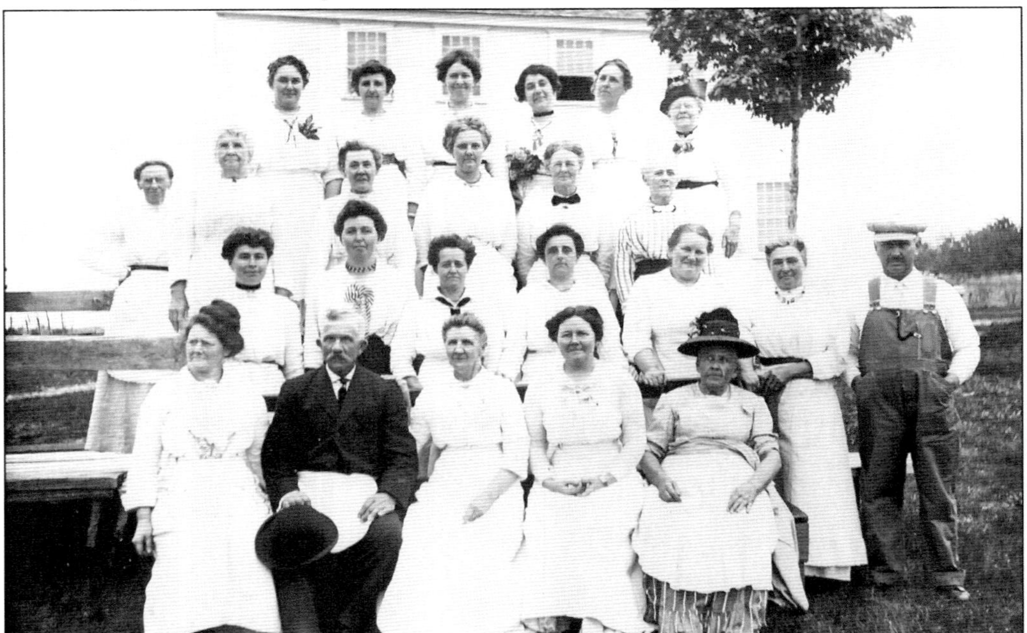

Rev. Lester Howard (right) attended Howard Hill School in town and Lapham Institute in Scituate. He was ordained on July 17, 1882, at 30 years old. On October 31 of the same year, he was named the first pastor of the Foster Center Church. He ended up leaving Foster in 1887. This photograph was made between 1900 and 1910. (Courtesy of Sandra Ball.)

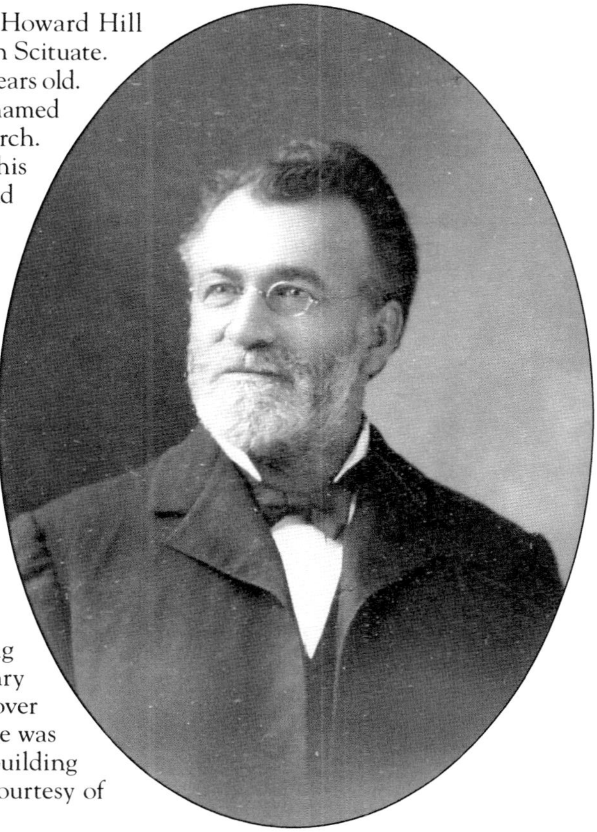

The Rockland Cornet Band is leading the Masons as they pass in front of Henry Bennett's store. The Masonic Hall was over the store, and at one time, the post office was located beside the store. In 1824, the building housed the Welcome Rood Tavern. (Courtesy of Mary Thoman.)

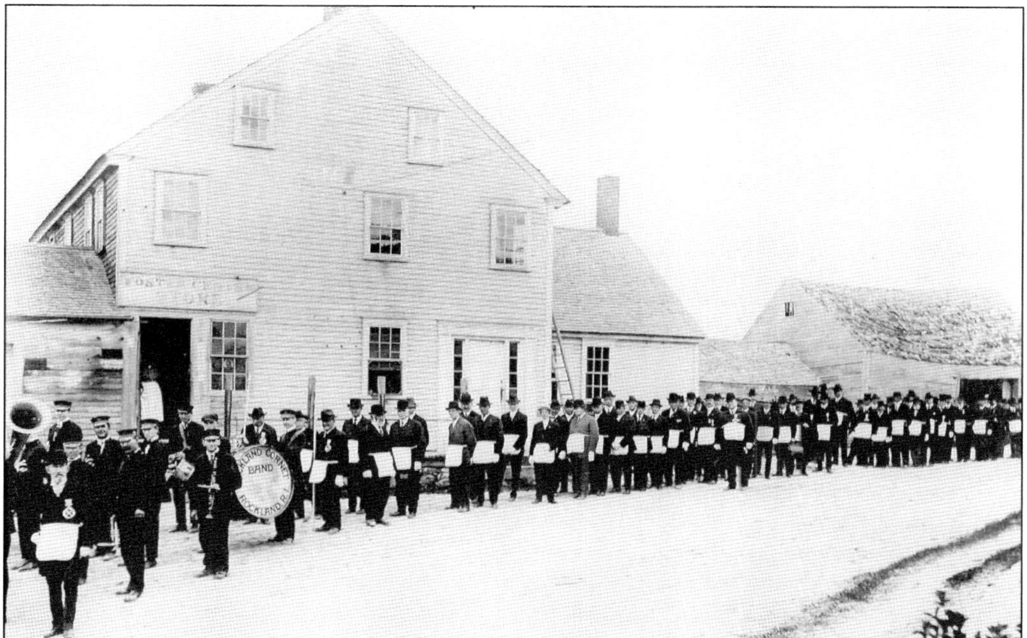

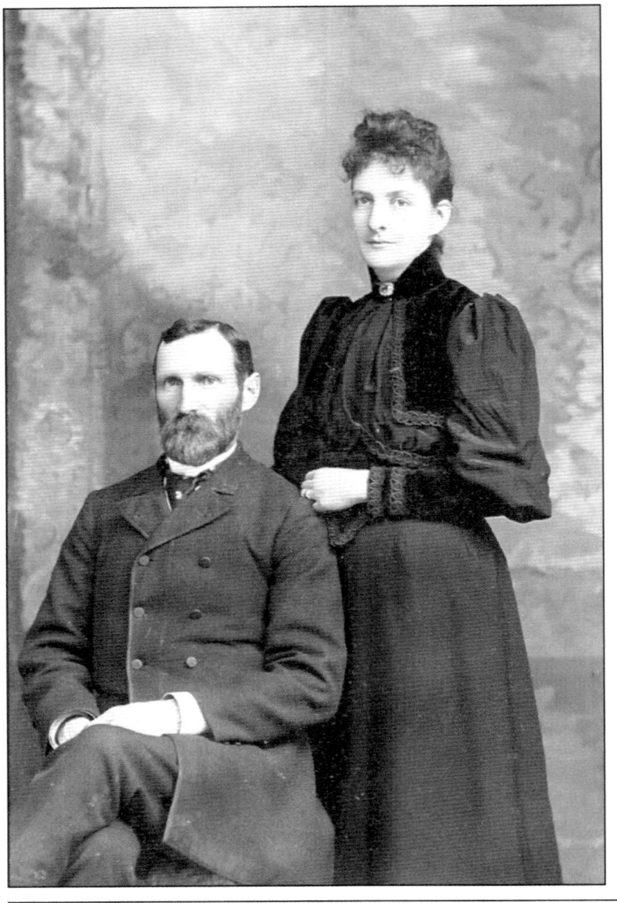

This photograph is labeled Dr. Henry Arnold and wife. He was born in 1855 and followed in his father's footsteps to become a doctor. Both father and son lived in the residence pictured below. The following verse is from "You Were My Valentine" by Helen O. Larson: "We announced our engagement, as the clock was striking seven / I was sure I had left the Earth, and was living up in Heaven." (Courtesy Sandra Ball.)

Andrew and Sally Hopkins built this beautiful farm in 1770. Dr. Mowry P. Arnold, with his second wife, Dorcas Peckman-Mowry, bought if from them in 1830. Dr. Arnold began his practice in 1828 and was a physician in Foster for over 60 years. His son Henry, shown on the left, also became a doctor. (Courtesy of Mary Thoman.)

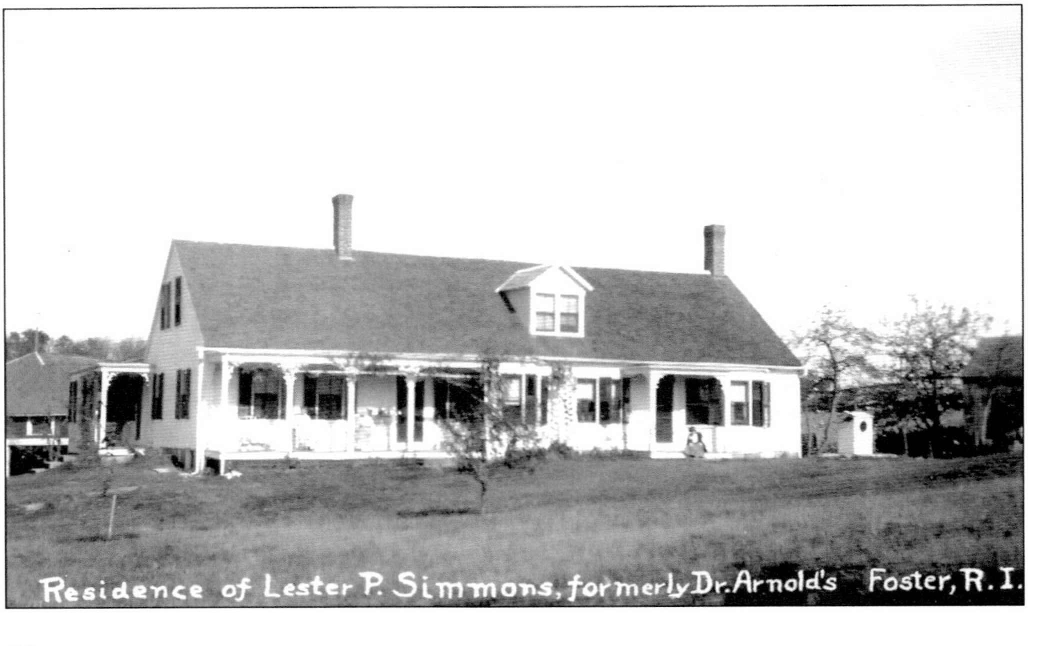

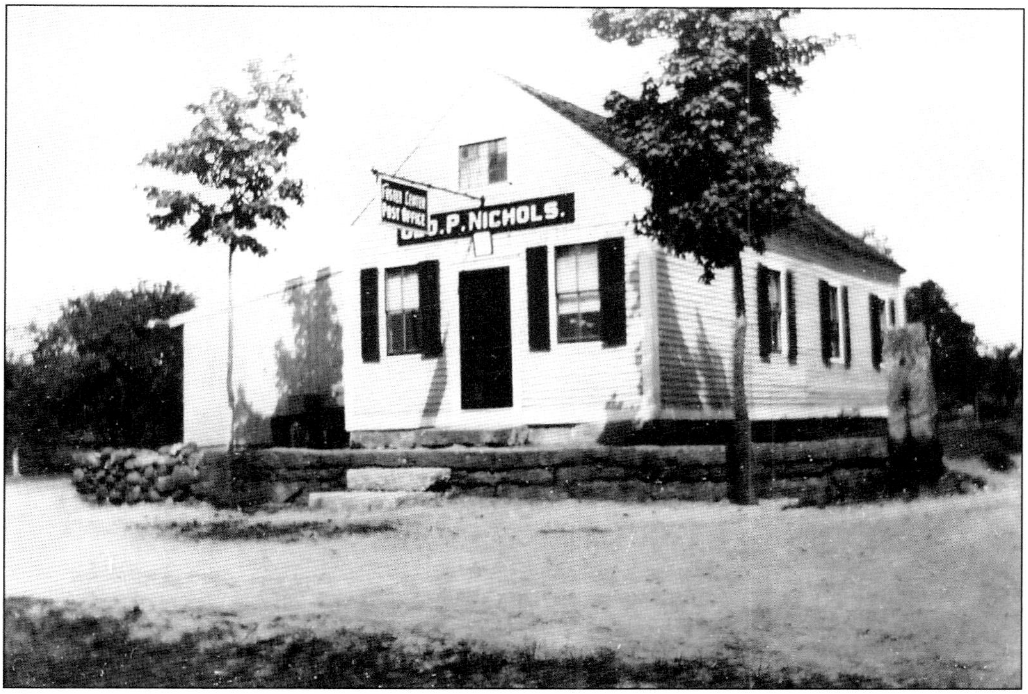

This postcard of George P. Nichols's first store on Foster Center Road was mailed on August 26, 1909. The sign hanging above the door announces it is also the Foster Center Post Office. The postcard below was mailed on September 5, 1913. This was after Nichols had moved the small building (above) across the road and built this larger store. He still provided the mail service. What a contrast—the horse and buggy unknowingly were doomed as the automobile was about to dominate the future of travel. (Both, courtesy of Mary Thoman.)

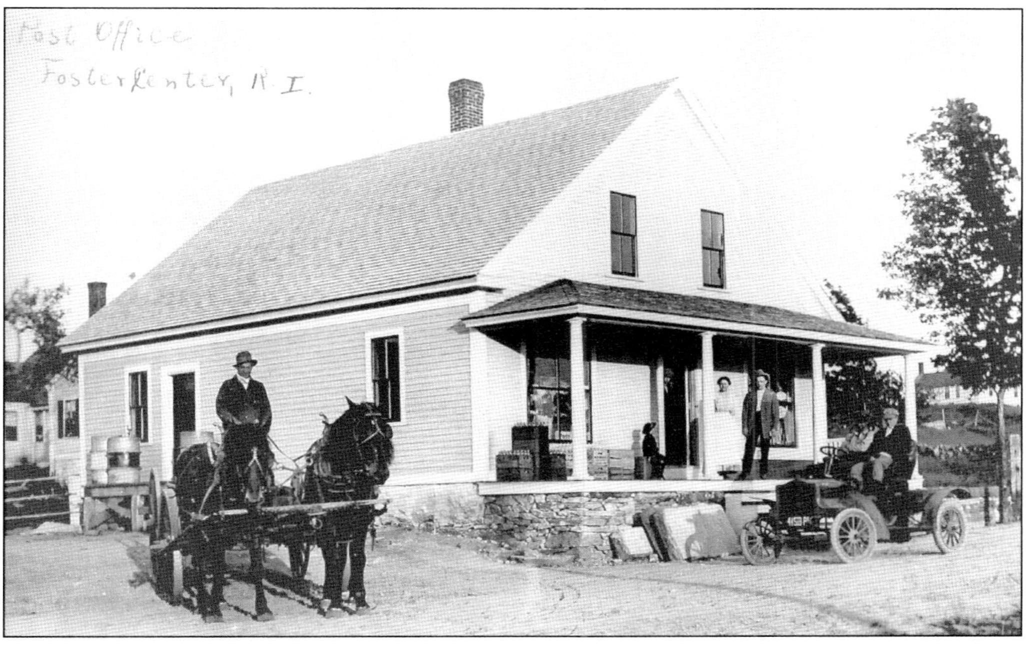

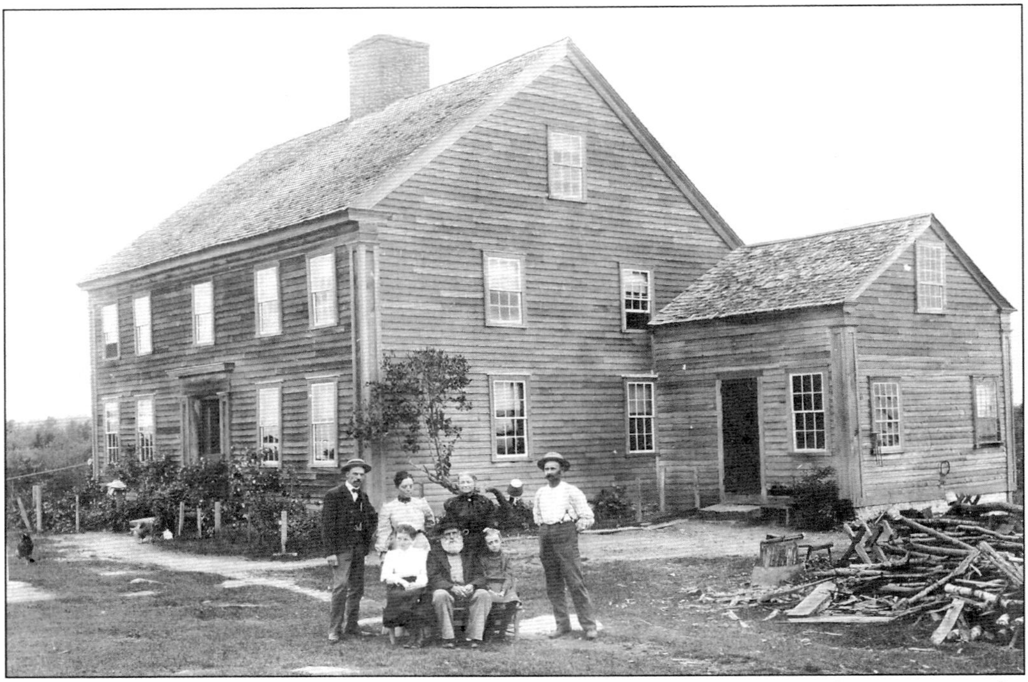

Thomas Hammond's tavern was built around 1755. When Foster broke away from Scituate, the first town meeting was held here on November 19, 1781. The tavern is pictured here on June 14, 1903. In 1796, Thomas's son John would be influential in the building of the Second Baptist Church, known as Elder Hammond's meetinghouse. (Courtesy of Mary Thoman.)

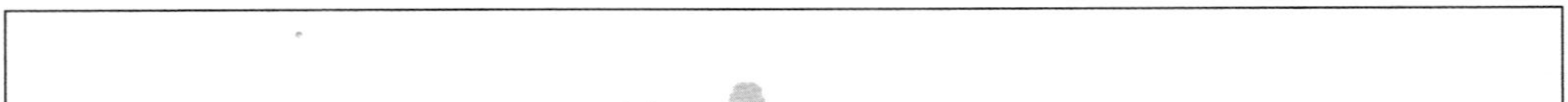

This photograph shows that Thomas Hammond's tavern had later become the private residence of James P. Nichols. It had been completely remodeled as pictured. The large center chimney had been replaced with two smaller ones, a third window was added to both first- and second-floor gables, and a small dormer and chimney were part of the addition.

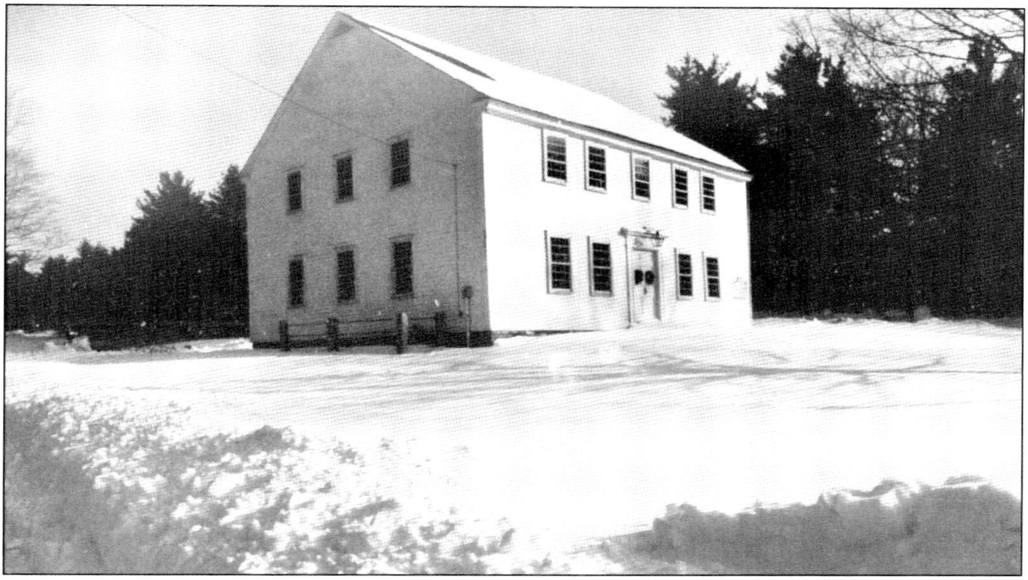

The Second Baptist Church broke off from the First Baptist Church in Hopkins Mills in 1780. It was incorporated in 1791 under the care of elder John Hammond. In 1796, the congregation, using funds from a lottery, built what became known as Elder Hammond's meetinghouse. By 1822, it needed repairs; therefore, the church deeded it to the town for $86. Town meetings had been held here since 1801. There are two stairways leading to the gallery occupying three sides of the structure. It has since become known as the Foster Town House, where town meetings continue to be held today. The following verse is from "Christmas" by Helen O. Larson: "You can hear the carolers singing, as they stand out in the snow / How sweetly their voices echo, singing all the hymns they know."

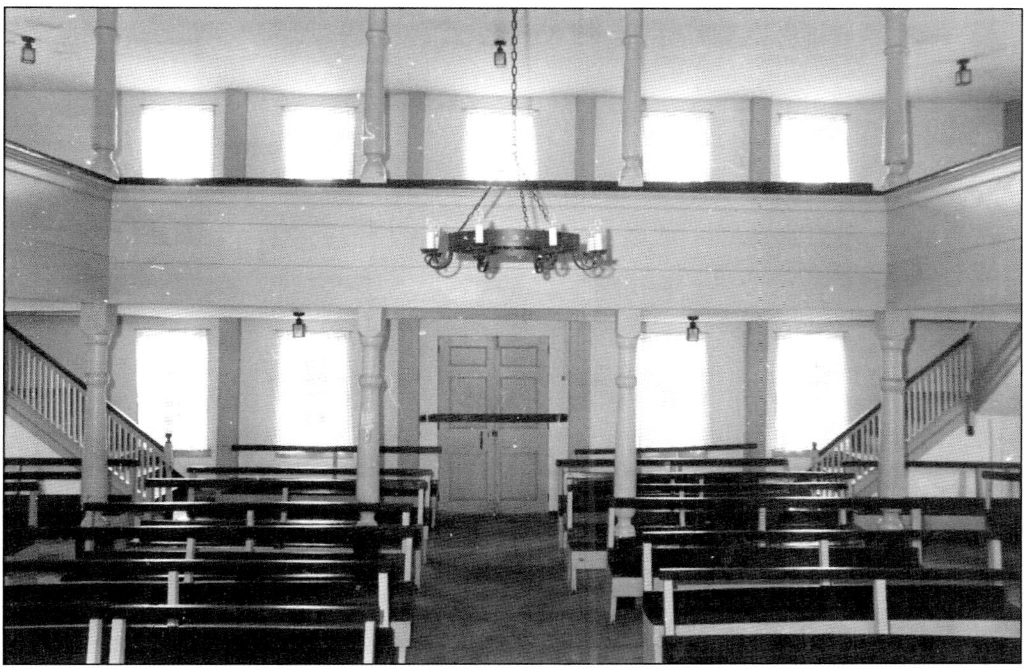

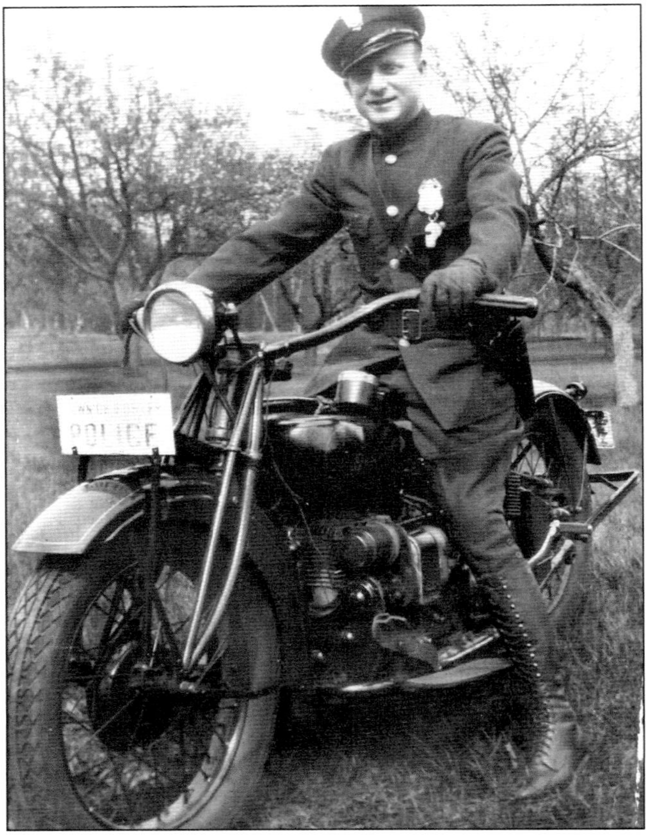

Thomas Chatterton Jr. is posing astride his new Indian motorcycle. It was the first one for the new all-volunteer Foster Police Department in 1928. The part-time four-man force also included William I. Wright, Chief James M. Wright, and George K. Read. The following verses are from "The Brave Policeman" by Helen O. Larson: "Don't run these brave men down, if tragedy should strike / They are the first ones you would call, on that fateful night."

Nehemiah Angell built this tavern around 1820. Eli Aylsworth bought the tavern in 1831 and ran it until 1841, at which time he sold it. Over the years, it went through a number of proprietors. The Town of Foster acquired it in 1960, and today, it houses the police department. (Author's collection.)

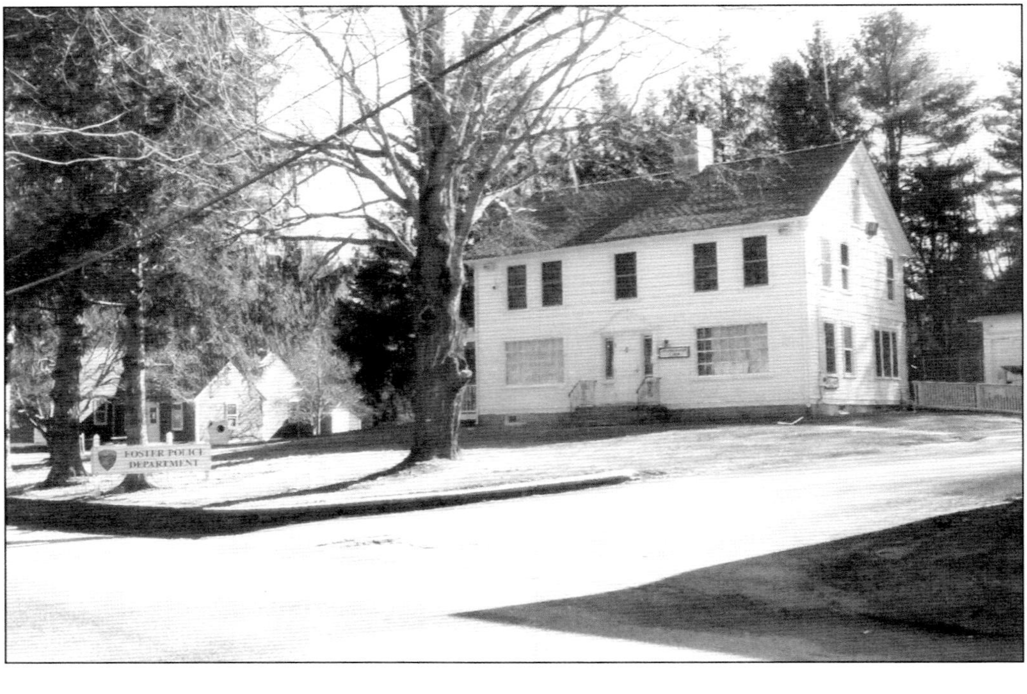

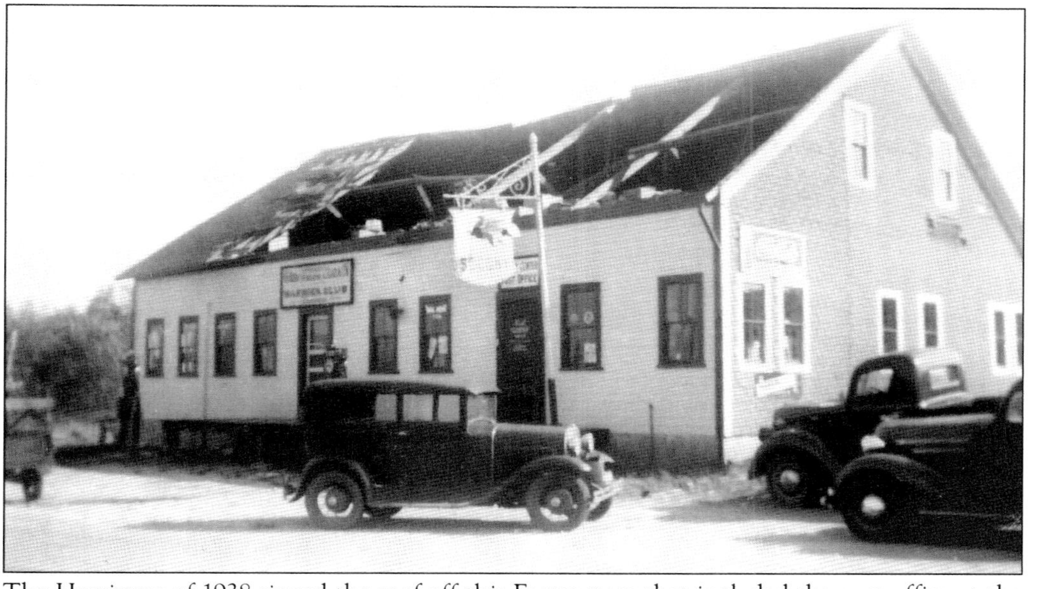

The Hurricane of 1938 ripped the roof off this Foster store that included the post office at the time. A sign above the car in the center is advertising Flying A Gasoline. The top of a pump can be seen above the car's roof; another pump is at the far end of the building. The sign on the nearest gable end of the building announces that the store has Warwick Club Soda inside. (Courtesy of Mary Thoman.)

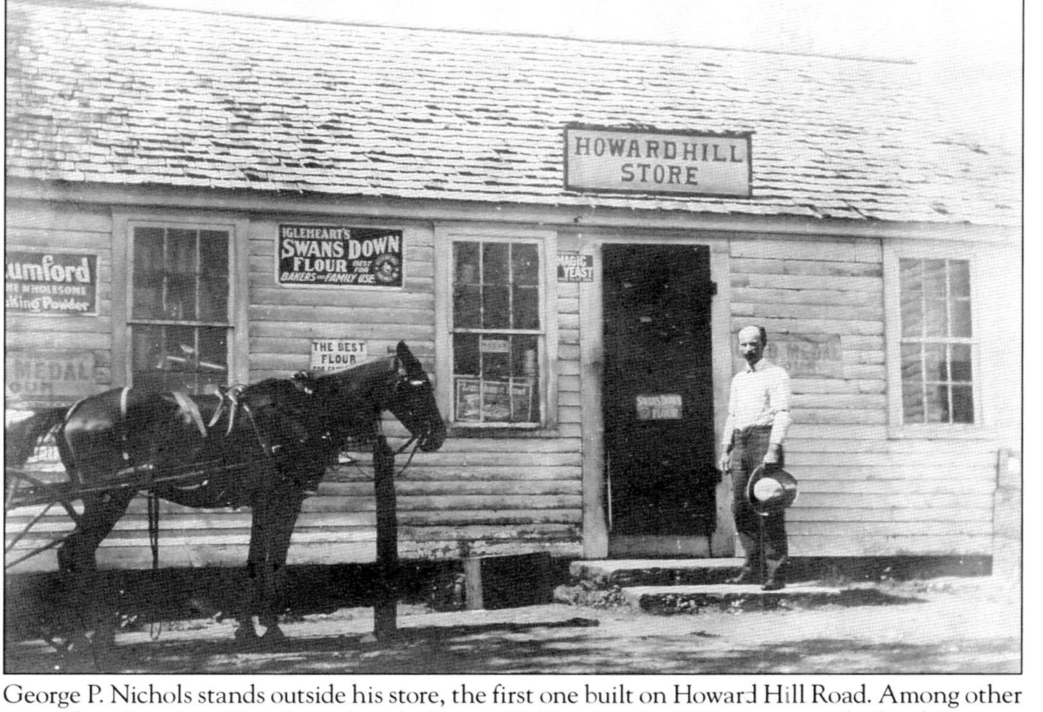

George P. Nichols stands outside his store, the first one built on Howard Hill Road. Among other items, he advertises "Rumford, the wholesome Baking Powder." The horse at the hitching post waits patiently for its owner to return. (Courtesy of Mary Thoman.)

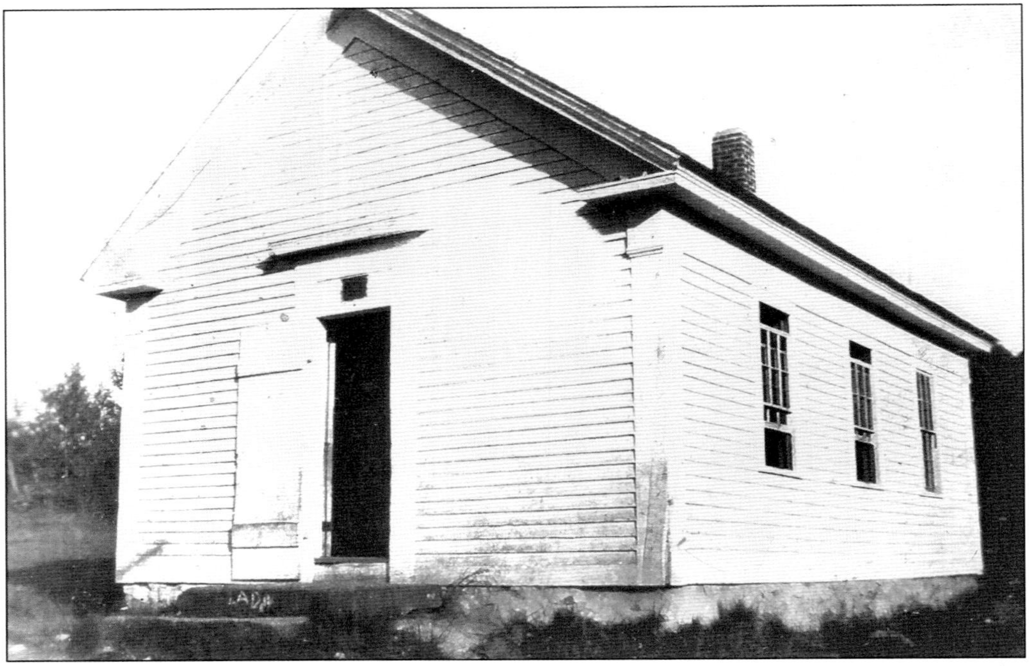

This view of the Wood School No. 10 was taken in 1932. It was tucked in the corner at the intersection of North Road and South Killingly Road. It was unusual to see an old school with only one entrance for both boys and girls. (Courtesy of Viola Ulm.)

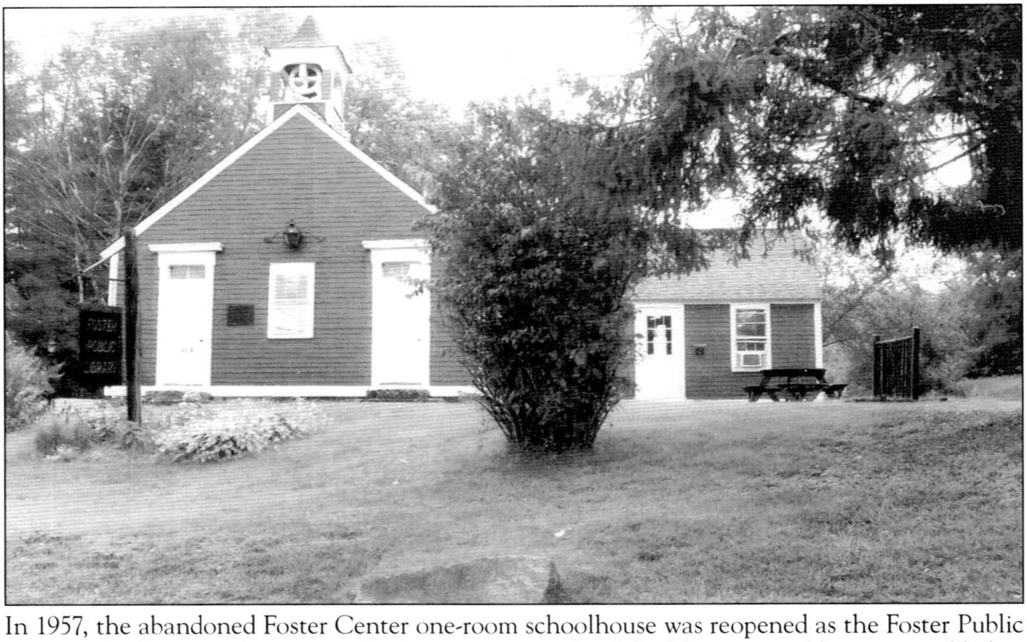

In 1957, the abandoned Foster Center one-room schoolhouse was reopened as the Foster Public Memorial Library. To keep up with the growing needs of the library, an addition was added in 1964 and another one in 1970. The old school belfry stands proudly on the end of the gable roof as a reminder of the past pictured in July 1971.

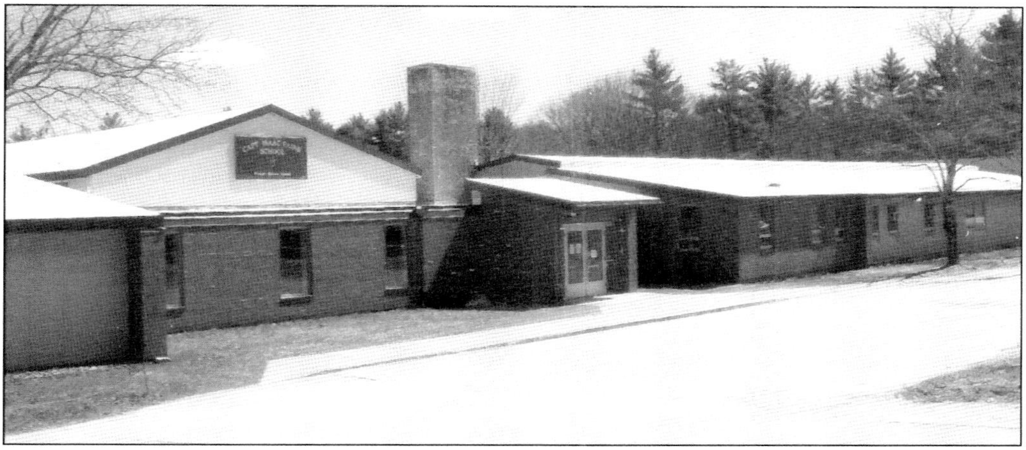

In June 1952, the following 13 students were the last graduates of the one-room school system: Ernest Andrews, Marian Correia, Alice Dort, George Harrington, Theresa Harvey, Richard Hopkins, Sarah Lamphere, Anne Law, Marie Morin, Patricia Peck, Barbara Perry, Heidi Schlaepfer, and Joan Wood. Graduation exercises were held at the newly constructed Capt. Isaac Paine School. When it opened officially for classes in the fall of 1952, it ended the era of one-room schools in Foster. (Author's collection.)

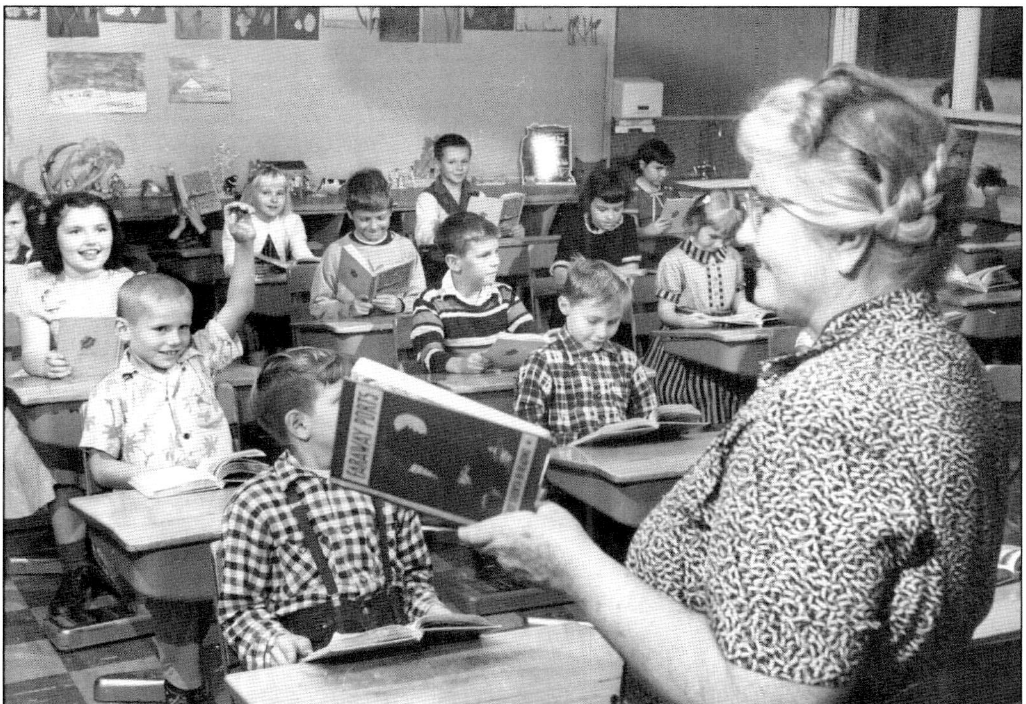

Ermina Harris is teaching her eager third-grade class from the reading book *Faraway Ports* on November 2, 1955. From bottom to top, from left to right, they are (first row) David Williams, Jeffrey Tucker, unidentified, and, ? Parent; (second row) Richard Belanger, Berrick Dewhirst, Paul Kanerva, and Sylvia Turnquist; (third row) Janice Sweet, Nancy Bell, and Robert Belanger; (fourth row) Gail Hallene.

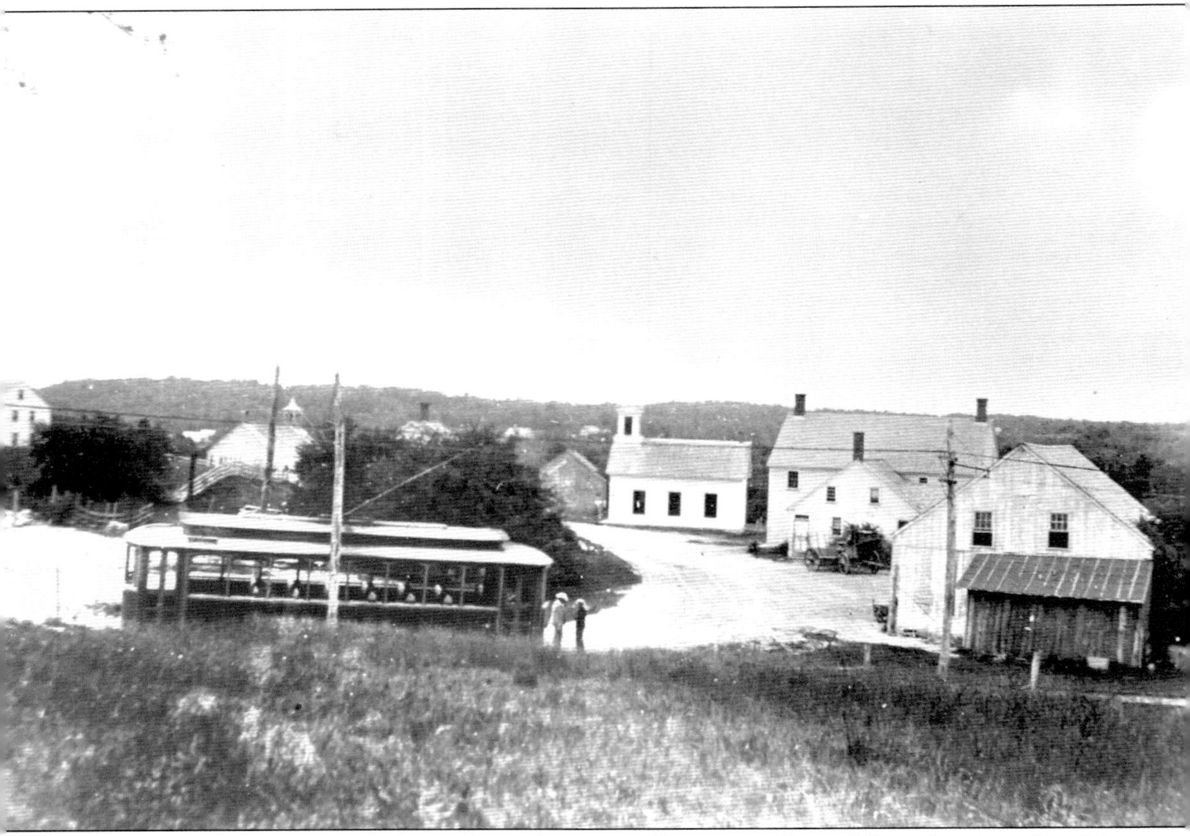

This view of Foster Center shows the Welcome Rood Tavern in the middle and to the right of the Foster Center Christian Church, before the church was turned to face the road. The Providence & Danielson Railway (P&D) is shown traveling on what is now Foster Center Road. On January 20, 1902, Gilbert Hopkins was walking north on these tracks when the trolley came around the corner from Clayville and started down the hill. The conductor rang his bell furiously for Hopkins to get off the tracks. When he realized the man was not responding, it was too late to stop the moving trolley. Hopkins felt the vibration underfoot and turned as the trolley struck and killed him. The conductor did not know what all the towns people knew, that Hopkins was deaf. He was the first fatality of the P&D. (Courtesy of Mary Thoman.)

Hon. James Manchester Wright was born in 1834 near the house he bought in 1873 (shown below). He was a Democrat until 1860, when he had issues with the party over slavery. As a Republican, he was a state representative, state senator, and chairman of the Republican Town Committee for 47 consecutive years. (Courtesy of Sandra Ball.)

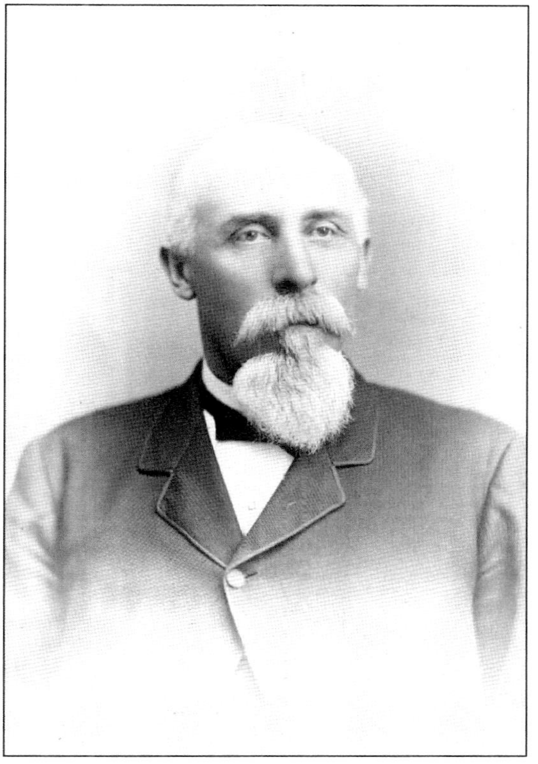

Jacob Phillips built this house in 1770. It was a typical center chimney house with an ell added after 1910. James M. Wright bought the property in 1873. He was born and grew up nearby. (Courtesy of Mary Thoman.)

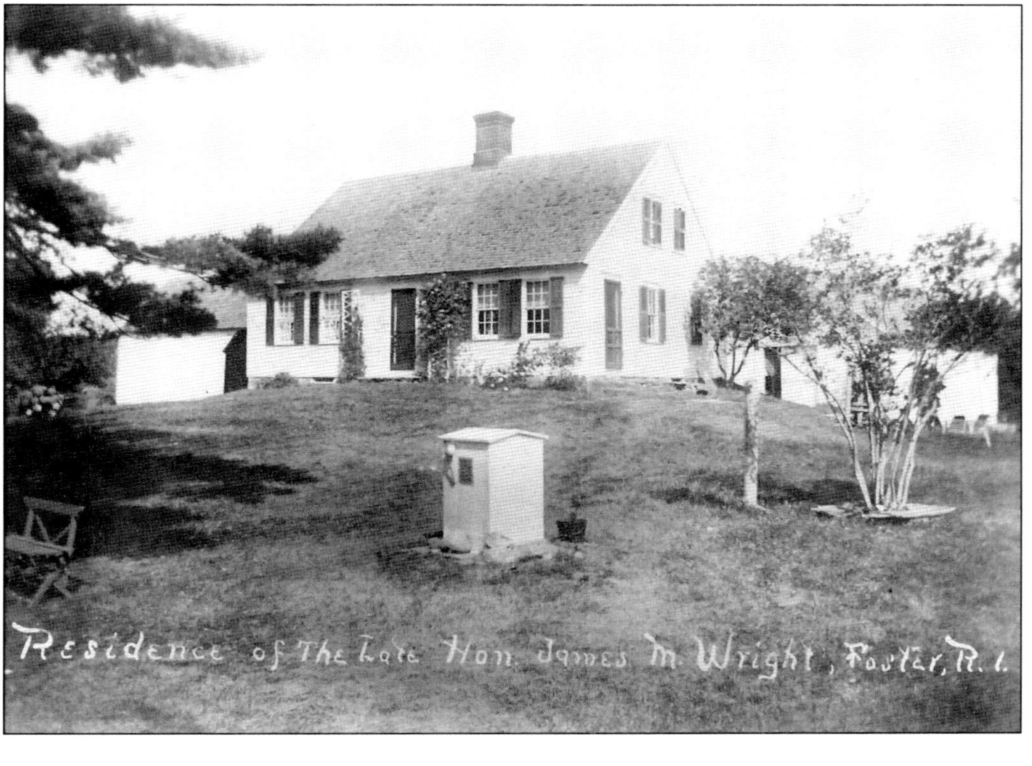

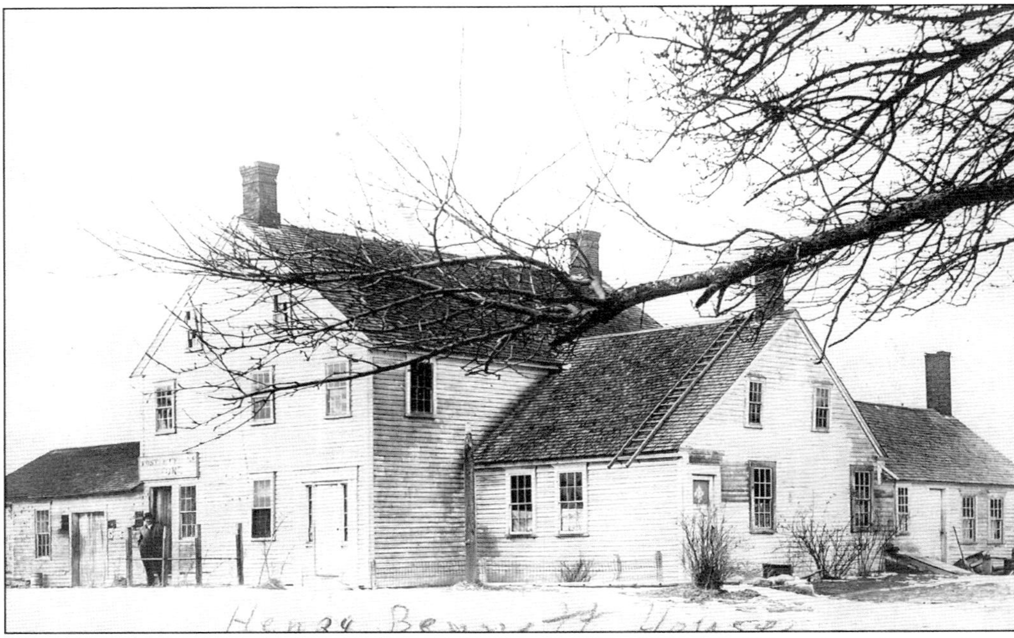

It is believed the original house to this complex is the ell built about 1780 to the right rear. Later, an addition was added to the front. Welcome Rood built the 2.5-story addition to the left in 1824 for his tavern and store. The second floor housed the Masonic Hall. The ell to the left was originally a grain shed. (Courtesy of Richard Siembab.)

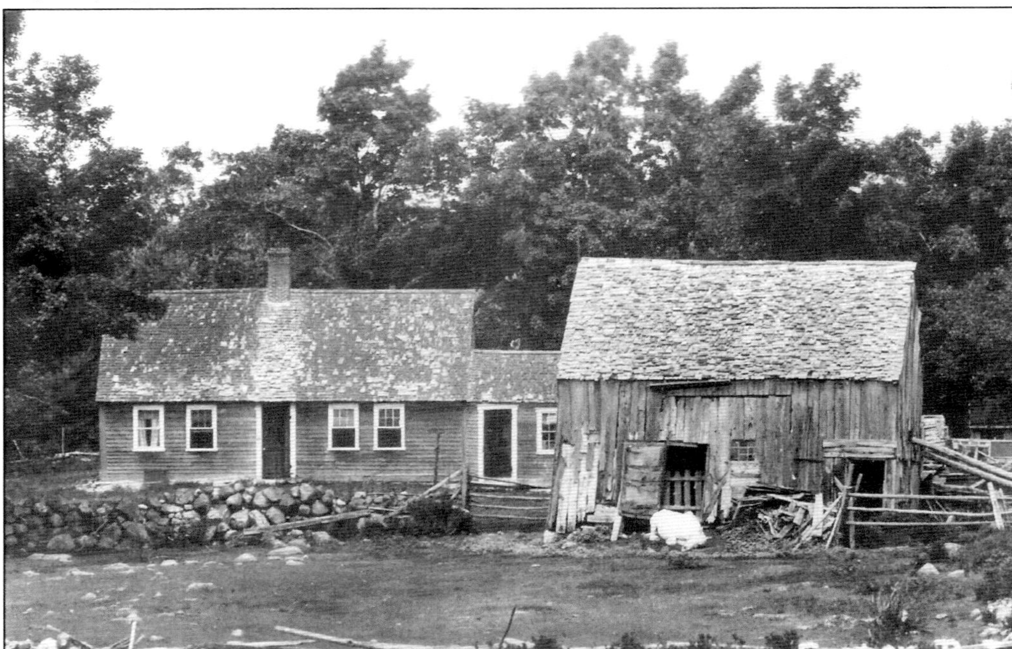

This postcard shows Henry Havens's farm on the corner of Foster Center and Mill Roads. He lived here with his wife, Hanna Cole-Havens. The kitchen area was destroyed during the 1938 hurricane and has been completely replaced. The rest of the original house remains.

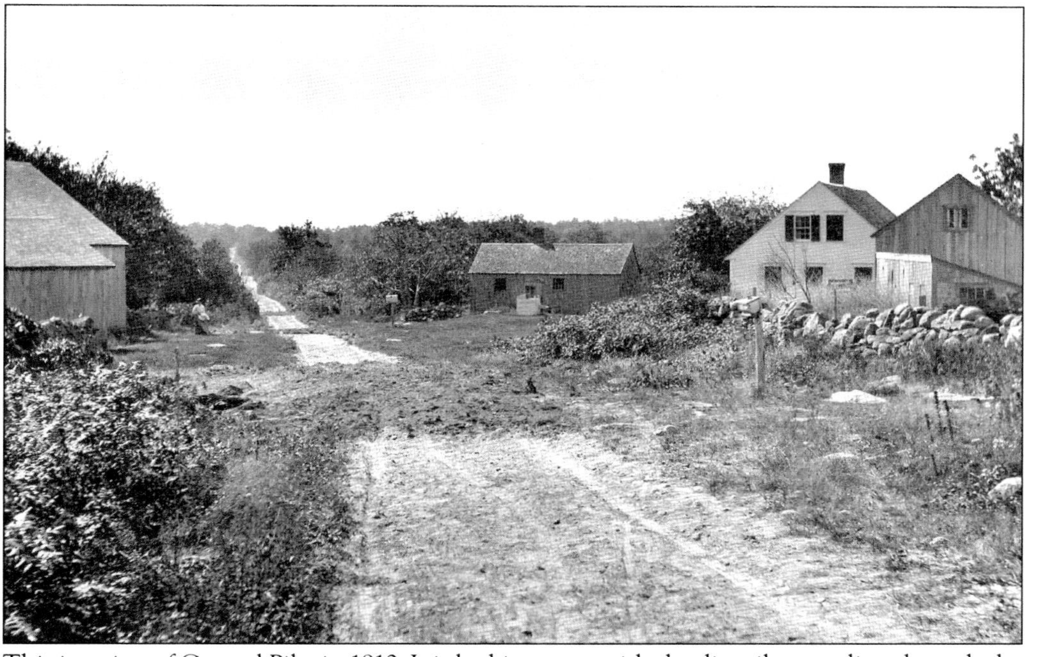

This is a view of Central Pike in 1910. It is looking west, with the dirt pike traveling through the Hopkins-Young farm. The farm was established in 1810 and included the house with a center chimney, an outhouse, sheds, and a barn on the opposite side of the pike.

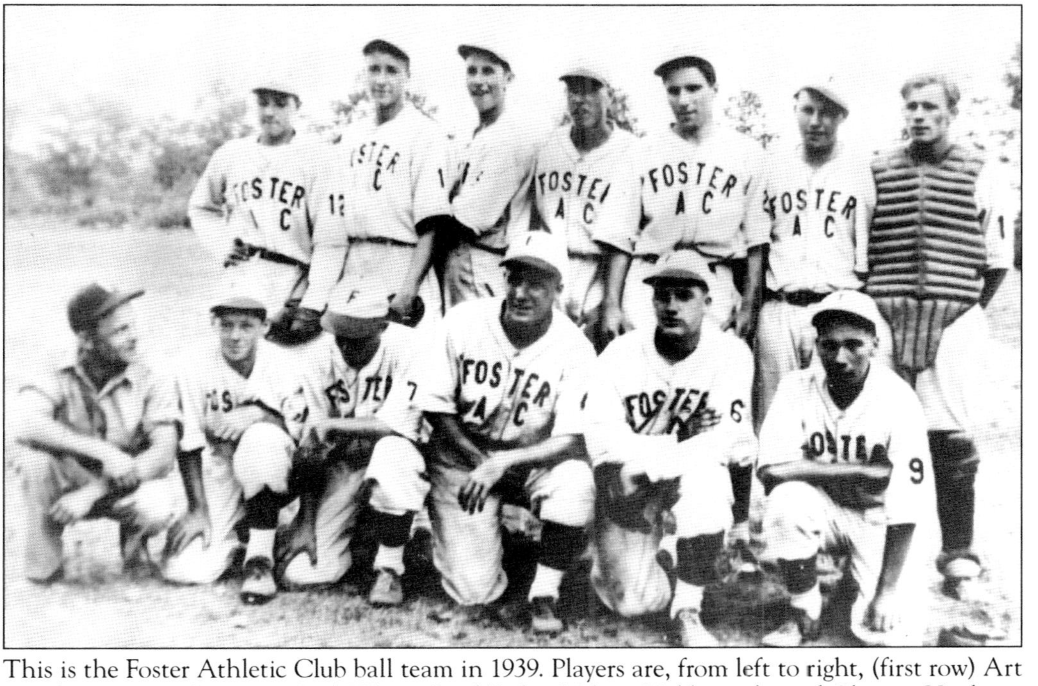

This is the Foster Athletic Club ball team in 1939. Players are, from left to right, (first row) Art Boucher, George Brayton, Carl White, Brad Rider, Milton Holdsworth, and Clinton Hopkins; (second row) Norman Tucker, Arthur Holdsworth, Leon Shippee, William Bellows, William Cummings, Ralph Pierce, and Robert Richard. (Courtesy of Dorothy Brayton.)

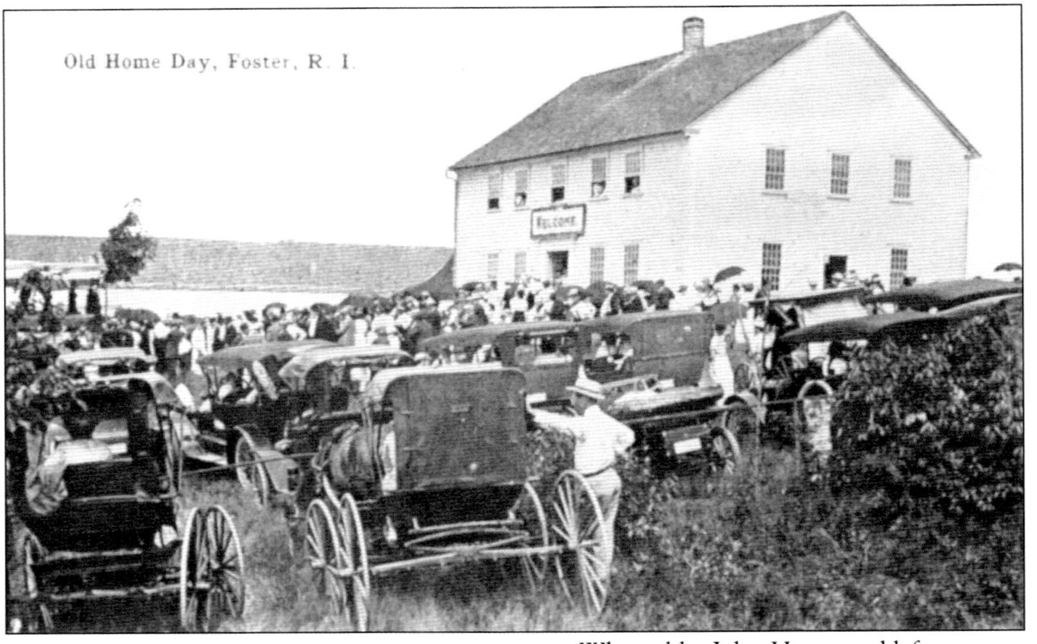

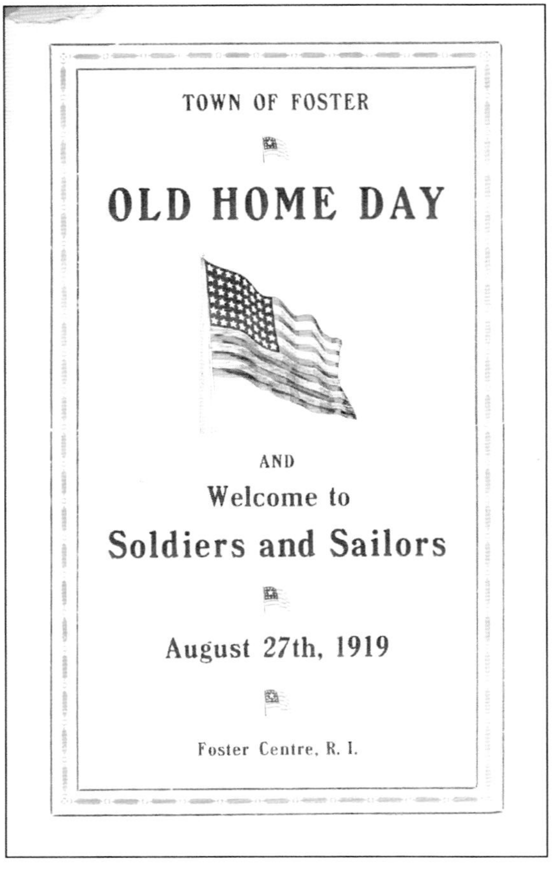
TOWN OF FOSTER

OLD HOME DAY

AND

Welcome to

Soldiers and Sailors

August 27th, 1919

Foster Centre, R. I.

When elder John Hammond left Foster in 1815, life went out of the Second Baptist Church, and over time, the meetinghouse fell into disrepair. However, the Ladies Home Mission Society of the Foster Center Christian Church organized the first Old Home Day celebration in 1904 to raise funds to repair it. The fair was a huge success, and the proceeds completely restored the meetinghouse.

This brochure was handed out to attendees of the Old Home Day celebration in 1919. Being the close-knit community they were, locals wanted to publicly extend a welcome home to their servicemen.

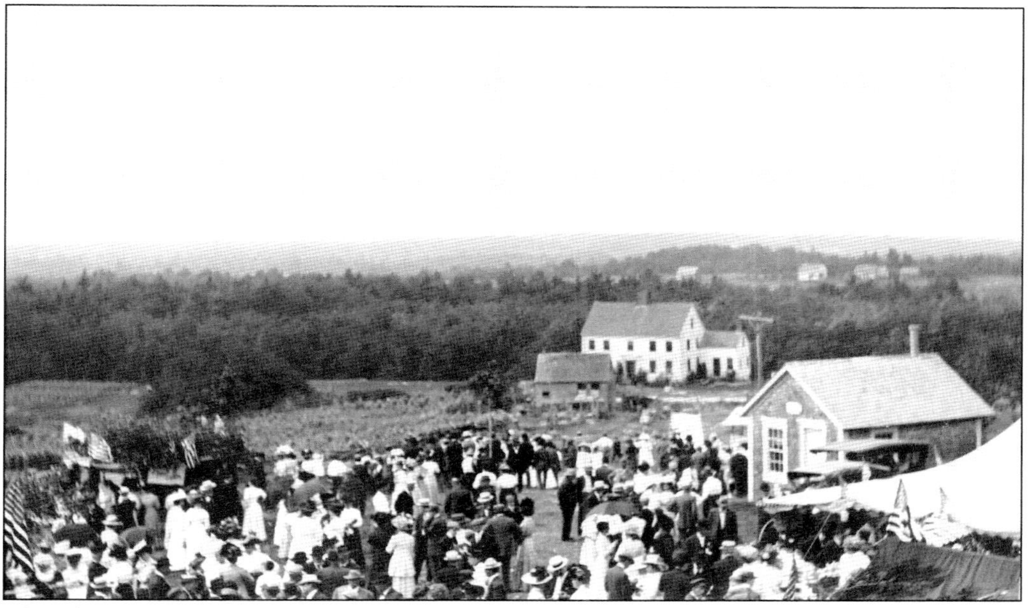

This photograph depicts the 1910 Foster Old Home Day celebration at the Foster Town House property. Looking to the northwest, it was taken from one of the windows on the second floor of the Foster Town House. The image not only shows a portion of the townspeople enjoying the day but also how much of the land was allotted to farming. James P. Nichols's large, white home can be seen in the distance and also on page 32.

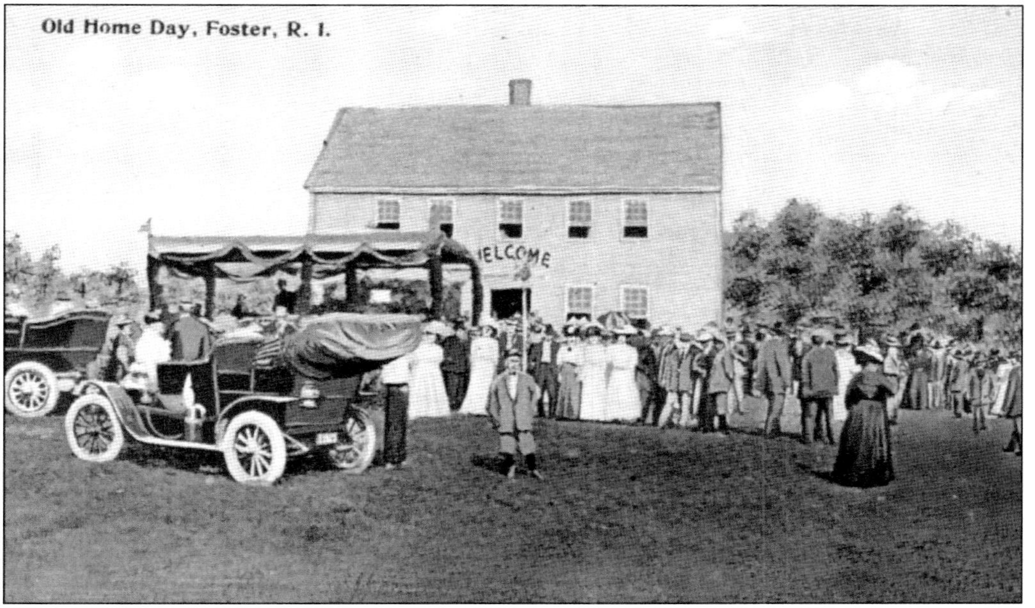

This postcard shows the 1912 Old Home Day gathering. It is on the grounds of elder John Hammond's original meetinghouse, known as the Foster Town House since 1822. The gathering has been discontinued from time to time, as during World War II. However, it is still going strong, and the celebration now spans the last Friday, Saturday, and Sunday of July yearly at the same place, Howard Hill Road in Foster Center. (Courtesy of Richard Siembab.)

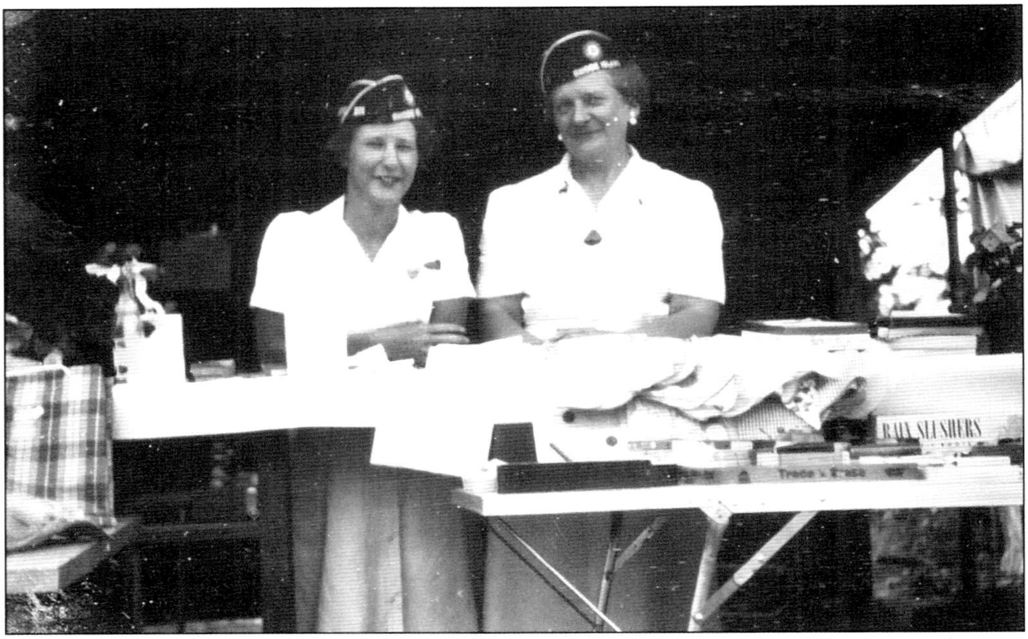

This photograph was taken on July 27, 1957, at Foster Old Home Days. Those pictured at the booth of the American Legion Auxiliary are Barbara Webster (left) and Ruth Keidel. (Courtesy of Michele Harris.)

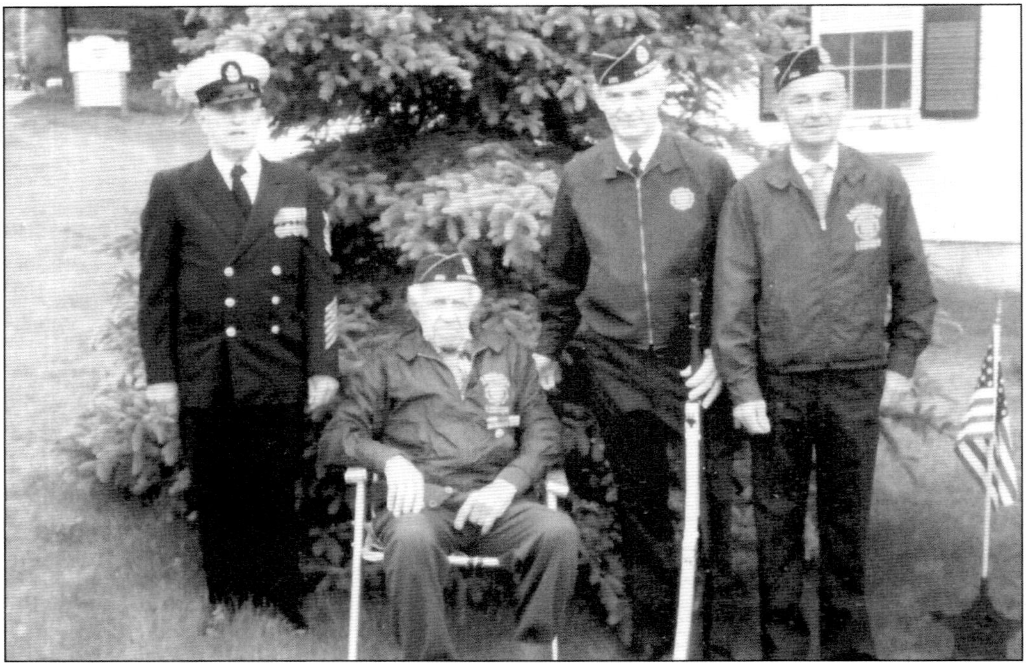

This photograph was taken after a Memorial Day parade in the 1990s. The servicemen pictured are, from left to right, Albert Thoman, Russell Wells, George Newman, and Gordon Mumford. Russell Wells always proclaimed he was in three wars: World War I, World War II, and the WWHW (the War With His Wife). (Courtesy of George Newman.)

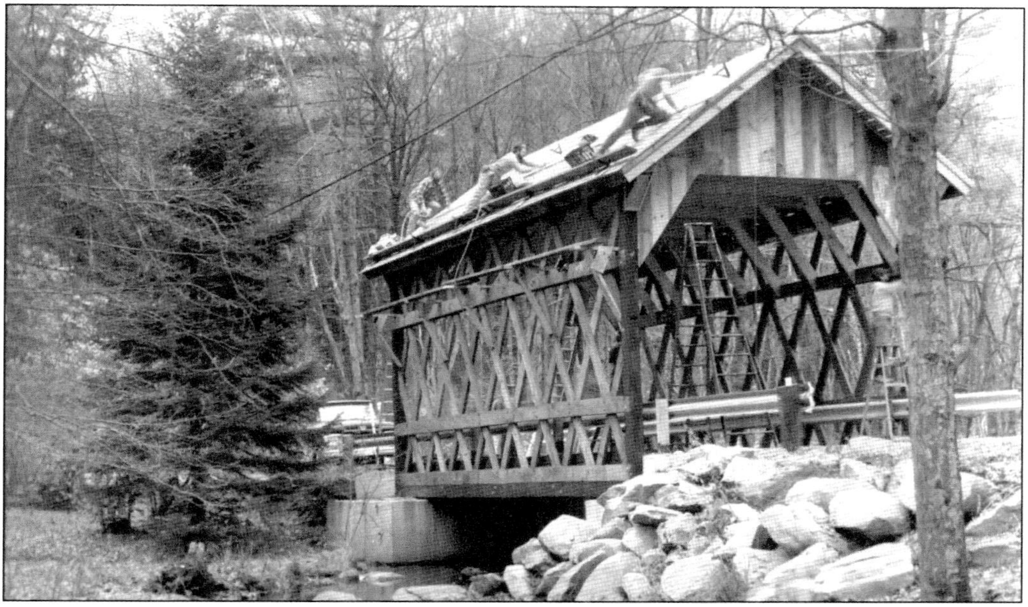

In 1986, Robert Salisbury suggested to the town council the idea of building the only covered bridge on a state road in Rhode Island. Six years later, Rhode Island Department of Transportation (RIDOT) finally agreed on a site where Central Pike crosses over Hemlock Brook. Charles Borders was appointed chairman of the bridge committee, and a call for volunteers was answered enthusiastically. Funds were donated by Citizen's Bank, and Providence Water gave the project timber from the reservoir property. No state or federal funds were used. The Swamp Meadows Covered Bridge (below) was dedicated on May 23, 1993. Rhode Island could now join with its five sister New England states (known for their covered bridges) because the folks of Foster had united and built their very own covered bridge. (Both, courtesy of Russ Benson.)

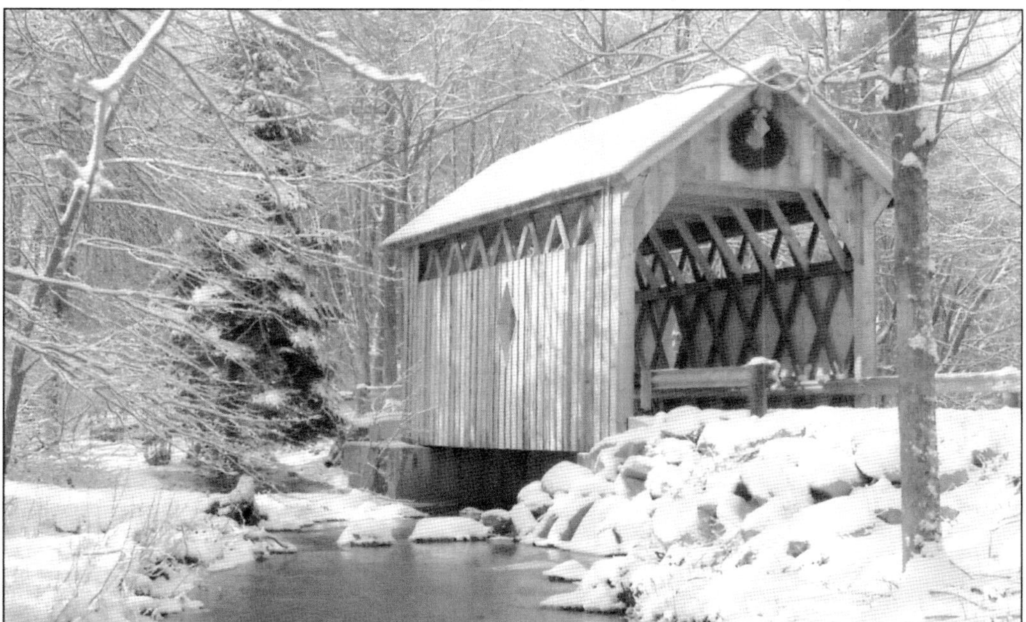

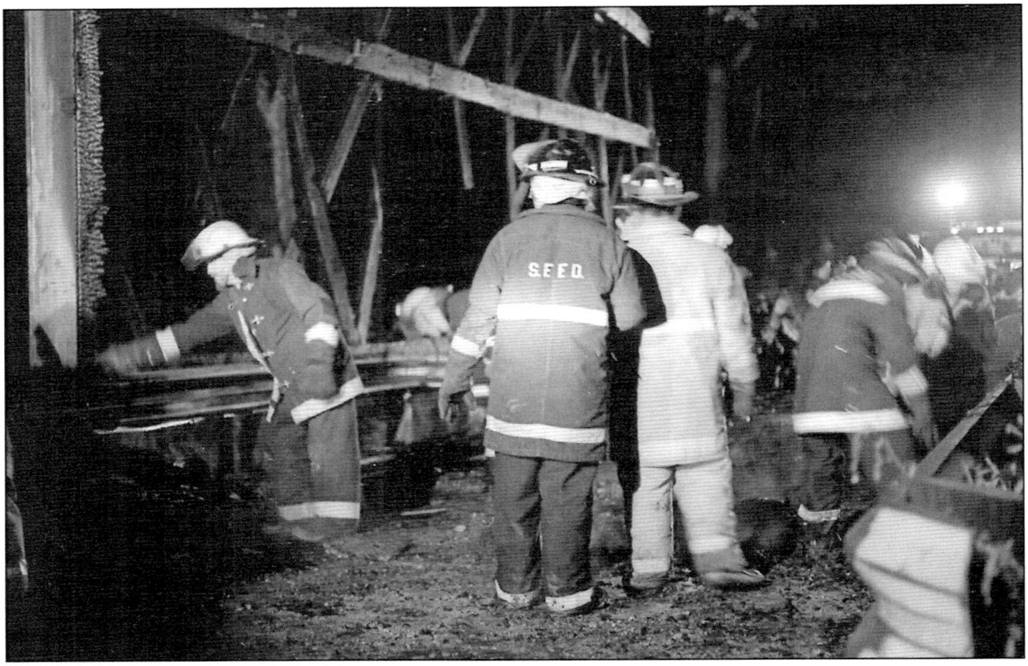

This photograph was taken on the evening of September 11, 1993, after vandals had set fire to the bridge, totally destroying it. By the time it was reported and the fire company arrived on the scene, the bridge was engulfed in flames that were out of control. (Courtesy of Rus Benson.)

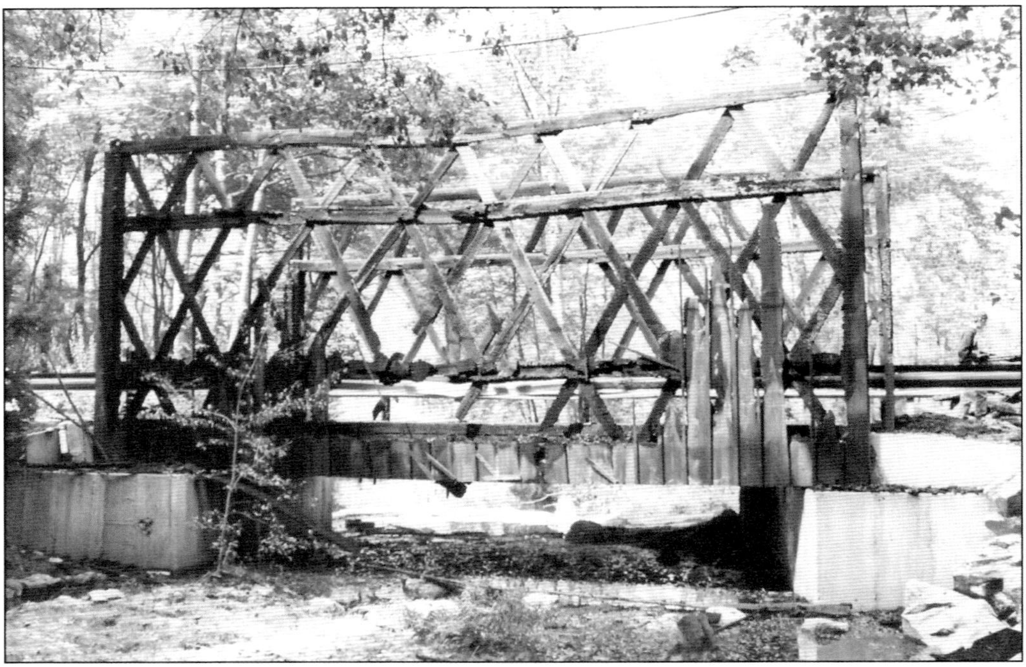

This photograph, taken the following day, shows the devastation of the vandals' actions. The townspeople were not sure they wanted to put the time and work into building a replacement. (Courtesy of Heidi Colwell.)

When money and volunteers poured in from all over the state, the townspeople made the decision to rebuild. That is exactly what they are busy doing in this photograph. Again, Rhode Islanders would have their own covered bridge. (Courtesy of Heidi Colwell.)

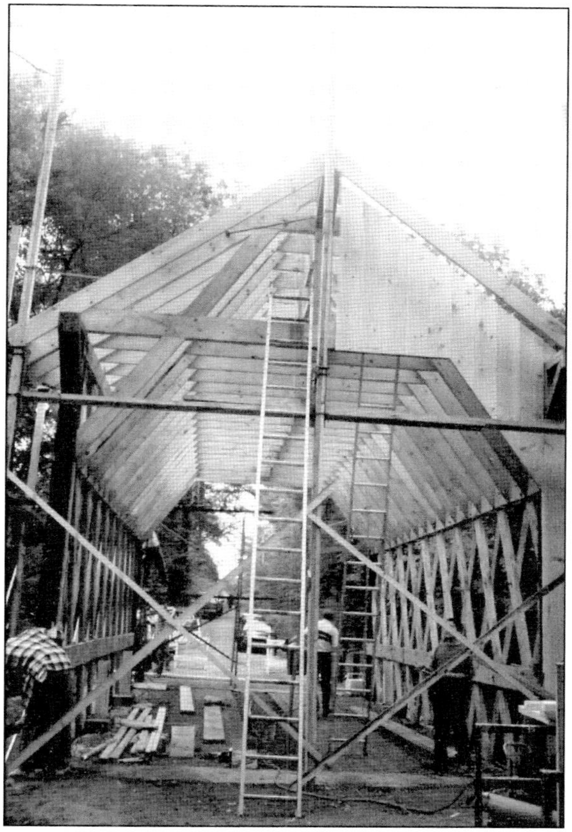

This photograph, taken in 2010, is of the second Swamp Meadows Covered Bridge, dedicated on November 5, 1994. The first person to have the honor of crossing the bridge was Lillian Stone, age 98. She lived to be 108 years old (see page 122). (Author's collection.)

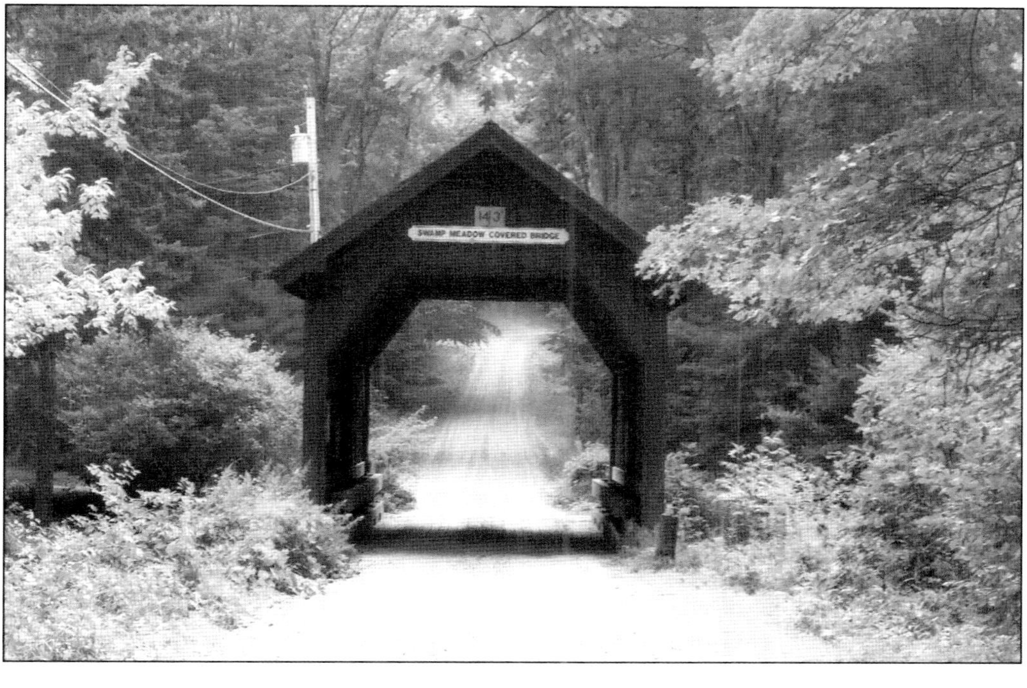

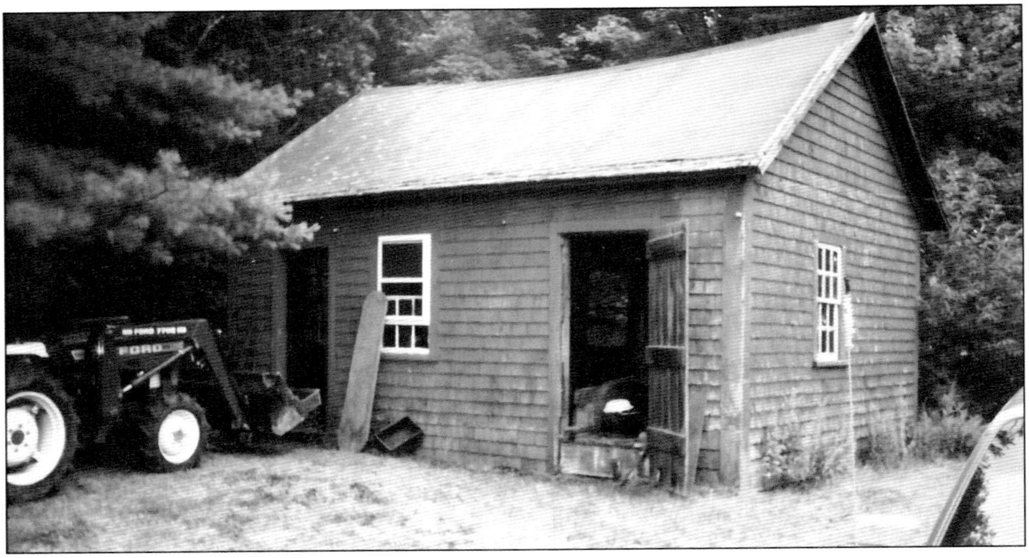

Ira Winsor built his blacksmith shop, pictured here, around 1860 on Winsor Road. It stayed in the Winsor-Hayfield family until 1992, when George Brayton was concerned it might be sold and taken out of town. Therefore, he and wife Dorothy bought it on September 23, 1993, and donated it to the Foster Preservation Society in 1994. More than 50 townspeople volunteered to dismantle the shop and transport it to the Foster town grounds, where it would be reconstructed in the spring. The shop was used mainly for shoeing oxen. However, oxen cannot stand on three legs while being shod and have to be supported. The oxen sling frame below is being removed from the building by Marshall Spaulding (left) as George Brayton observes. A new leather sling was made and donated by the La-Salle Harness Company in Scituate. (Both, courtesy of George Brayton.)

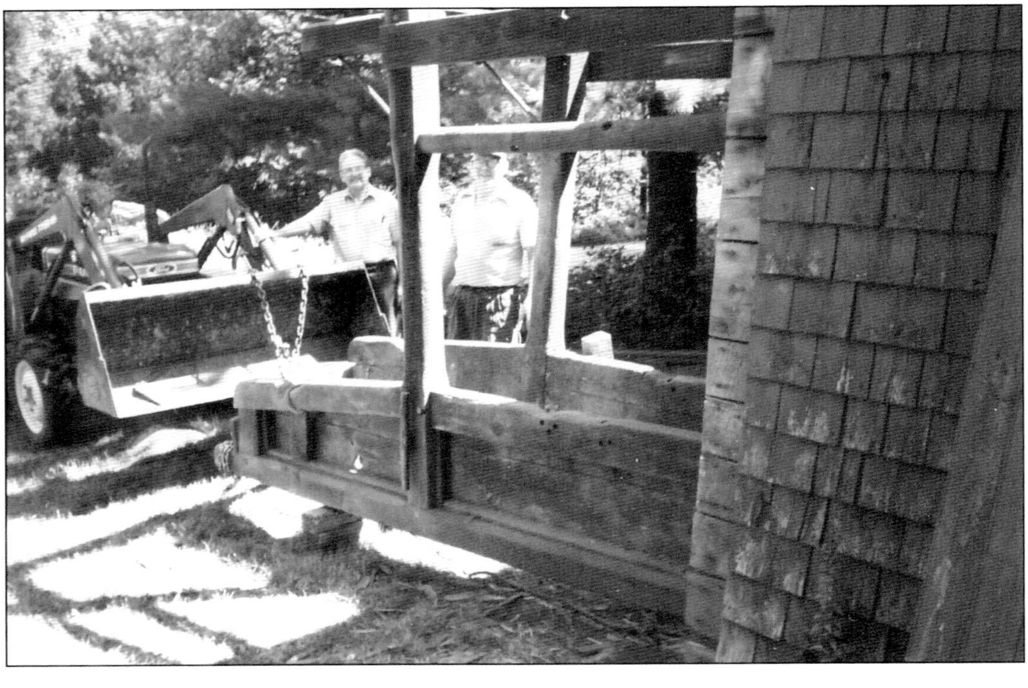

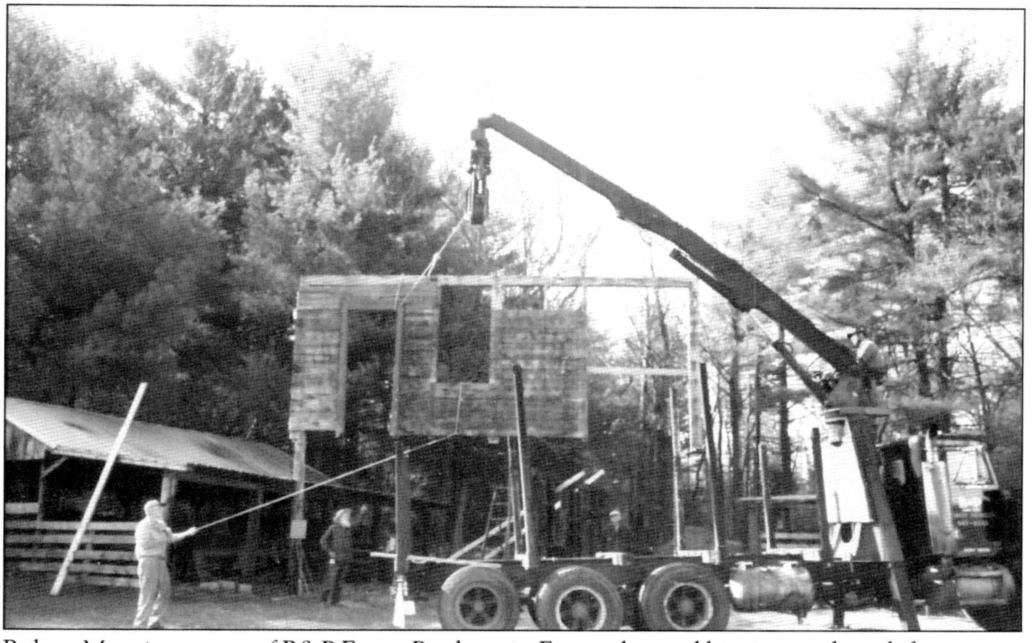

Robert Maguire, owner of B&P Forest Products in Foster, donated his time and truck for moving the sections of the shop that had been dismantled. He not only moved them to the Foster Town House grounds in the fall but also came back in the spring to reassemble them. (Courtesy of Heidi Colwell.)

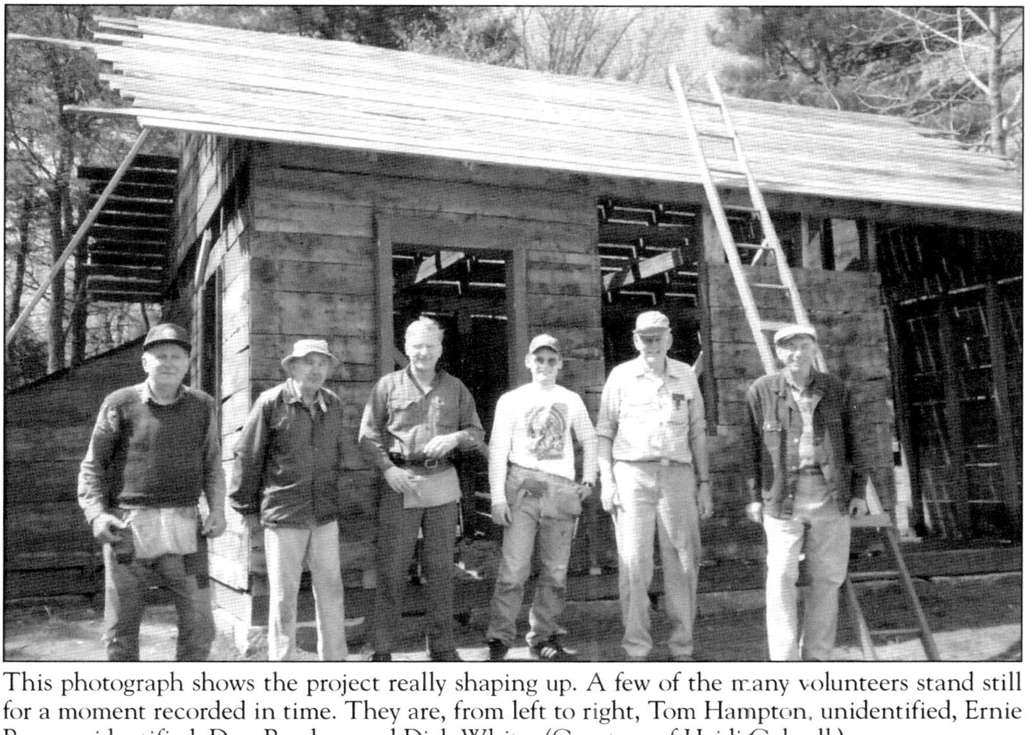

This photograph shows the project really shaping up. A few of the many volunteers stand still for a moment recorded in time. They are, from left to right, Tom Hampton, unidentified, Ernie Ross, unidentified, Don Boyden, and Dick White. (Courtesy of Heidi Colwell.)

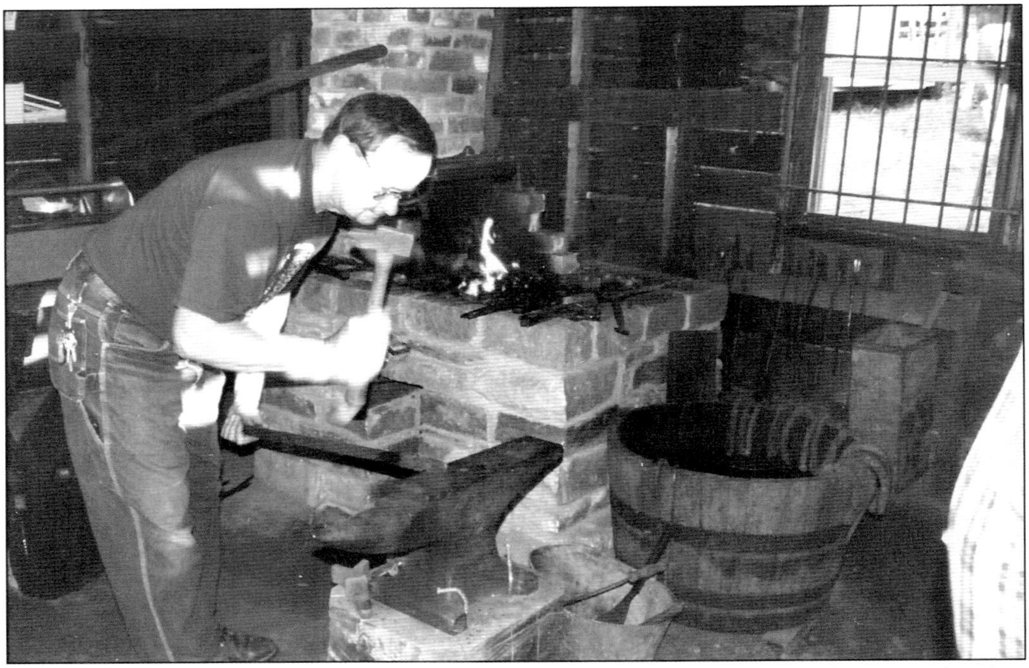

This photograph, taken in 1995, shows the Ira Winsor Blacksmith Shop totally restored and in working order. Fred Mikkelsen shapes an iron bar as the fire roars beside him. Below, George Brayton (left) is probably saying, "We did it." James "Bud" Heaton (standing in the doorway) was a retired welder from Scituate whose hobby was blacksmithing. At a special ceremony on April 1, 1995, the Rhode Island Historical Preservation Commission presented a Preservation Award to the Foster Preservation Society. It is shown displayed by the door. (Both, courtesy of George Brayton.)

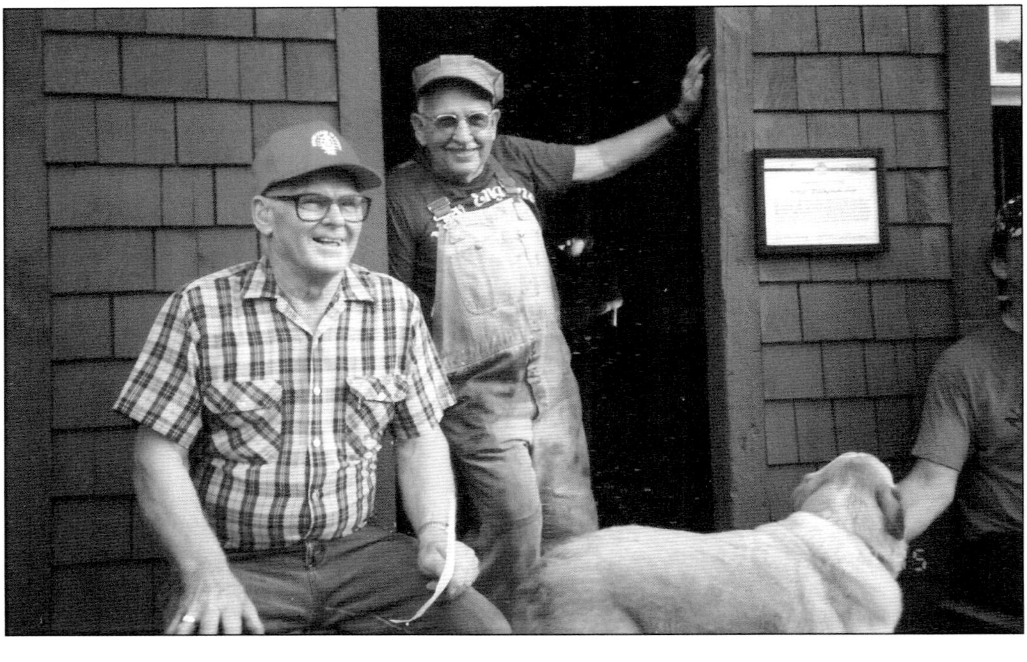

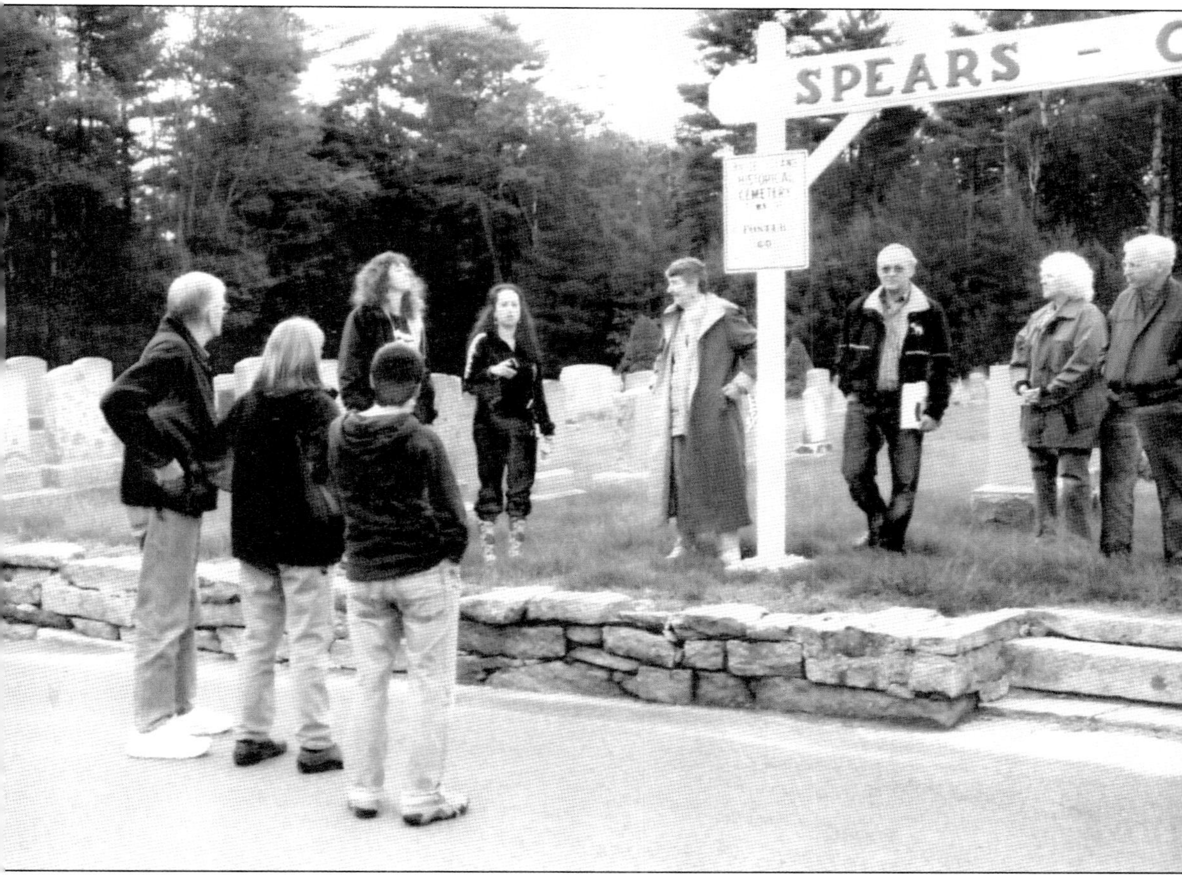

This photograph was taken June 14, 2011, at the Spears Cemetery on North Road. The Gravestone Girls are giving a lecture on images carved on old gravestones for the Foster Preservation Society (FPS). They also give lectures on cemetery art, history, and symbolism as well as teach gravestone rubbing classes. Their stated mission is to "Keep Our Dead Alive." On October 7, 1905, Henry Nye was appointed by the town council to procure a lot for burial of poor soldiers, sailors, and marines who were Civil War veterans. There are 393 inscriptions through the cemetery, dated from 1816 to 1991. Standing in the road are, from left to right, Richard Walls, Cathy Walls, and Tracy Mahaffey. Those standing in the grass are, from left to right, the Gravestone Girls, Maggie White and Brenda Sullivan; Janet White; Raymond A. Wolf, the author of this book; Maggie Fennessey; and Ernie Ross. The following verse is from "There's Room in Heaven" written by Helen O. Larson at age 83: "There's always room in Heaven, for one more Angel so fair / So let us live for the day, when God will take us there." (Courtesy of Ed Robinson.)

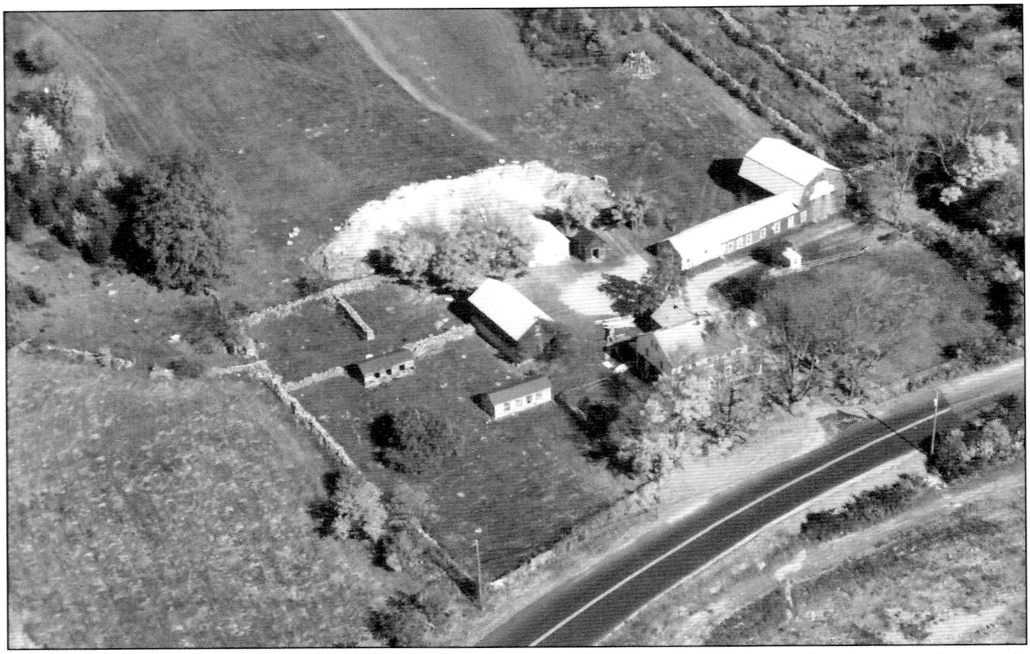

This is an aerial view of the Paine-Bennett Farm on Old Plainfield Pike at the intersection with Victory Highway (Route 102). The Paines owned the farm until after 1862; the Bennetts held it until 1895. Over the next 90-plus years, the farm became run-down for lack of attention. Then, in 1987, Richard and Cathy Walls viewed it, bought it, and started a love relationship of restoring it. Over the last 14 years, they have refurbished six of the nine buildings, and it is one of the most complete farms in Foster. To the left of the large gambrel-roofed shingled barn (below) is an attached cobblestone dairy house, built in 1888. Seen next to the wall is a beautiful three-seater outhouse. The farmhouse pictured on the next page is to the left of the field. (Both, courtesy of Cathy Walls.)

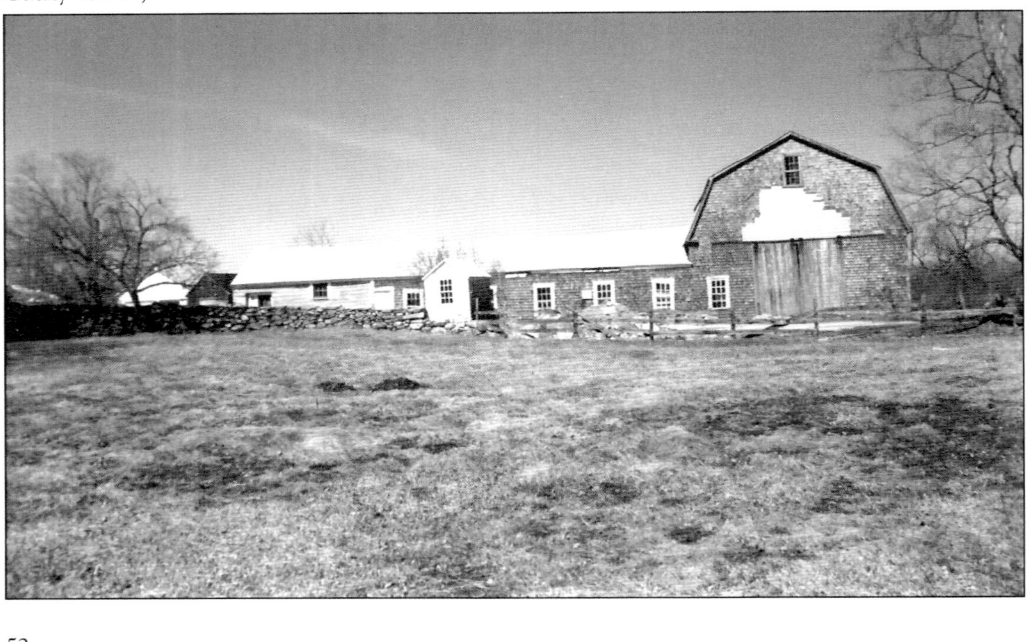

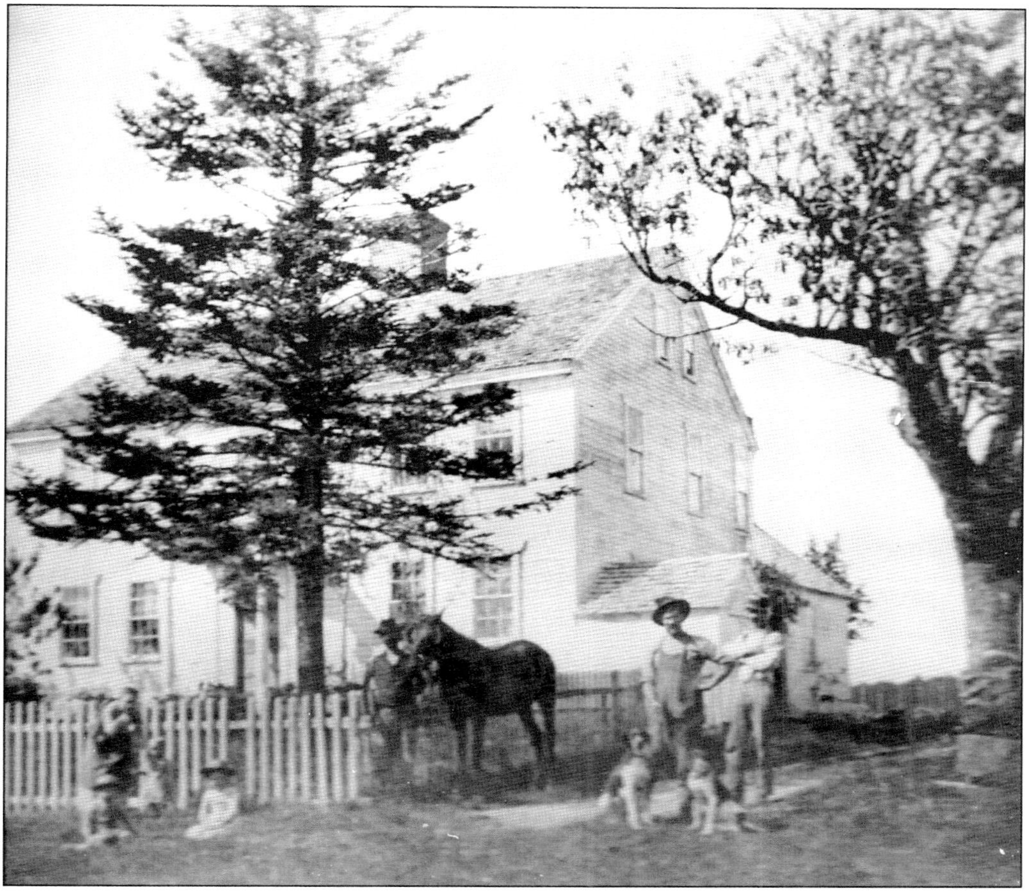

This photograph, taken in 1893, shows one of Foster's finest Federal-style farmhouses. It belonged to the Bennett family and is five bays wide and three bays deep. The 2.5-story house has a 1.5-story ell set at a right angle in the rear. The Bennetts pictured are, from left to right, Etta L. with Walter M. and James E., Leroy A., with his horse, Eilia H., and Warren W. with his hunting dogs. The final man is unidentified. The back of the deed below records that another Bennett, Barnard, bought the farm on October 5, 1889, as it is recorded in Book 17 on page 379 in the Town of Foster's records. (Both, courtesy of Cathy Walls.)

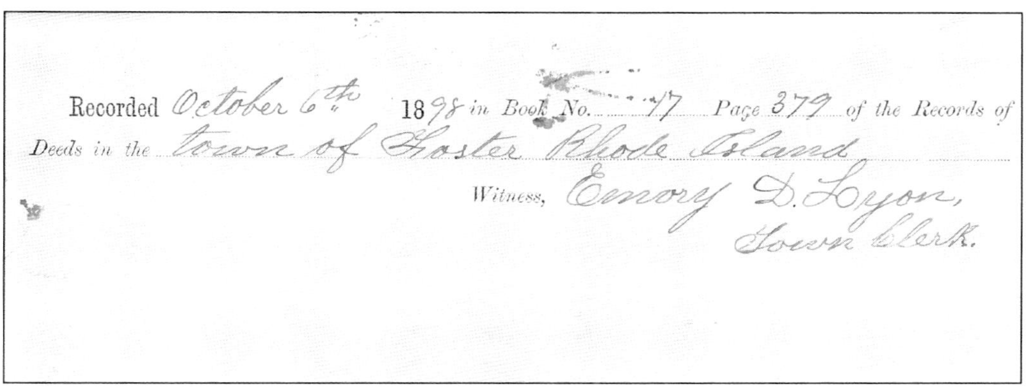

Recorded October 6th 1898 in Book No. 17 Page 379 of the Records of Deeds in the town of Foster Rhode Island

Witness, Emory D. Lyon, Town Clerk.

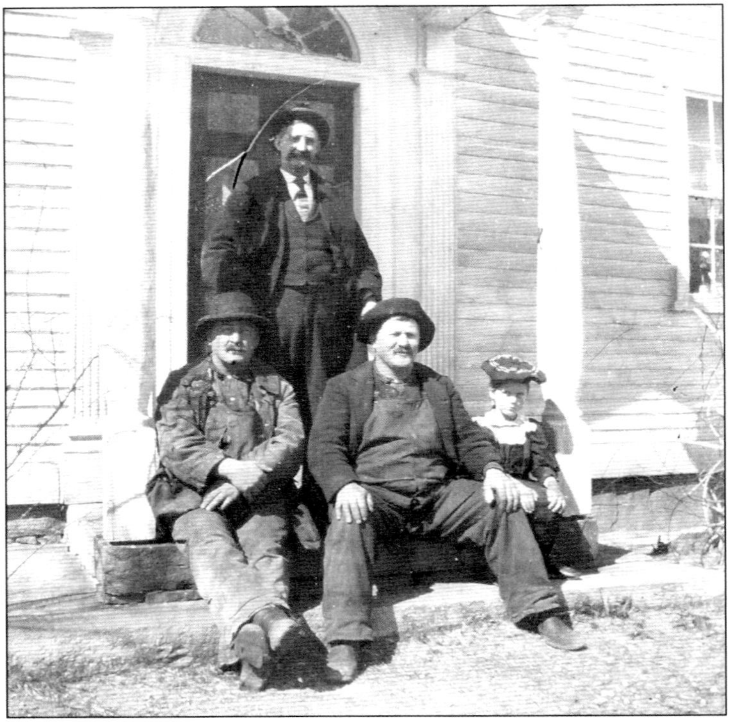

It is not clear where or when this photograph was taken. The little girl and the man standing look like they are ready to attend church. The two men seated are more casually dressed. (Courtesy of Cathy Walls.)

This stone dairy house was built in 1888. A shingled addition appears to have been added at a later date. (The large barn—approximately 30 feet by 40 feet—that was added even later is seen on page 52). (Courtesy of Cathy Walls.)

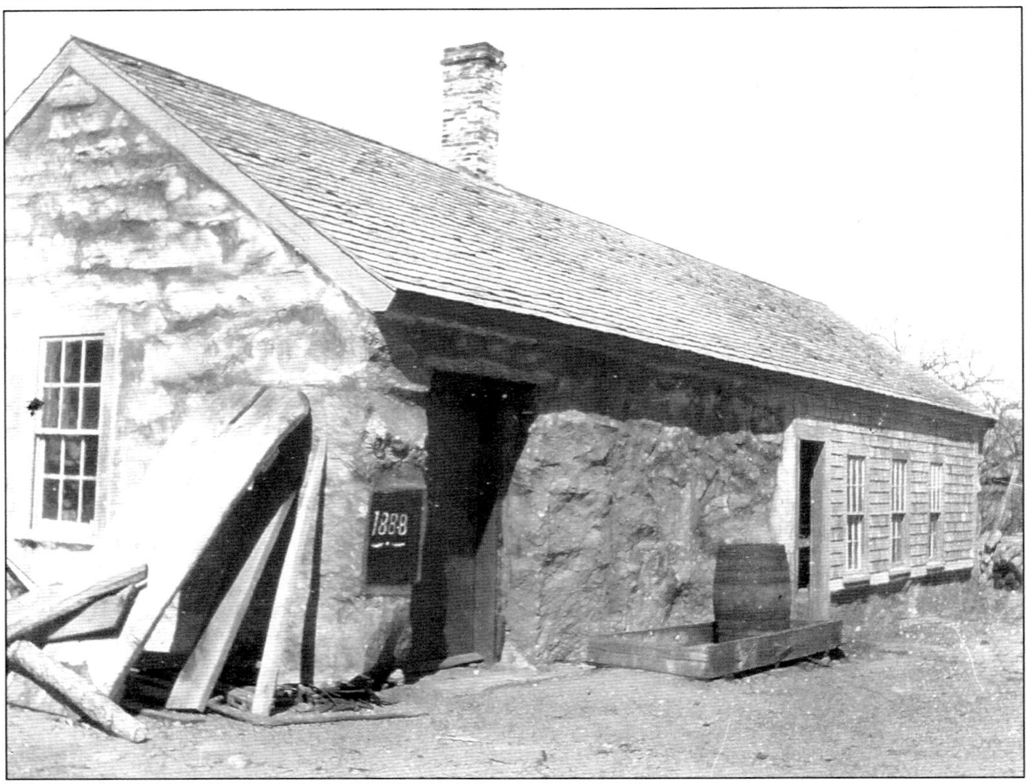

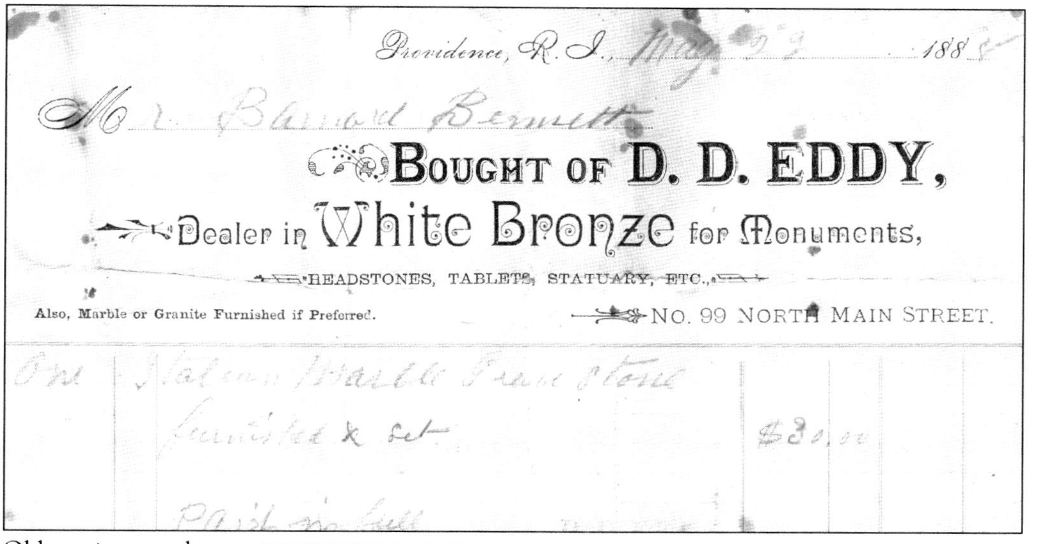

Providence, R.I., May 22 1888

Mr. Barnard Bennett

BOUGHT OF D. D. EDDY,

Dealer in White Bronze for Monuments,

HEADSTONES, TABLETS, STATUARY, ETC.,

Also, Marble or Granite Furnished if Preferred.

No. 99 NORTH MAIN STREET.

One | Italian Marble Grave Stone furnished & set | $30.00

Paid in full

Old receipts can be fascinating. This one, dated May 22, 1888, is for one finished Italian marble gravestone. Barnard Bennett paid $30 for it from D.D. Eddy, located at 99 North Main Street in Providence. (Courtesy of Cathy Walls.)

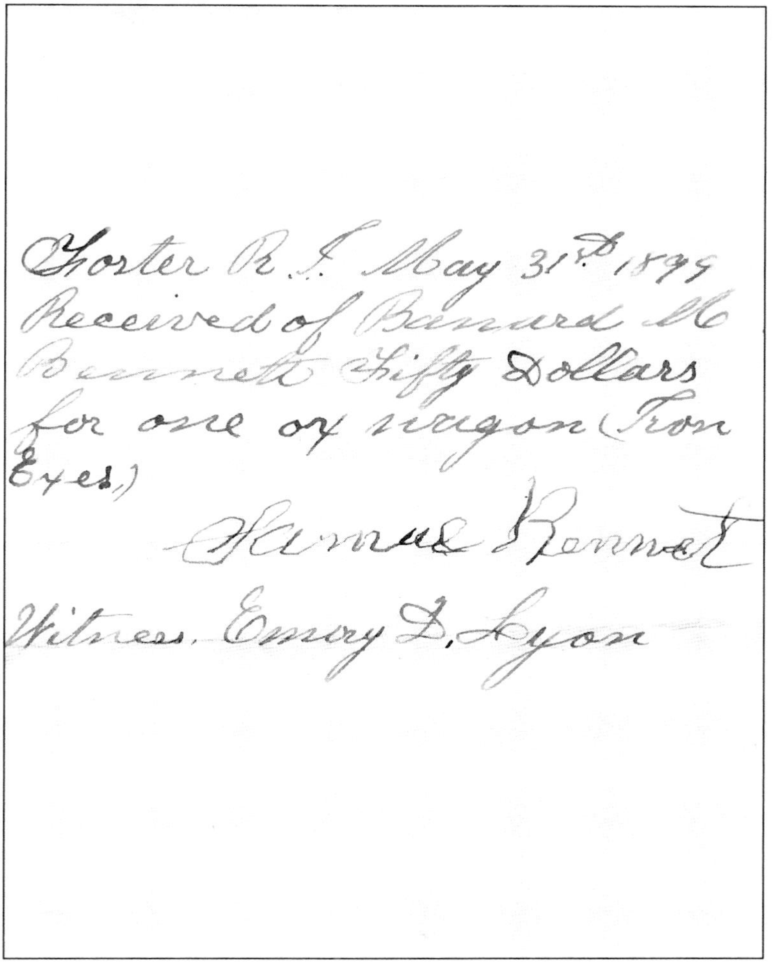

Foster R.I. May 31st 1899

Received of Barnard M Bennett Fifty Dollars for one ox wagon (Iron Eyes.)

Samul Bennett

Witness. Emory D. Lyon

This receipt is interesting. Samul (his spelling) Bennett sold one ox wagon to Barnard Bennett on May 31, 1899, for $50. Even though the receipt states he received payment, he still had it witnessed by the town clerk, Emory D. Lyon (see the bottom of page 53.) (Courtesy of Cathy Walls.)

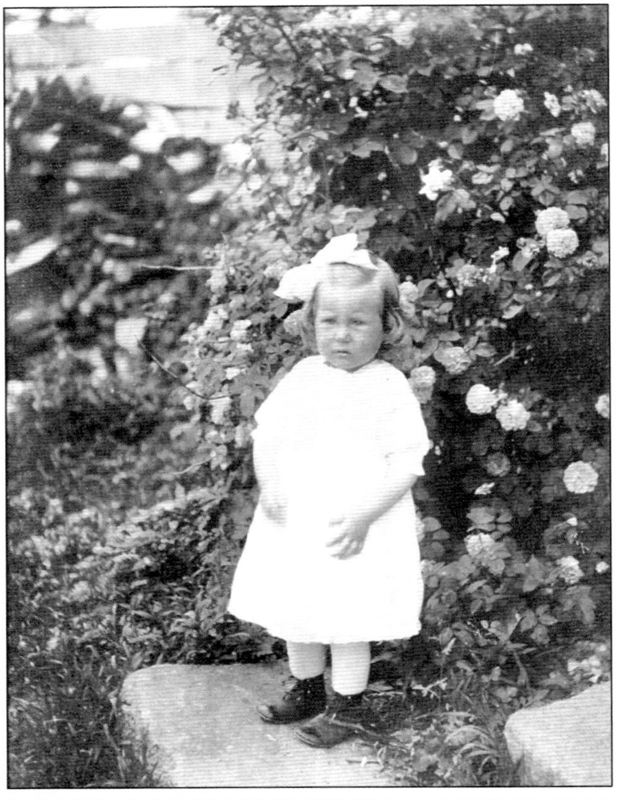

A book about Foster would not be complete without mentioning Viola Ulm, who has earned the title of town historian. The picture on the left of Viola was taken on the Walker farm when she was only three years old. (Courtesy of Viola Ulm.)

Viola is shown in front of the Ancient Chamber on Howard Hill Road in 1999. Today, in 2011, at the age of 93, she is as sharp as a tack and a wealth of knowledge about the days gone by. (Courtesy of Viola Ulm.)

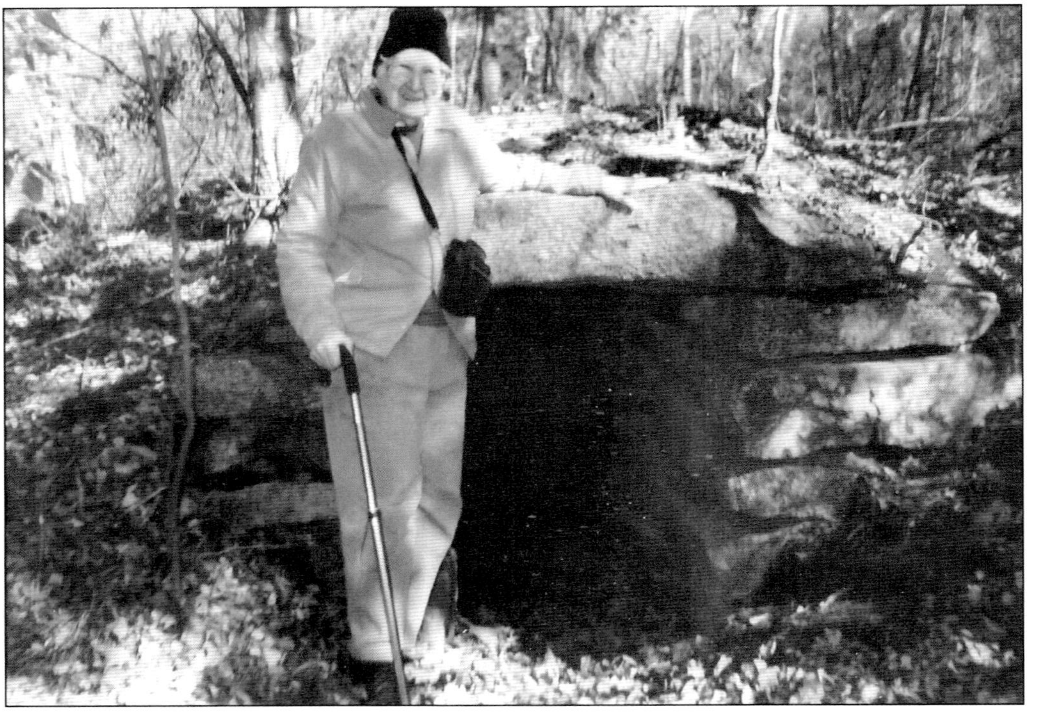

This is a photograph of Viola Ulm's grandparents. Adelbert Earl Card was born in 1857 and married Amy Viola Taylor on August 25, 1883. Amy was born in 1867. One of their children was Viola's mother, Lena Card (pictured below). Amy's father, John Taylor, was the author's great-great-grandfather. John's mother-in-law was Melissa Ann Hopkins-Burchard (pictured on page 124). (Courtesy of Viola Ulm.)

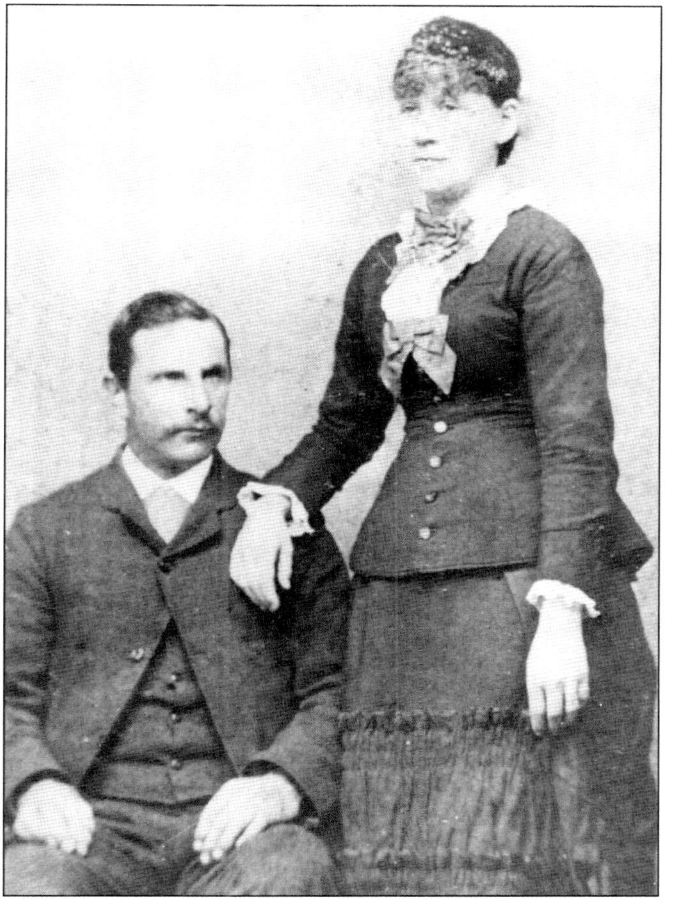

This photograph, taken in 1917, shows Lena Card Walker cultivating corn on the Bennett Hill Farm. Lena was pregnant with Viola at the time. This was a time when people did what needed to be done. (Courtesy of Viola Ulm.).

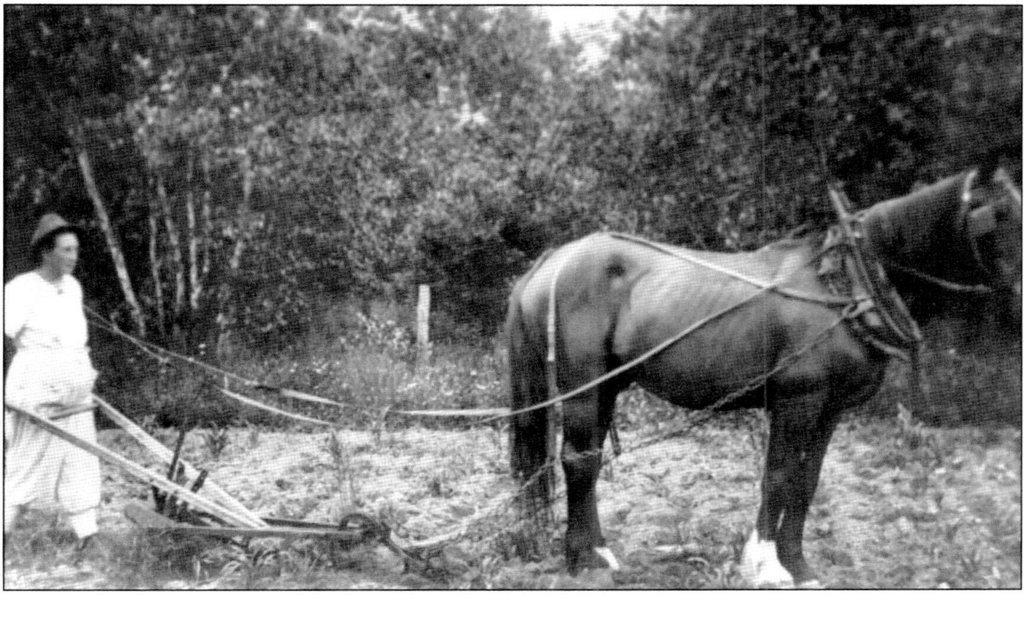

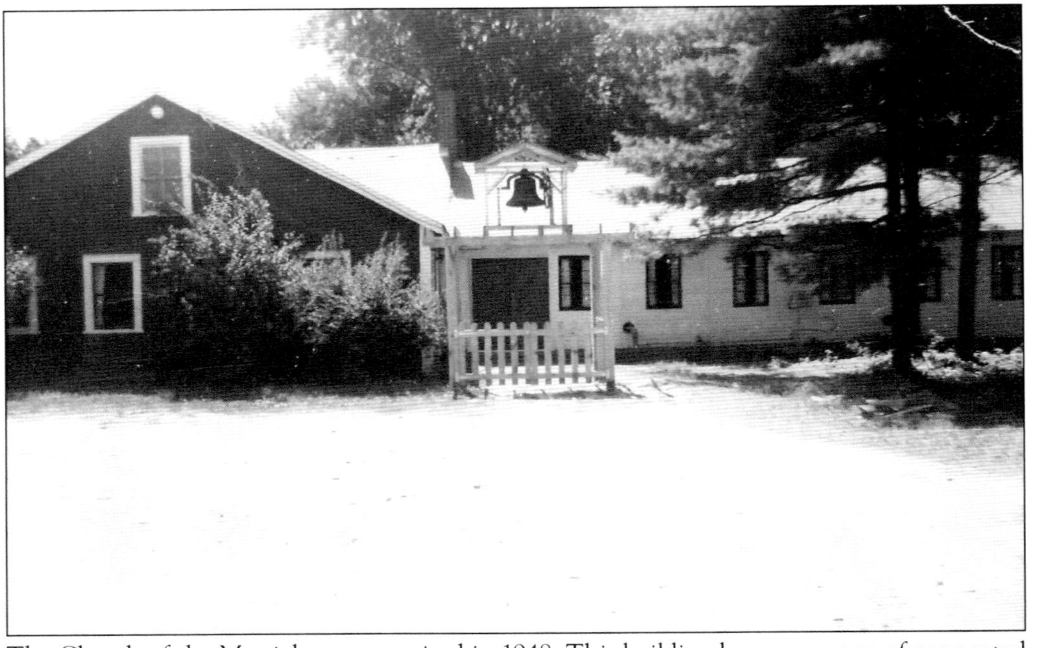

The Church of the Messiah was organized in 1948. This building began as a row of connected cabins. There was a lunchroom in this structure, and a dental clinic was located in the back. In 1956, part of the Christ Church building from Coventry was added, and this church was complete. Pews came from St. Ansgarius in Providence. (Courtesy of George Newman.)

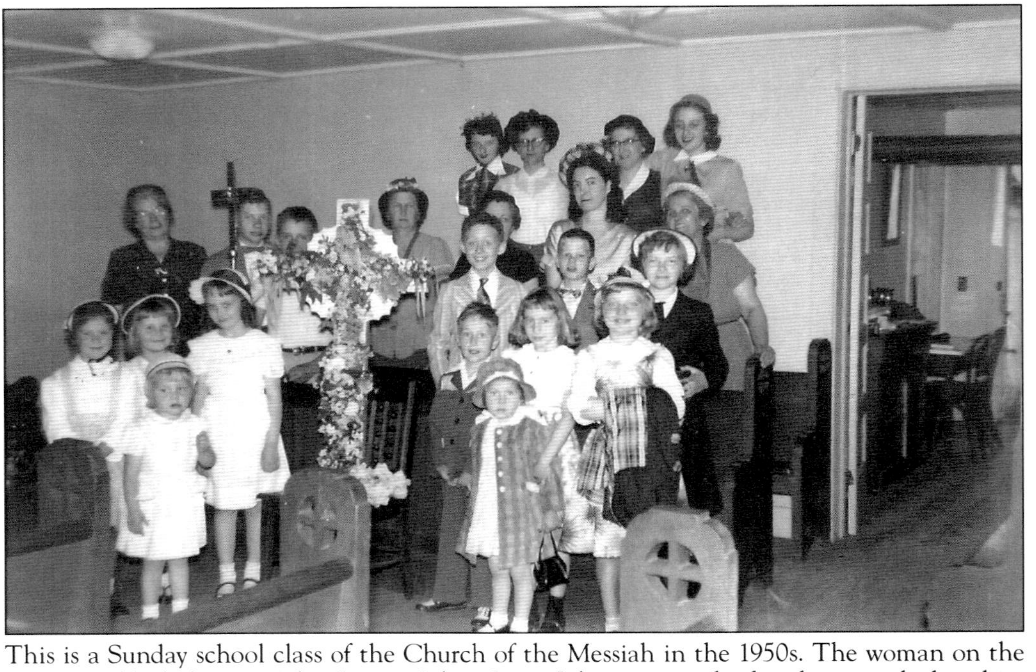

This is a Sunday school class of the Church of the Messiah in the 1950s. The woman on the left in the black dress is Helen Bemis. Sylvia Corey-Johnson is in the fourth row with the white blouse (third from right), and Lee Pray-Niles is beside her in the black dress (second from right). Everyone else is unidentified. (Courtesy of Mildred Arline Corey.)

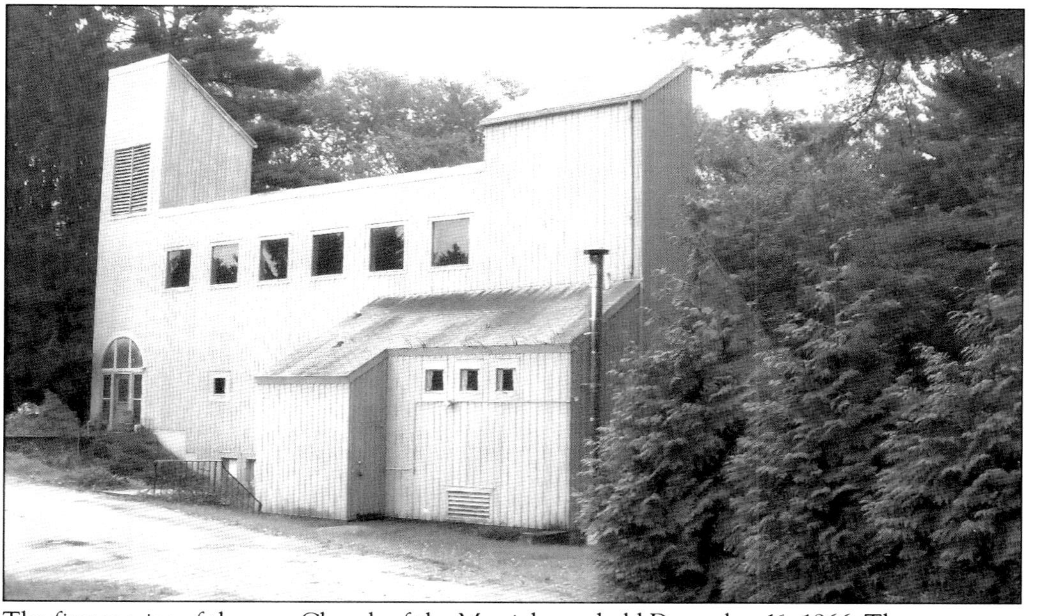

The first service of the new Church of the Messiah was held December 11, 1966. The organ was played by 14-year-old Donald Dame. The church is located on the corner of Foster Center Road and Danielson Pike. The following verse is from "He's the Same Messiah" by Helen O. Larson: "Ask someone to pray, and the healing will be done I know / By the same Messiah that, walked on the earth so long ago." (Author's collection.)

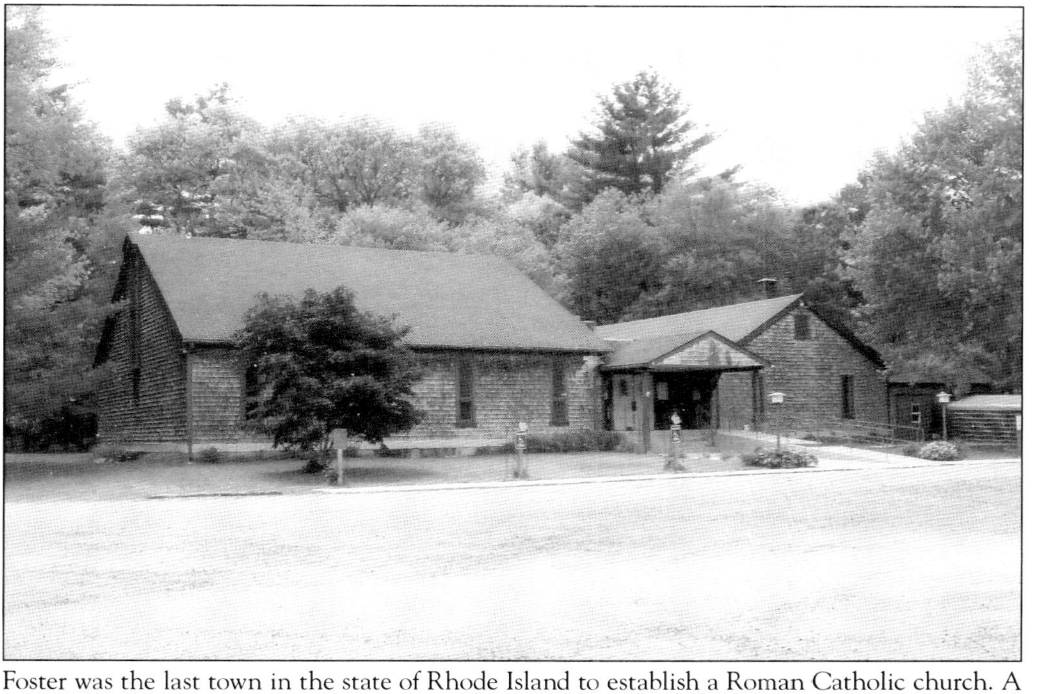

Foster was the last town in the state of Rhode Island to establish a Roman Catholic church. A mission was established here in 1970, a parish in 1972, and St. Paul the Apostle Church (pictured here in June 2011) was completed on March 3, 1973. (Author's collection.)

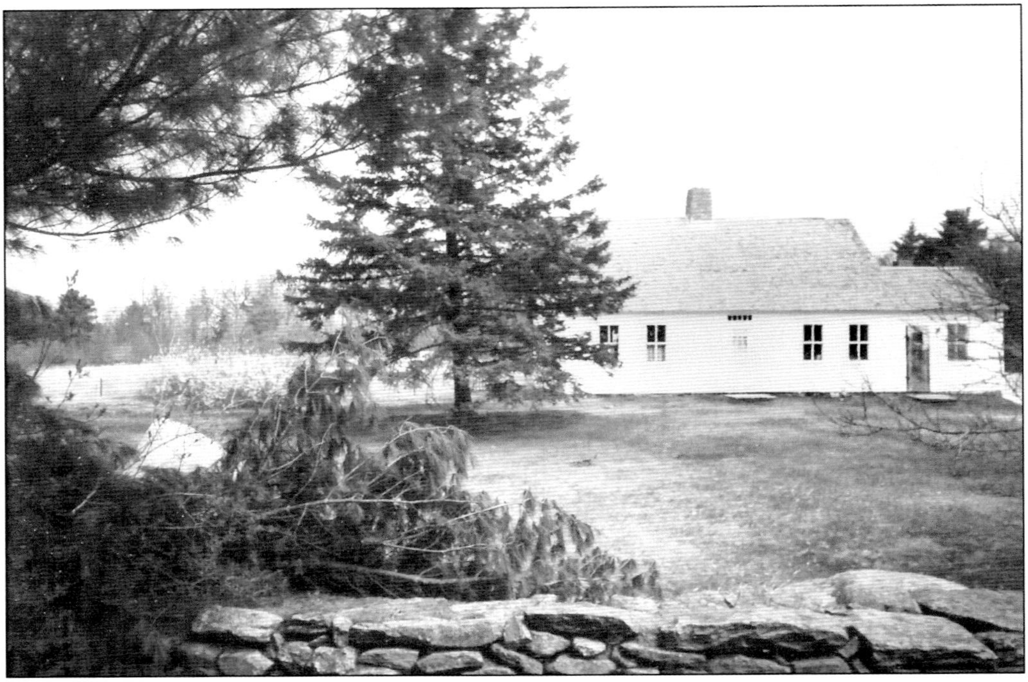

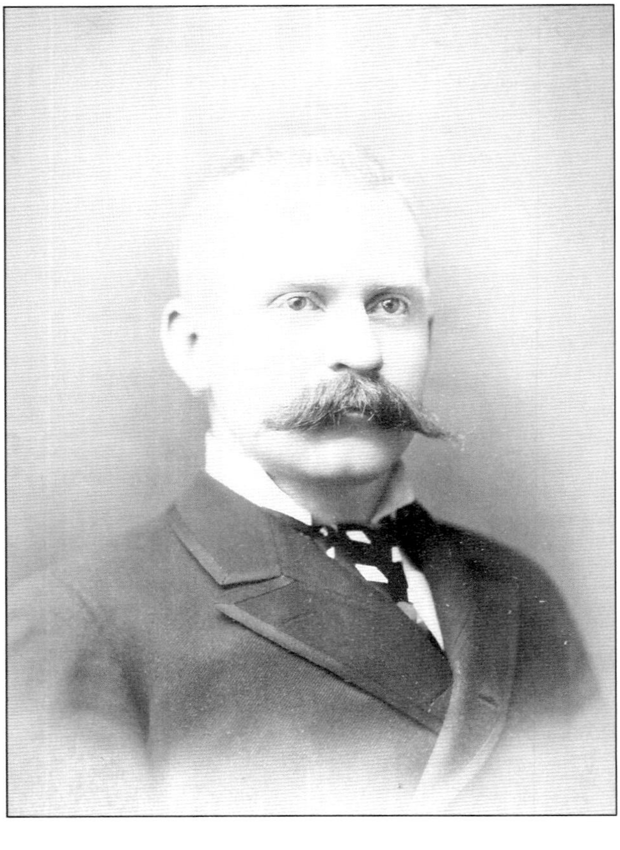

This is a photograph of the Randall Farm on Foster Center Road. It was built in the 1780s, and Zephaniah Randall was born here in 1791. He and his wife, Marcy Tillinghast-Randall, raised seven children here, one of the children being Thurber Randall, born on March 16, 1828. Thurber and his wife, Celia, would have three children. The middle child, William R. Randall, is pictured at left. (Courtesy of Ed Robinson.)

William R. Randall was born on August 14, 1858. He married Minnie Albert Goff, and they lived on the Randall Farm for many years. William died on March 21, 1933, while living in East Providence. (Courtesy of Sandra Ball.)

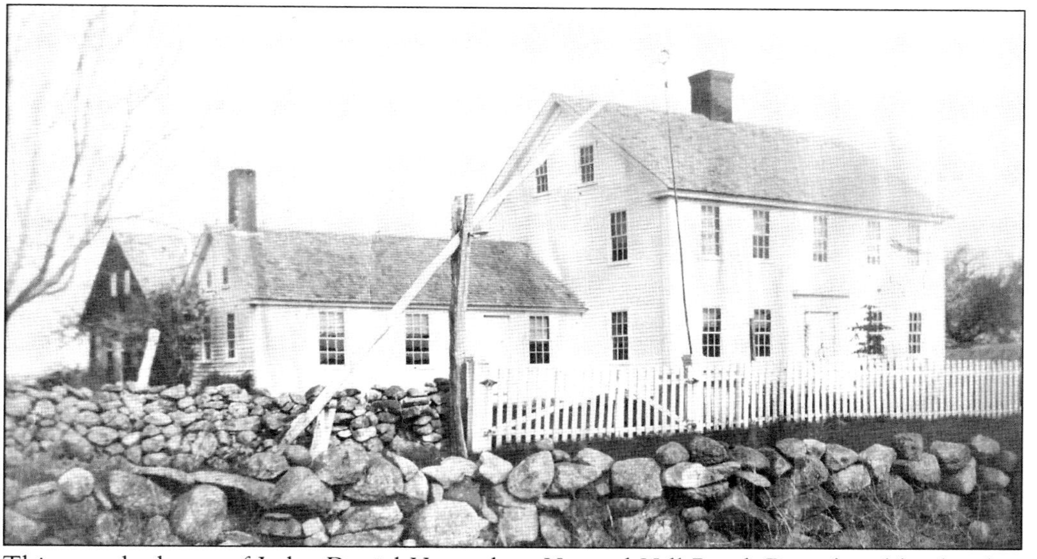

This was the home of Judge Daniel Howard on Howard Hill Road. Daniel and his brother Gorton built it in 1805. In 1811, Daniel bought his brother's share and rebuilt the farm in 1856. The photograph below shows, from left to right, William R. and Minnie Randall along with Judge Howard's grandson Daniel Howard and his wife, Hannah. The families are on vacation at Niagara Gorge in New York in 1888. They most likely traveled by stagecoach and train. (Both, courtesy of Sandra Ball.)

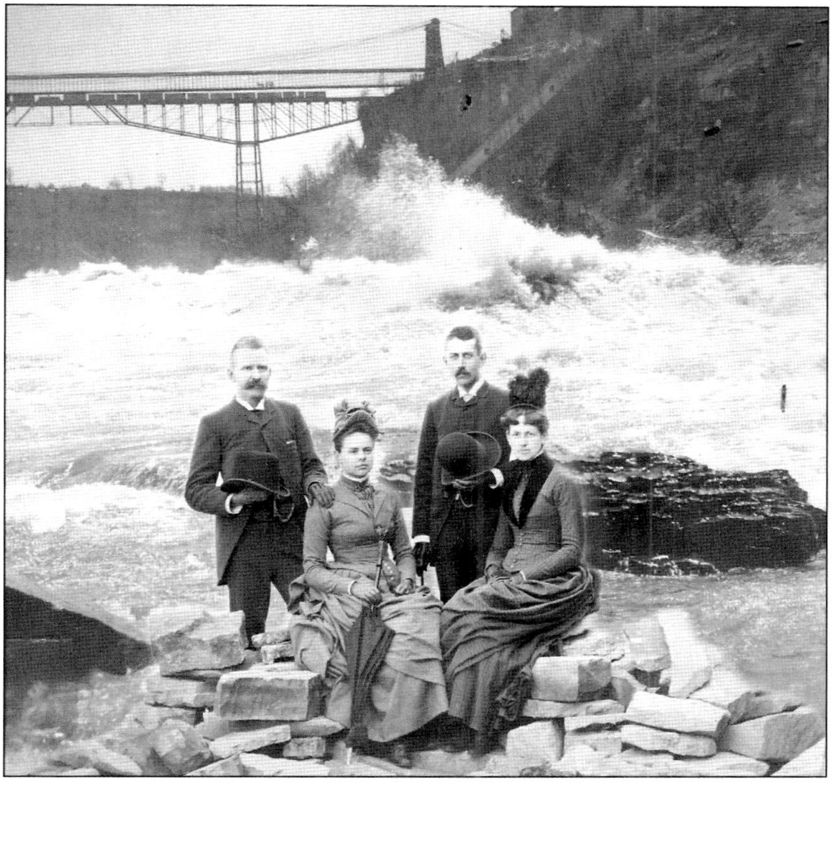

FOSTER TAX BOOK.

1870.

NAMES.	Real.	Person'l	Real Tax.	Pers'al Tax.
Adams Lillis R	1200	......	12 00	......
Aldrich Jonathan, jr	600	......	6 00	......
Anderson Nathaniel	200	......	2 00	......
Angell Joshua	2400	......	24 00	......
Aldrich Nelson W	150	......	1 50	......
Arnold Cyrus, for wife	400	......	4 00	......
Arnold Mowry P	3900	3000	39 00	30 00
Arnold Piercy and Hill Rachael	100	......	1 00	......
Arnold Welcome	600	......	6 00	......
Arnold Mowry P. jr	......	500	....	5 00
Aylsworth Cyrus, for wife	1000	......	10 00	......
Austin Henry	1200	......	12 00	......
Austin John F	400	......	4 00	......
Austin Joseph R	1100	......	11 00	......
Austin Thirsa, for third	200	......	2 00	......
Aylesworth Darius R., for wife	......	700	......	7 00
Baker Wm. I. P., for wife	1100	......	11 00	......
Baldwin John, for wife	1000	500	10 00	5 00
Balcome Alfred W	2500	......	25 00	......
Barden Harley P	1700	200	17 00	2 00
Barden Isadore F. and Eliza Ann.	200	......	2 00	......
Barden Job W	900	......	9 00	......
Barden John H., and Steere Alanson	1600	......	16 00	......
Barden John H., & others f. Wil'x fm.	700	......	7 00	......
Barden Henry C., and wife	1500	......	15 00	......
Barnes Albert K	600	......	6 00	......
Battey Daniel	150	150	1 50	1 50
Battey Henry	1600	......	16 00	......
Battey James F	150	......	1 50	......
Battey Sampson	150	......	1 50	......
Baxter Edward B	......	400	......	4 00
Bennett Albert F	......	200	......	2 00
Bennett Abraham	450	......	4 50	......
Bennett Arnold	2600	......	26 00	......
Bennett Arnold, for small lot	150	......	1 50	......
Bennett Asher, 2d	1700	......	17 00	......
Bennett Benjamin, 3d	100	......	1 00	......
Bennett Charles for wife	100	......	1 00	......
Bennett Francis	2500	500	25 00	5 00
Bennett George, heirs est	750	......	7 50	......
Bennett James	2300	800	23 00	8 00

This fascinating Foster tax booklet dates from it being a separate town for 90 years. For example, Dr. Mowry P. Arnold (see page 30) was paying the highest tax listed, a whopping $39 on his real estate. Plus, he was paying $30 on his personal property at a time when many people were not paying any personal tax because they did not own any personal property. On the other end of the spectrum, Benjamin Bennett III and Charles Bennett and his wife hold the record on this list for paying the lowest real estate taxes of $1 on land valued at $100.

Three

Hopkins Mills Area

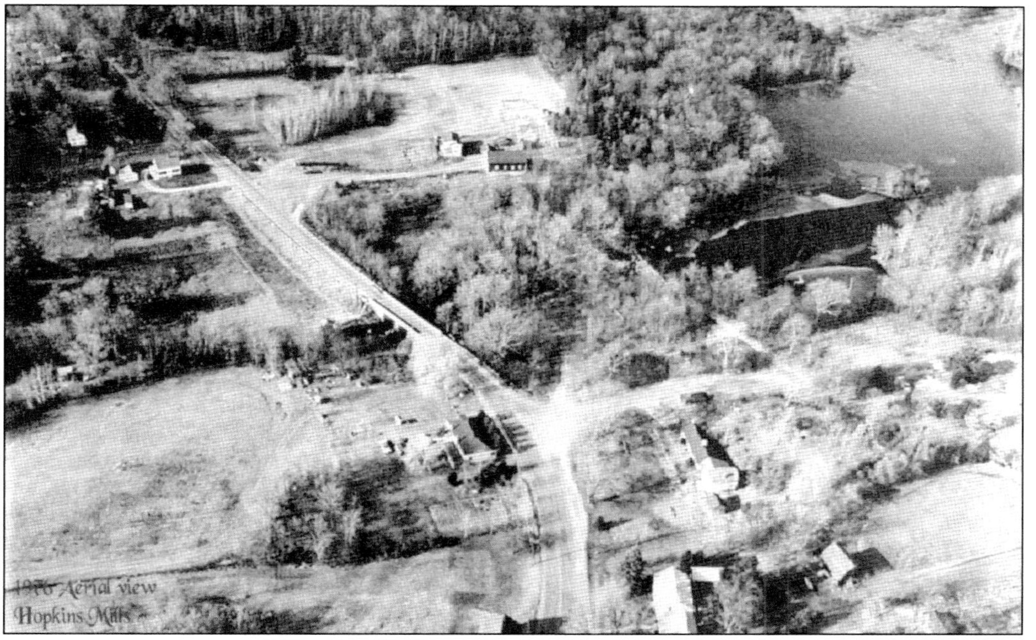

This aerial view of the old Danielson Pike traveling through Hopkins Mills was taken in 1976. The bridge shown crossing Ponagansett River can also be seen on the bottom of page 72. The Andrew-Shippee Farm is shown in the upper left, and the Grace Cook Farm is on the opposite side of the pike. (Courtesy of George Newman.)

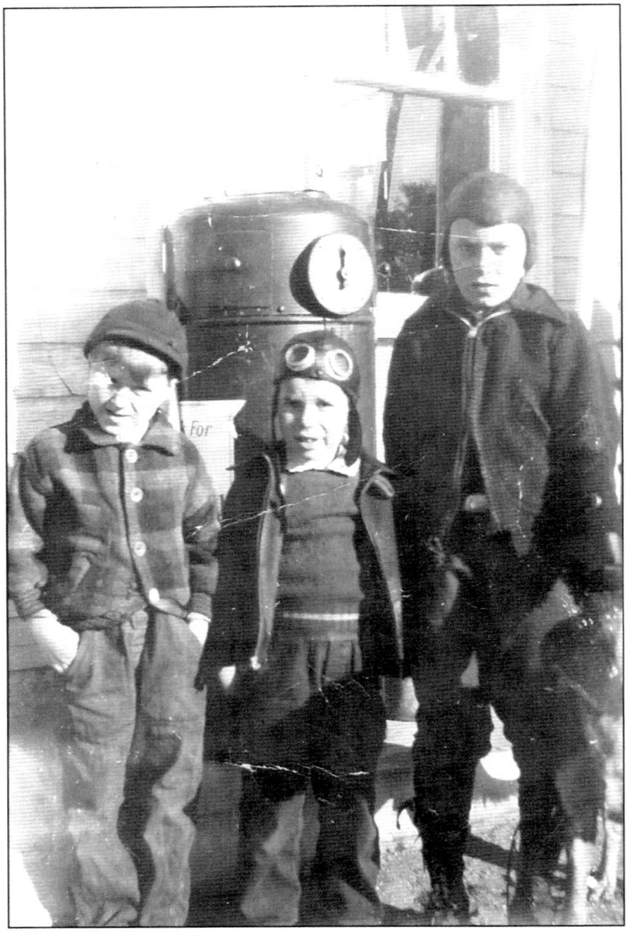

These three boys and their dog are standing in front of a gas pump at Ernest Hopkins's store in 1940. (The store is shown on the facing page.) They are, from left to right, Glen Hopkins, Dale Hopkins, and Robert Tucker. The following verse is from "Winter Wonderland" by Helen O. Larson: "The children were sliding, and were as happy as could be / Because the world looked like, a land of fantasy." (Courtesy of Glennis Beltram.)

These Hopkins Mills children stopped sliding for a moment the day after Thanksgiving 1940. They are, from left to right, (sitting) Marilyn Hopkins, Alta Hopkins, Diane Hopkins (behind), Avis Cole, June Peck, and Dennis Hopkins; (standing) Robert Cole, Mary Joan Hopkins, Creighton Cole, Keidel Hopkins, Glennis Hopkins, Robert Tucker (rear), and Earl Peck. They are lined up under the tree to the left of the Hopkinses' store seen on the next page. (Courtesy of Glennis Beltram.)

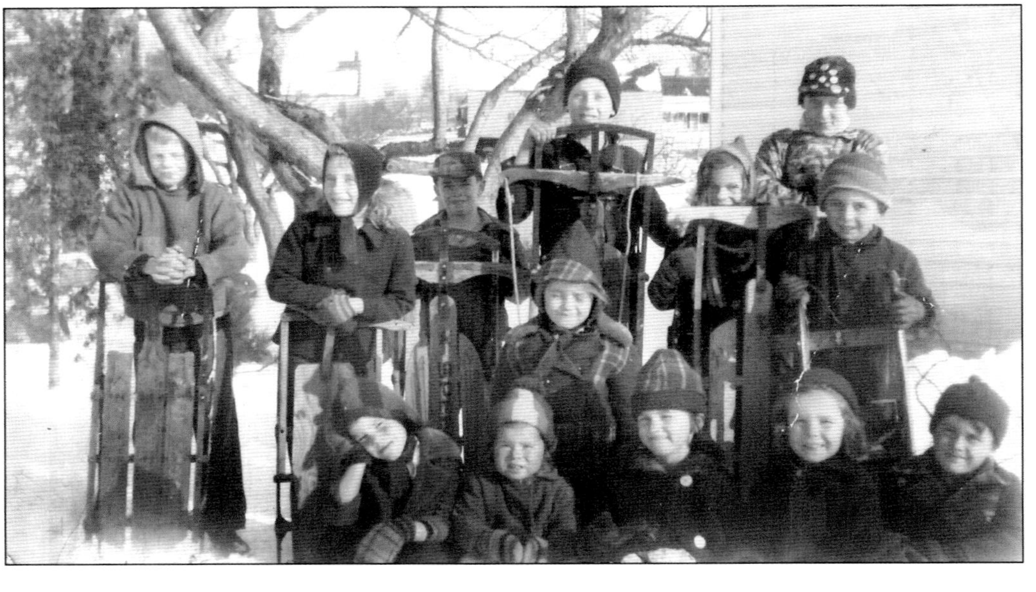

As this 1947calendar shows, Lytle Hopkins had come up with an idea to increase the income from the family store. She created the Hopkins Snack Shop inside the store. It served hamburgers and frankfurters along with soda and ice cream. This is most likely the last one of these calendars in existence. (Courtesy of Glennis Beltram.)

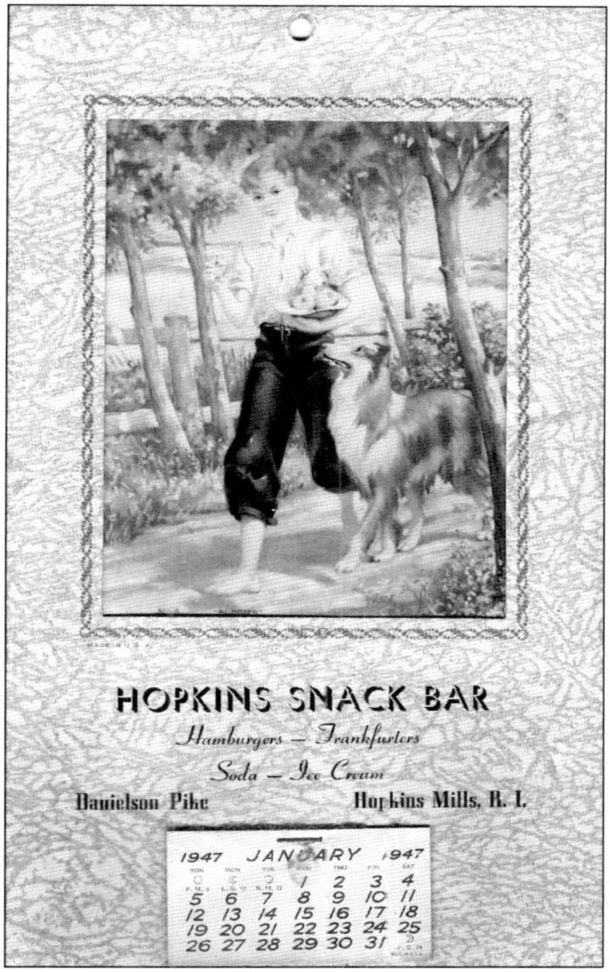

This view on the day after Thanksgiving 1940 is from Hopkins Mills Cemetery looking across the old Danielson Pike at the store belonging to Ernest and Lytle Hopkins. Behind it is the house belonging to Arthur and Ethel Hopkins; it once was a stagecoach stop. The following verse is from "Thanksgiving Day" by Helen O. Larson: "We'll get dressed in our very best, because we're going away / We'll go to our Grandma's, on this special day." (Courtesy of Glennis Beltram.)

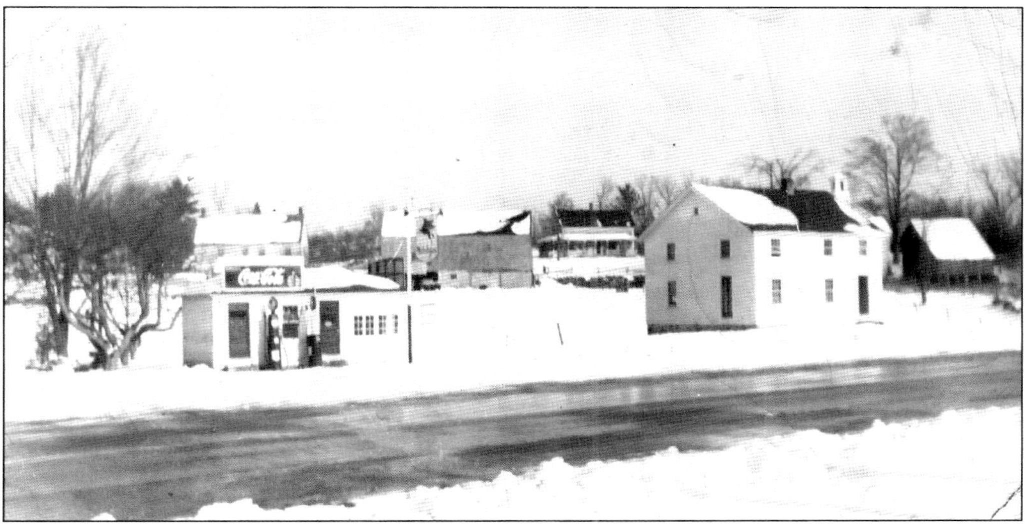

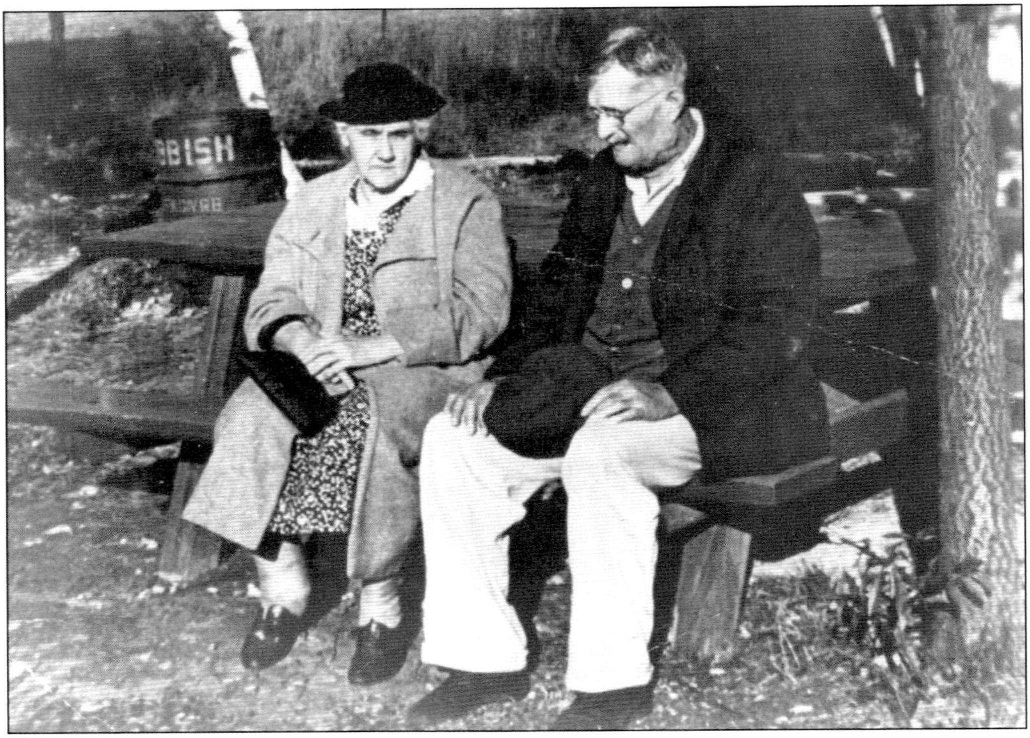

This photograph shows Rowena Marie Tyler-Cole and her husband, Leander Enos Cole, relaxing on a picnic table bench. They met when they were very young and as a result were married on Rowena's 15th birthday, February 7, 1883. Leander was 19. They were married over 59 years and had eight children. Rowena died September 14, 1942, and Leander joined her three months later on December 30, 1942. They are both buried in the Hopkins Mills Cemetery on Rams Tail Road, shown below on July 22, 2011. (Above, courtesy of George Newman; below, author's collection.)

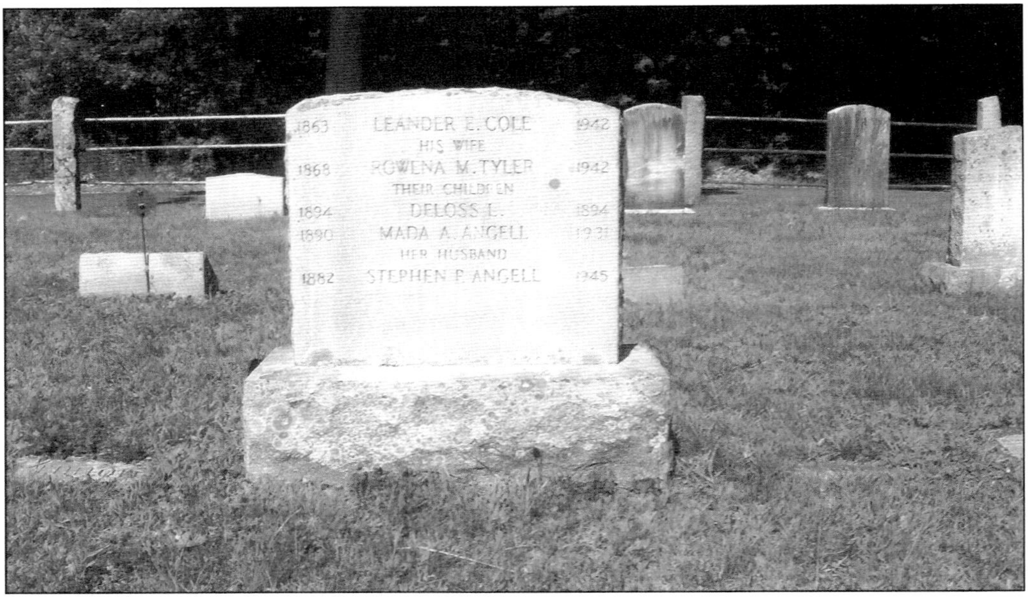

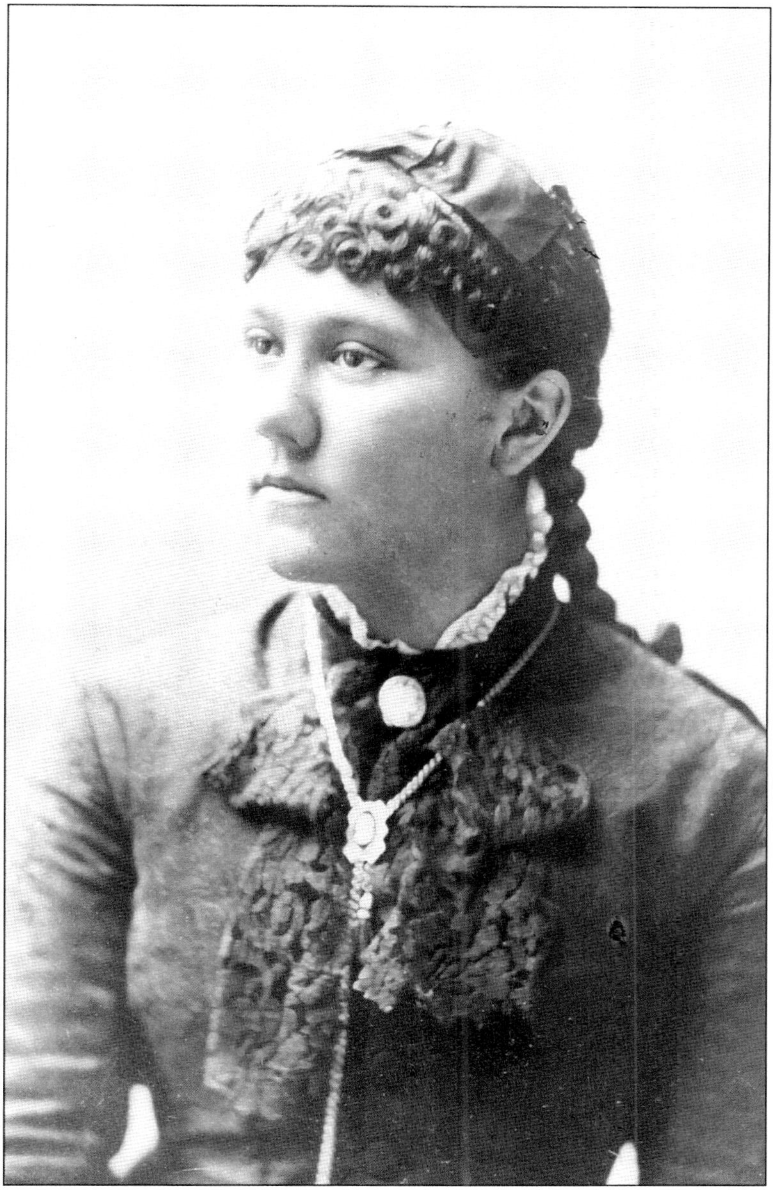

This photograph of Rowena Tyler-Cole, age 31, was taken on February 12, 1899. Rowena was born in Tylerville, now Moosup Valley. Her future husband, Leander Cole, lived in Hopkins Mills at the opposite end of Foster. They may never have met until fate took over. When her mother divorced, Rowena went to live with her aunt in the village of South Foster, located next to Hopkins Mills. Rowena and Leander met, fell in love, married, and the rest is history. The following verses are from "You Were My Valentine" by Helen O. Larson: "I met you at a valentine dance, we were in our teens / You had golden hair, and you were not wearing jeans. Later I walked you home, you were my valentine / I knew I couldn't rest, until I made you mine. Now your hair is silver gray, my love for you still grows / If ever I were to lose you, how I'd live no one knows. And so my silver haired sweet heart, I'll say good-night to you / And thank God in Heaven, that I found a love so true." (Courtesy of George Newman.)

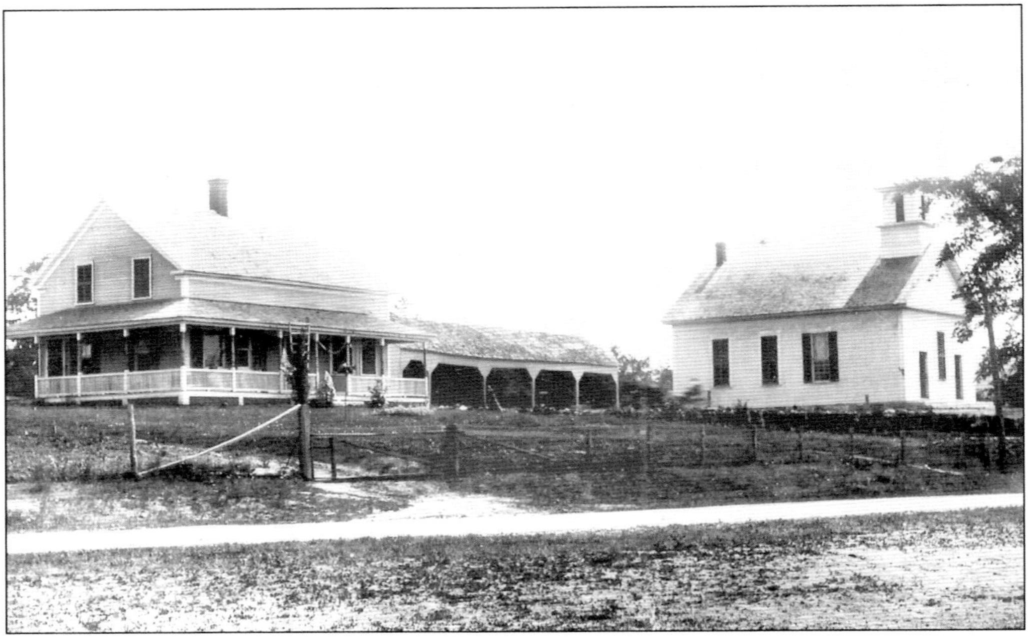

Pictured here is the Hopkins Mills Union Chapel on Old Danielson Pike (also shown on page 73). The house to the left belonged to John and Josephine Hopkins. John was born in 1877, and Josephine was in 1880. They spent many happy years here raising their six children and running their J.F. Hopkins village store (see page 82). The barn with the cupola on the roof in the picture below was located to the left of the Hopkinses' house, and the fire station was in front of it. Heuy Davis lived in the white house across the pike. This photograph was taken in 1941. (Both, courtesy of George Newman.)

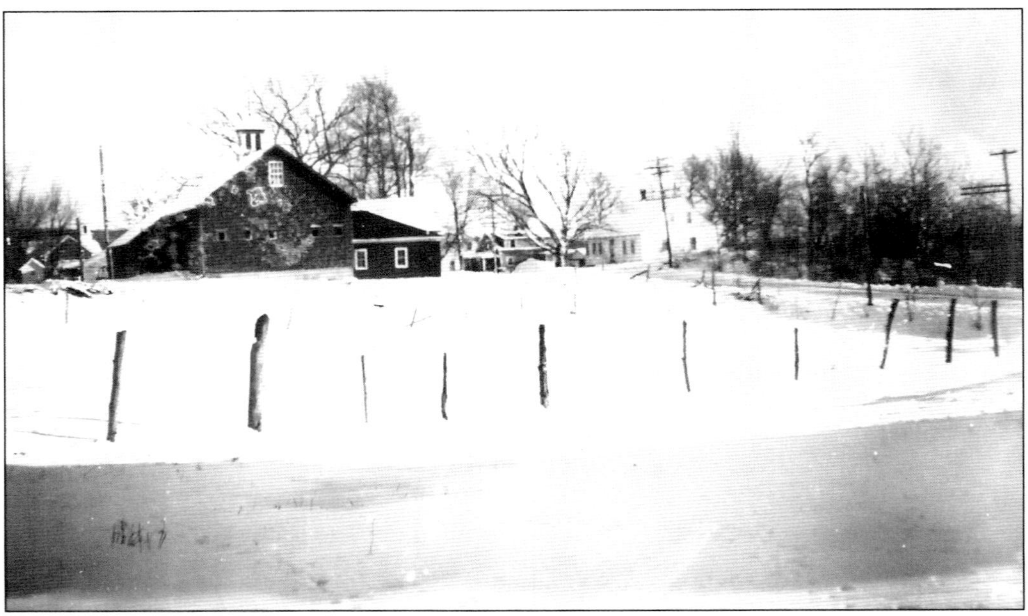

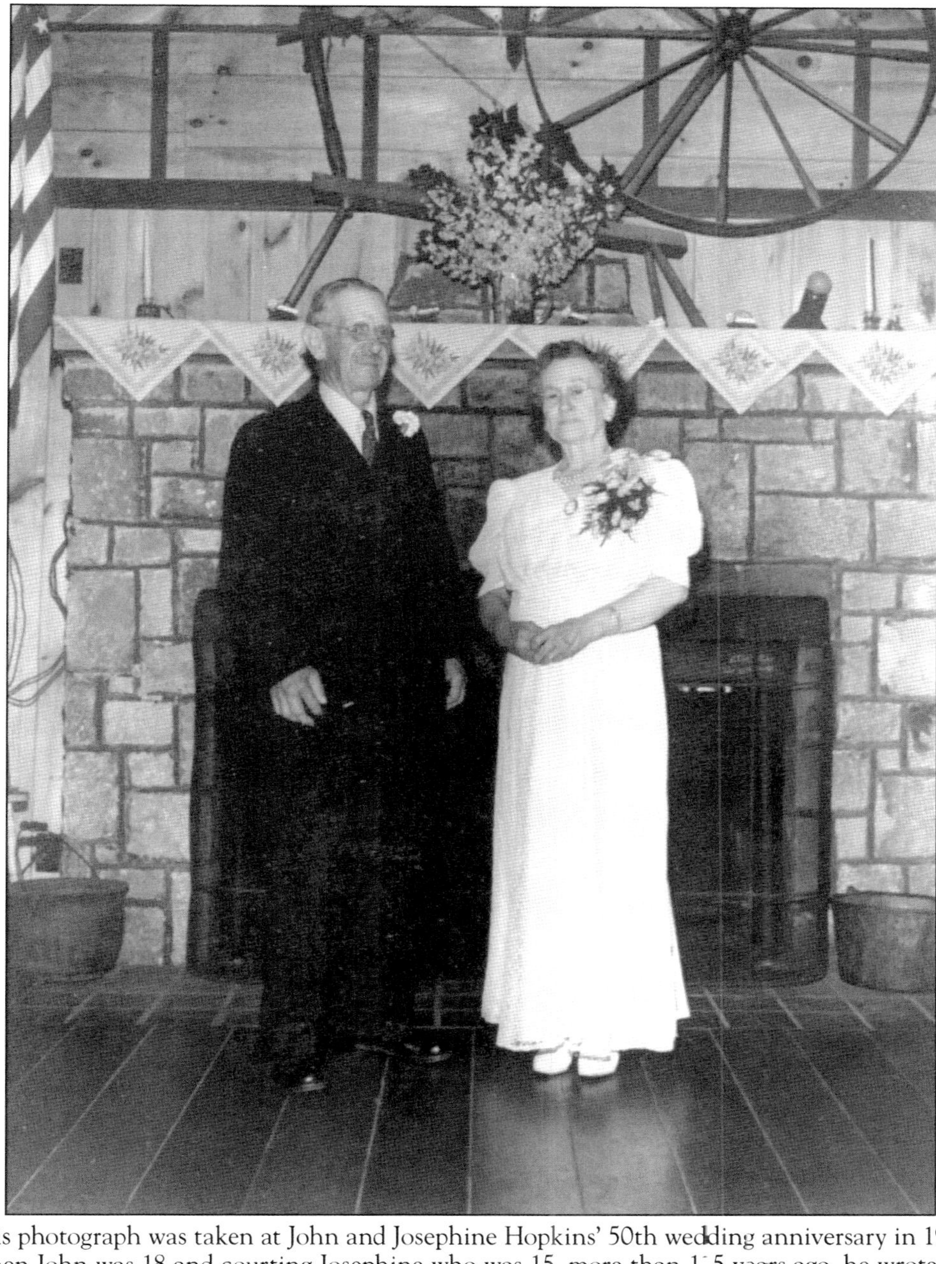

This photograph was taken at John and Josephine Hopkins' 50th wedding anniversary in 1946. When John was 18 and courting Josephine who was 15, more than 115 years ago, he wrote her the following untitled poem: "As I was walking out today, I found a flower by the way / Sweet its odor and pale its hue, I plucked the little flower for you. Take it Josie and let it tell, slight as it is I love you well / Put it between the leaves of a book, press it and sometimes on it look. When the years have fled like summer flowers, let this recall our happy hours / When we two loved to go side by side, where wild flowers grew. Flowers must wither they will not last, let not our friendship fade as fast / Let us each other's faults forgive, and love each other as long as we live." At age 19, John Fenner Hopkins married Josephine Eliza Bishop, who was 16 years old. Together, they raised six children. (Courtesy of Michele Harris.)

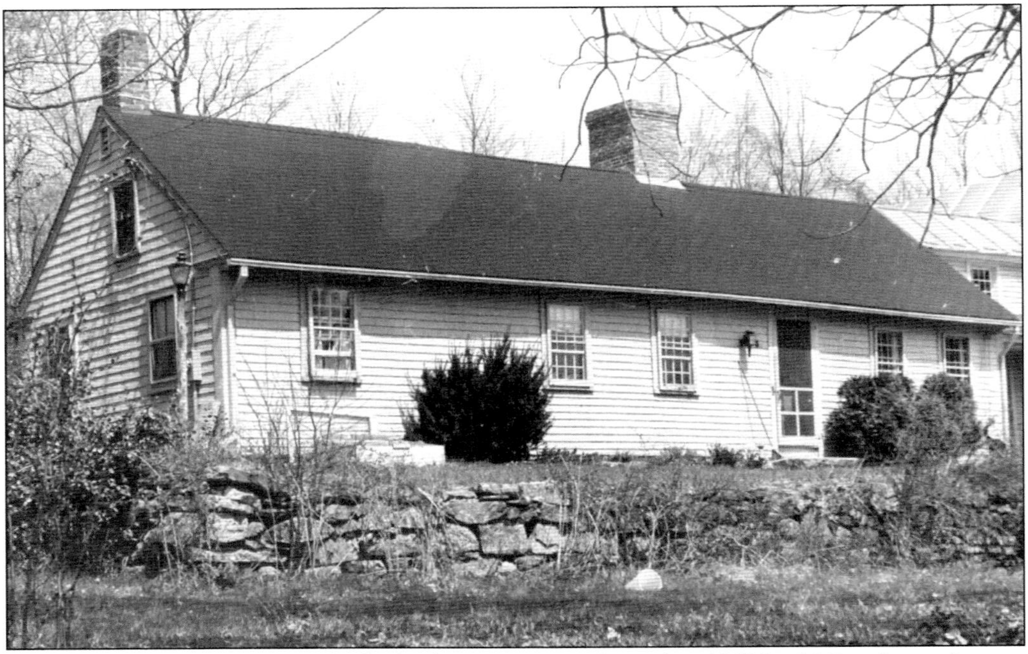

Ezekiel and William Hopkins built this house in 1720 along the old "North" Road, now known as the Old Danielson Pike. They also established a sawmill and a gristmill around 1723. The Providence & Danielson stage line stopped in Hopkins Mills daily into the late 1800s.

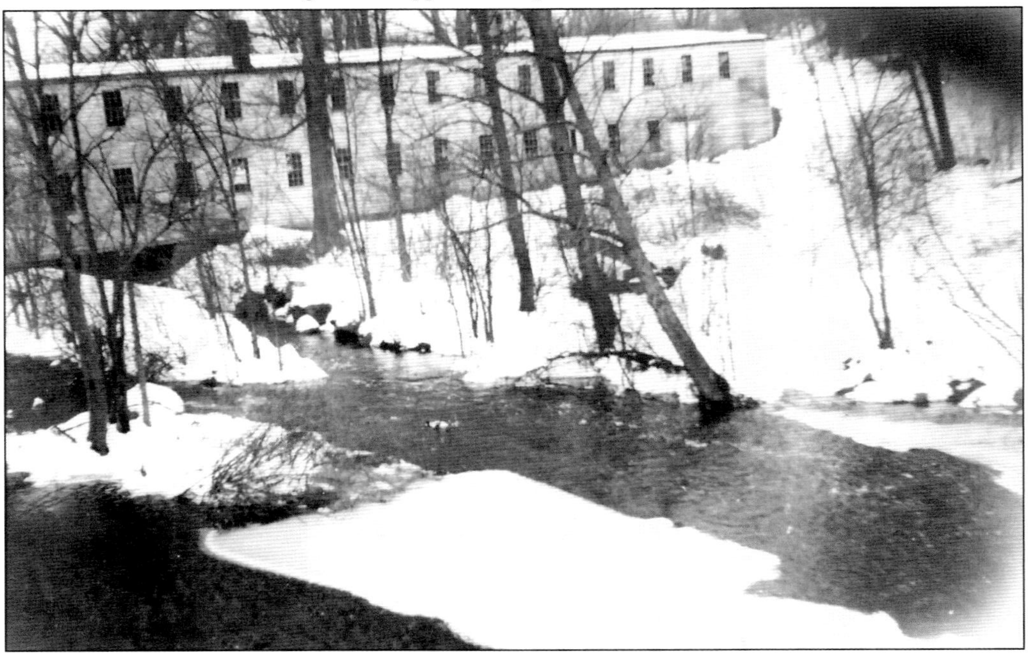

This photograph shows Simmons Braid Mill in 1941. Fred A. Simmons built the mill in 1910 on the Ponagansett River. It was producing shoelaces in the 1950s and shut down in 1960. Danielson Pike had received a new alignment in 1932 that encouraged the traffic to bypass Hopkins Mills. (Courtesy of George Newman.)

Marcus, son of Fred and Sally Simmons, is posed pointing his rifle with an unidentified hunting buddy and his trusty hunting dog. It appears they are well equipped for the hunt. The following verse is from "Old Nell" by Helen O. Larson: "Pa said Old Nell we can never, go hunting together again / So I must sell you to this man, please go and hunt with him." (Courtesy of Rus Benson.)

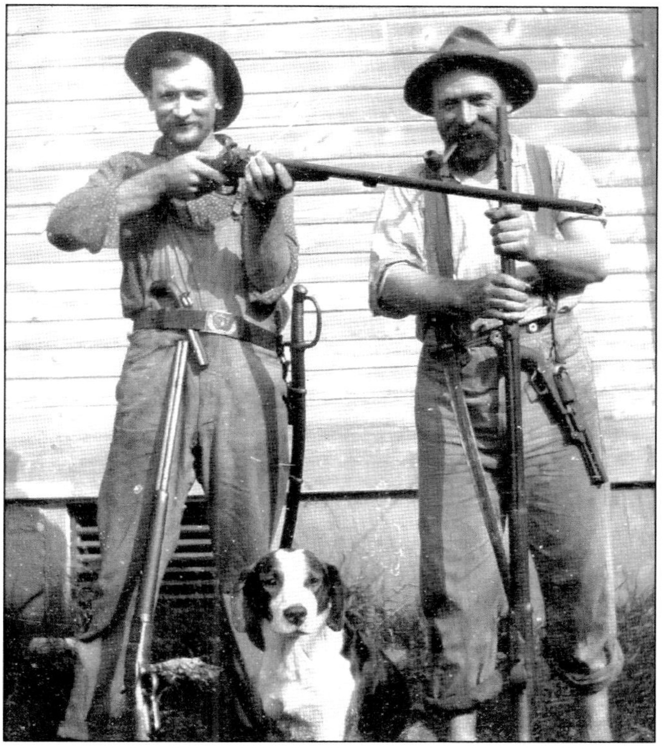

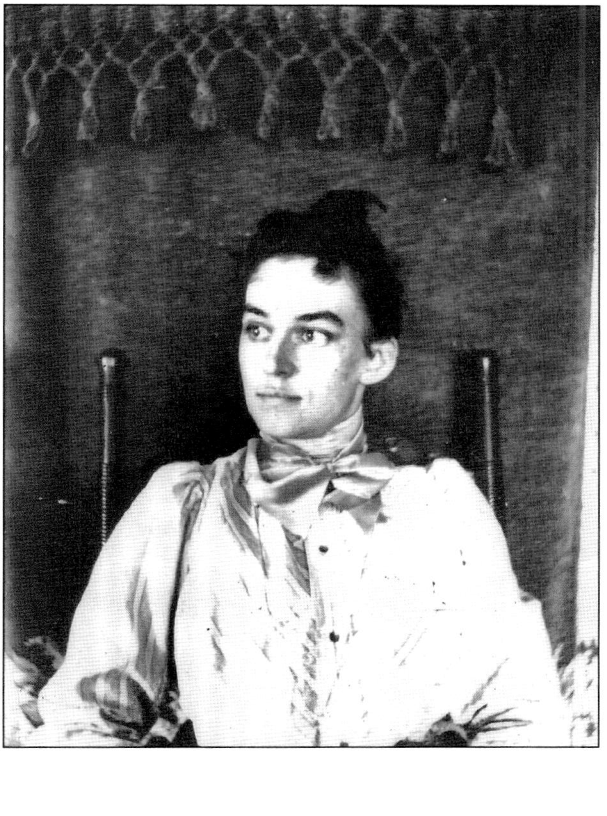

This photograph shows Edna Simmons posing for the camera. She was the wife of Marcus Simmons. (Courtesy of Rus Benson.)

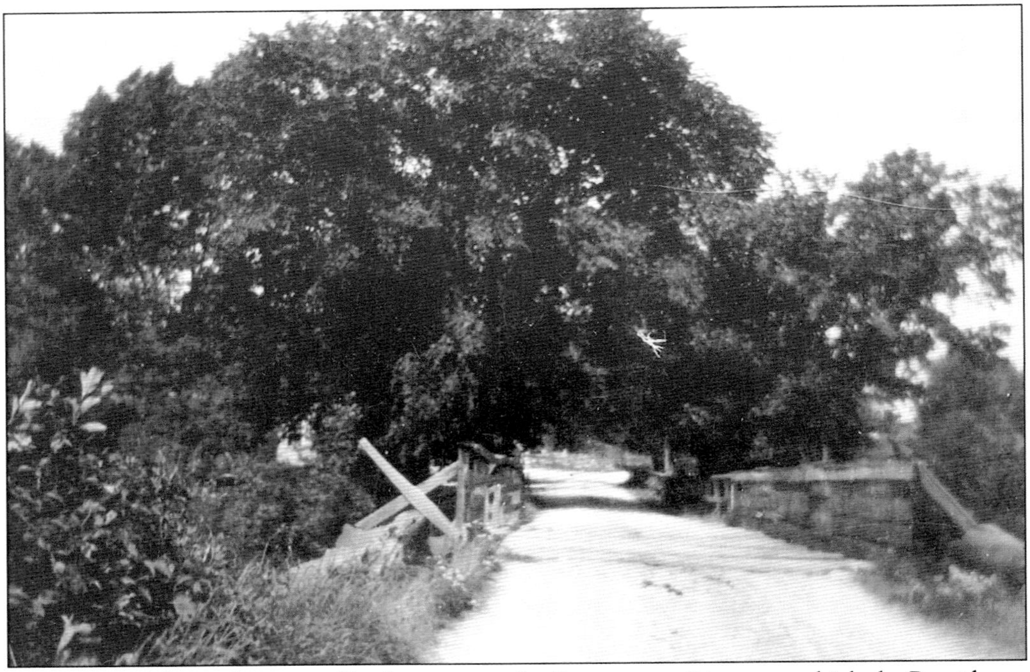

This postcard shows the original bridge crossing the Ponagansett River over which the Providence & Danielson stage traveled daily. This view is looking in an eastward direction. The bridge was eventually replaced with the one shown below. (Courtesy of George Newman.)

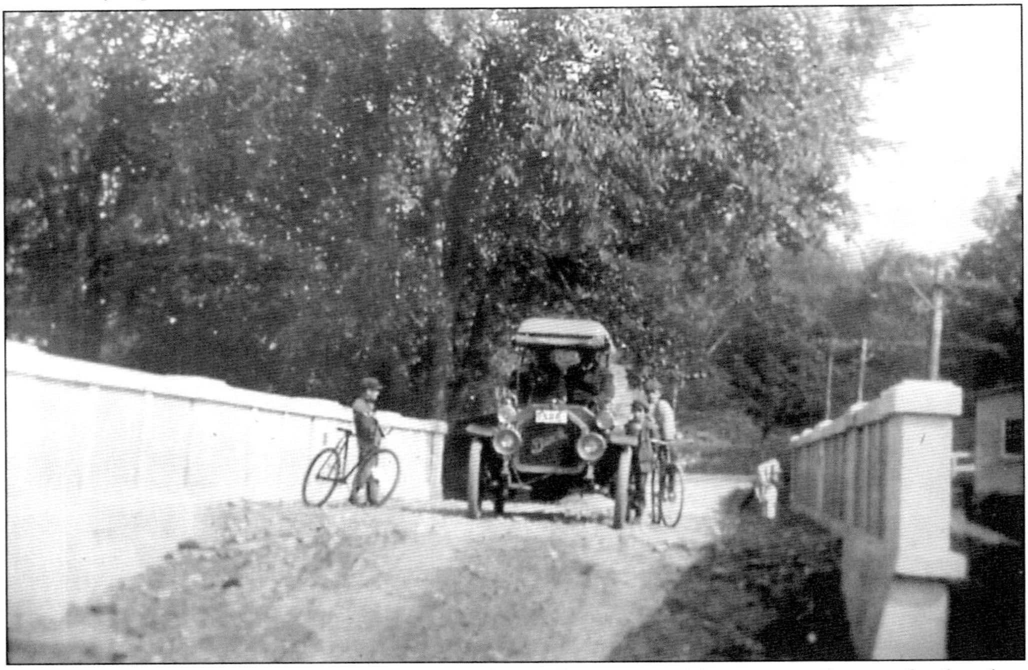

Here, three boys are admiring the unexpected site of an automobile crossing the new bridge that was built in 1932. Hopkins Mills was bypassed with the realignment of Danielson Pike. Today, the bridge has been barricaded to traffic and can only be used by pedestrians or cyclists.

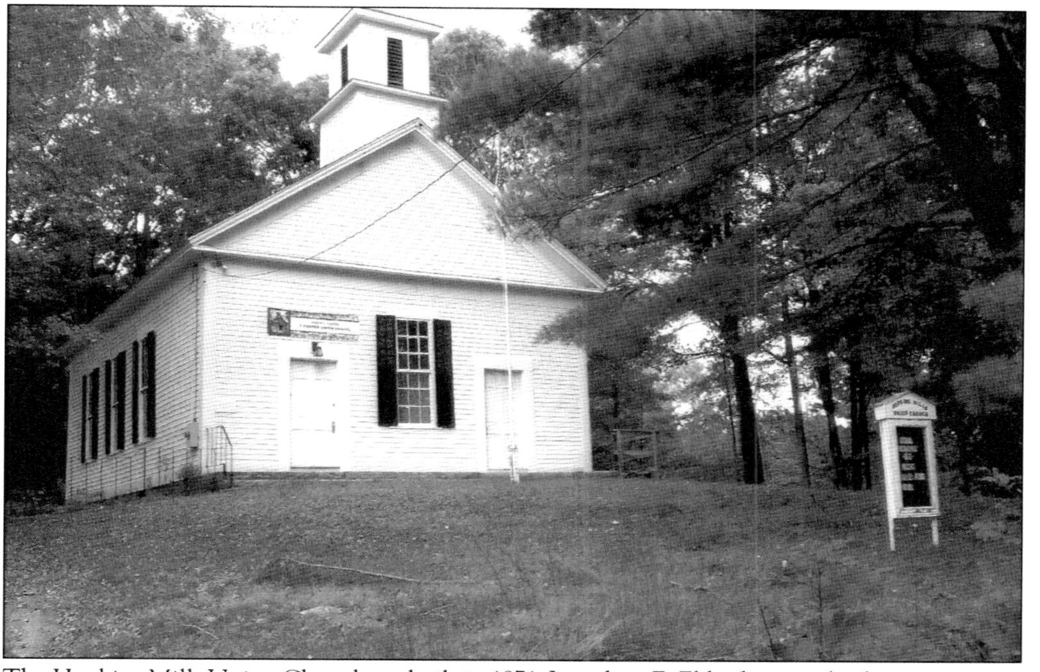

The Hopkins Mills Union Chapel was built in 1871. Jonathan E. Eldredge was the first permanent pastor. In 1926, on the 55th anniversary, a bronze plaque was dedicated: "In memory of Jane Walker through whose efforts and tireless energy this house was built and dedicated to the worship of God." (Author's collection.)

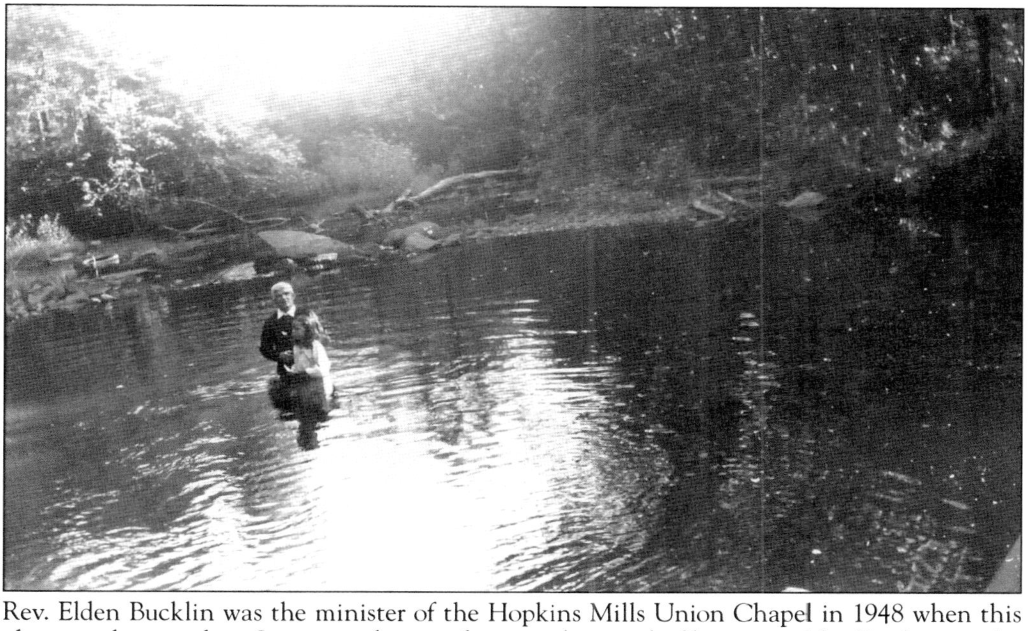

Rev. Elden Bucklin was the minister of the Hopkins Mills Union Chapel in 1948 when this photograph was taken. It pictures him performing the ritual of baptizing Alta Hopkins in the Rams Tail Pond. (Hopkins is also seen on page 64.) (Courtesy of Glennis Beltram.)

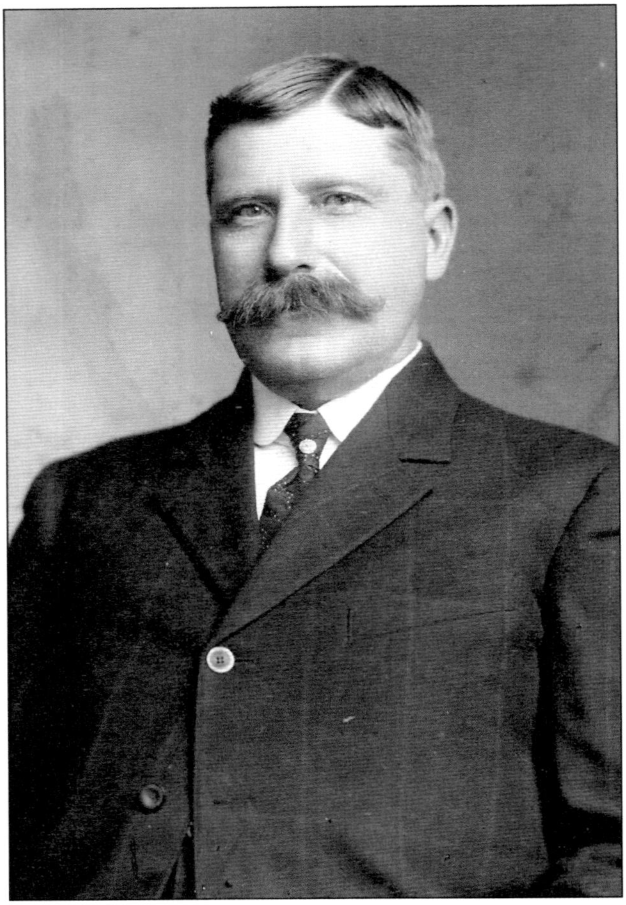

Arthur Hopkins was born October 4, 1863, and became very prominent in Foster in his 68 years. He served as Foster tax collector and was a charter member of the South Foster Fire Company. He was also elected a state representative in Rhode Island. He maintained membership in the Masons as well as the Independent Order of Odd Fellows. However, Glennis Hopkins (pictured on page 64) felt that above all, he was her grandfather. (Courtesy of Glennis Beltram.)

This photograph of the Providence & Danielson stage line was taken in 1880. The stage stopped once a day in Hopkins Mills on Danielson Pike, dropping off or picking up passengers. The fare from Providence to Foster was 75¢, and the trip took three hours. This was the last stage line operating in Rhode Island; it ended service shortly after the Providence & Danielson Railway began operation in June 1901.

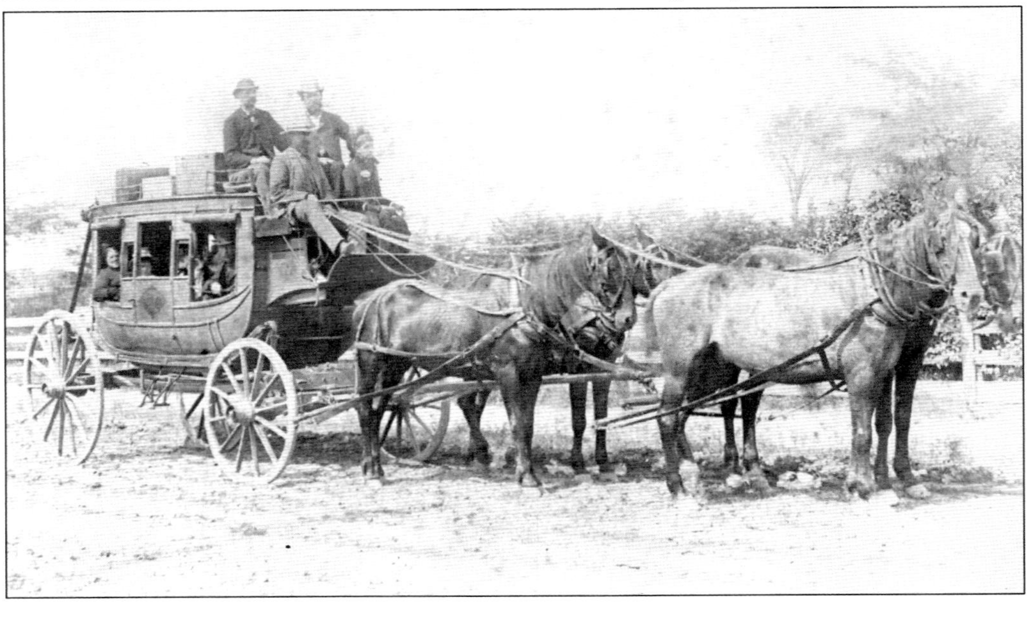

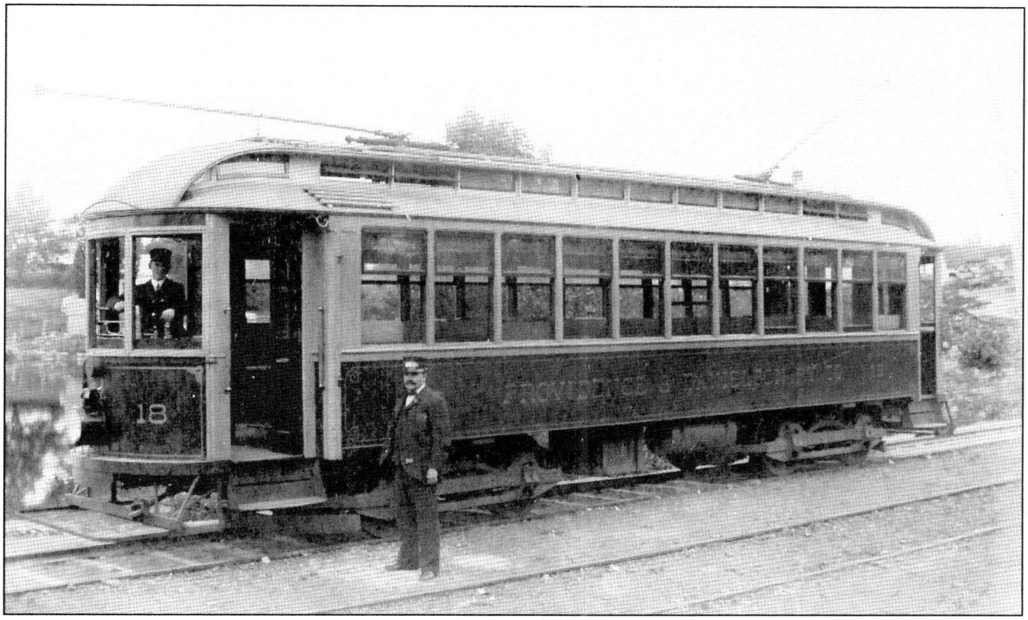

The Providence & Danielson Railway operated service through Foster from 1901 until 1920. This ended when the company decided not to replace the tracks that were displaced because of the building of the Scituate Reservoir. William Brown is the motorman at the controls, and Harry Hayden looks on. (Courtesy of Louis McGowan, president, Johnston Historical Society.)

PROVIDENCE and DANIELSON RAILWAY COMPANY

WINTER SCHEDULE: IN EFFECT JANUARY 1, 1906

(Subject to change without notice)

WEST BOUND — From Market Square, Providence.

FOR DANIELSON and way points,
5.45 A. M and hourly thereafter to and including 3.45 P. M., then 5.45 P. M.

FOR CLAYVILLE and way points,
5.45 A. M. and hourly thereafter to and including 7.45 P. M., then 9.45 and 11.15 P. M.

EAST BOUND — To Market Square, Providence.

FROM DANIELSON and way points,
6.40, 8.40 A. M and hourly thereafter to and including 6.40 P. M.

FROM CLAYVILLE and way points,
5.55 A. M. and hourly thereafter to and including 8.55 P. M., then 10 25 P. M.

On week days a car will leave North Scituate Post Office for Providence at 5.35 A M.

J. E. THIELSEN, Superintendent.

J.E. Thielsen, superintendent of the Providence & Danielson Railway Company, issued this winter schedule of trolley departures to and from Market Square, Providence, in 1906. This was the fifth year of operation through Foster. After arriving in North Scituate, the trolley would travel to Rockland, Clayville, Foster Center, and then swing north to Central Pike, finally turning west to its final destination, Danielson, Connecticut. The trolley did not travel through Hopkins Mills as the stage line did.

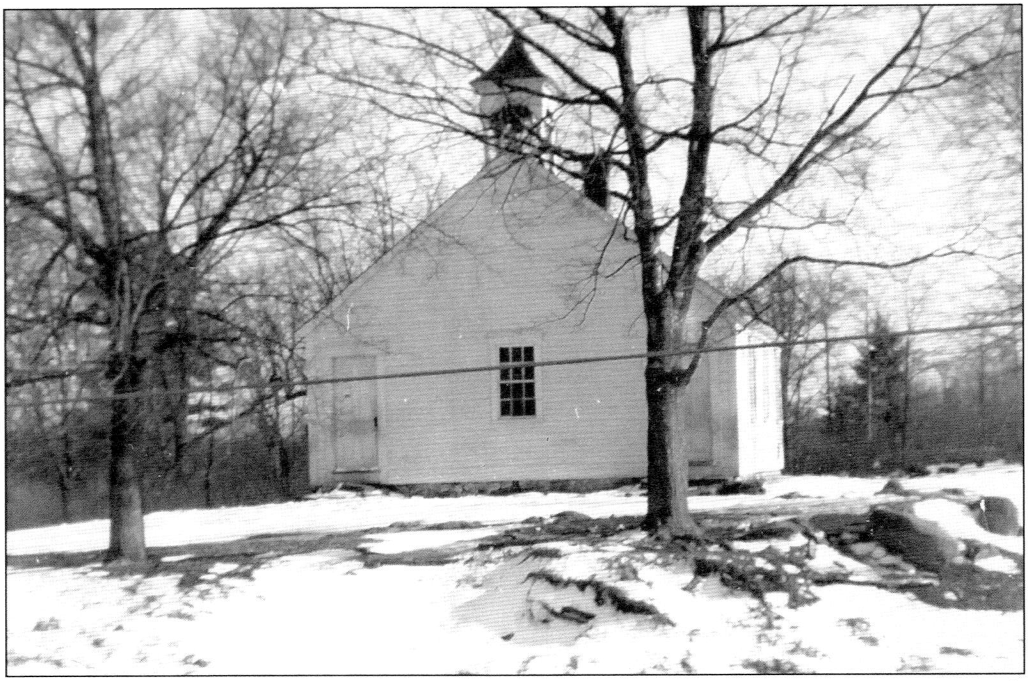

Hopkins Mills Schoolhouse was built in 1820. It was a typical one-room school of the time, with separate boys' and girls' entrances and a belfry at the front of the gable roof. Out of view behind the building were individual boys' and girls' outhouses. (Courtesy of Glennis Beltram.)

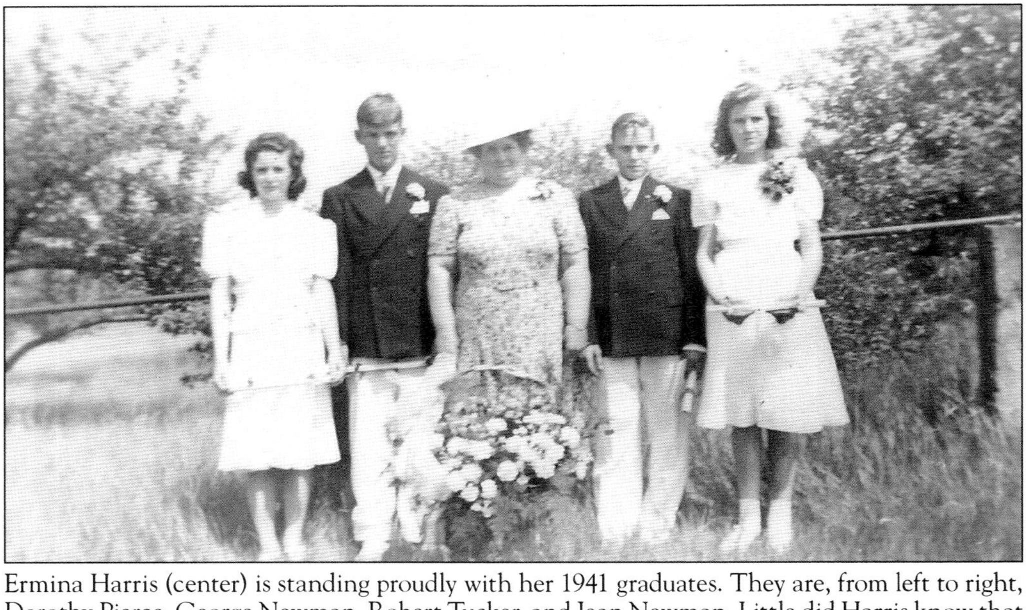

Ermina Harris (center) is standing proudly with her 1941 graduates. They are, from left to right, Dorothy Pierce, George Newman, Robert Tucker, and Jean Newman. Little did Harris know that 11 years later she would be teaching in the new Capt. Isaac Paine School, and her one-room school would be part of an era never to return. (Courtesy of Dorothy Pierce-Brayton.)

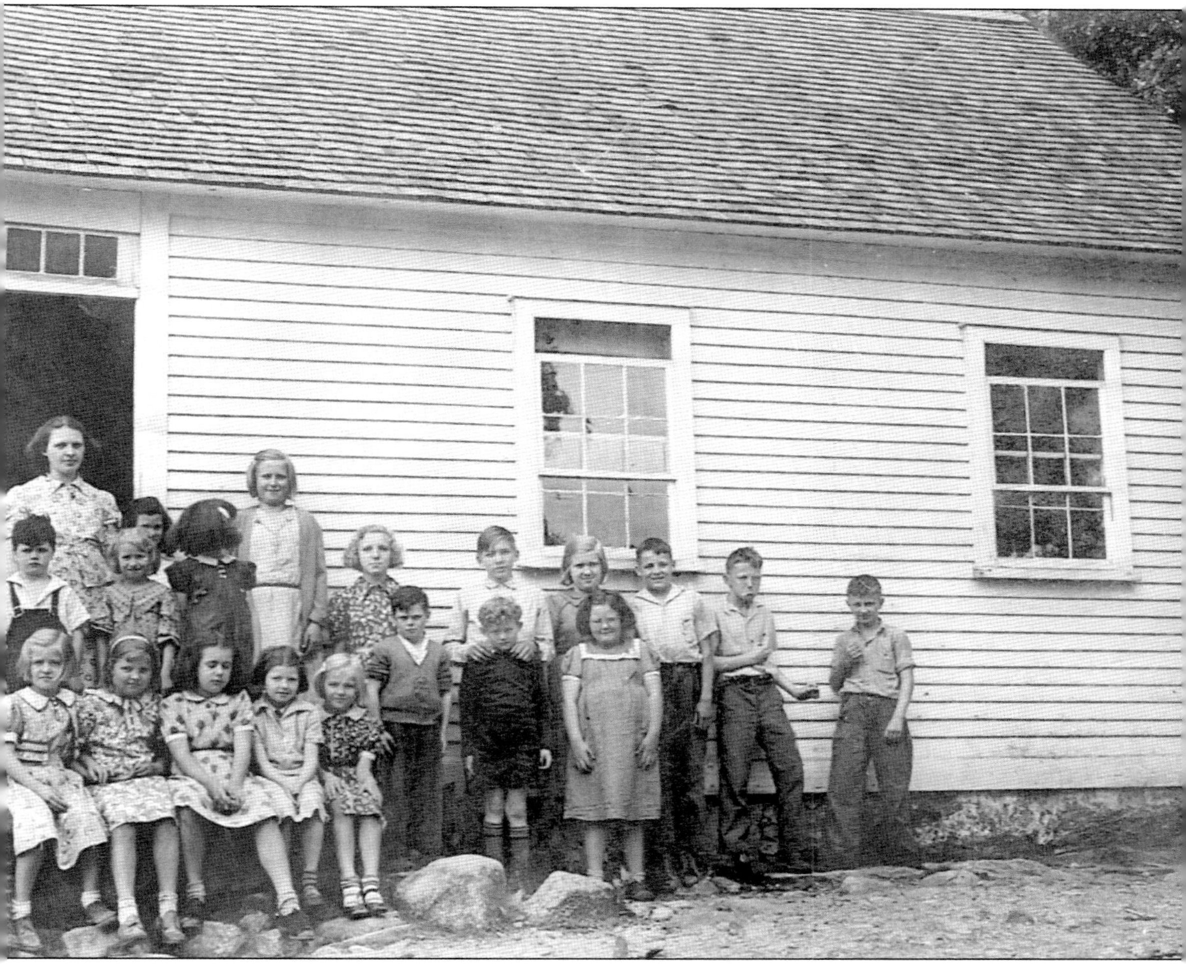

These are the students who attended the one-room Harmony School on East Killingly Road. In this 1937 photograph, all but one girl are looking very intently at the camera. From left to right are (first row) Olney Oksanen, Eleanor Perkins, Esther Oksanen, Lillian Bjork, Helen Shippee, Irene Bruis, Foster Simmons, unidentified, and Rosey Littlefield; (second row) Russell Simmons, unidentified teacher, unidentified, Delores Simmons (behind), unidentified (head turned), unidentified, Velma Young, Walt Grass, Dot Young, Pink Shippee, Red Shippee, and Newt Perkins. Again, the girls outnumber the boys 12 to 8. (Courtesy of George Newman.)

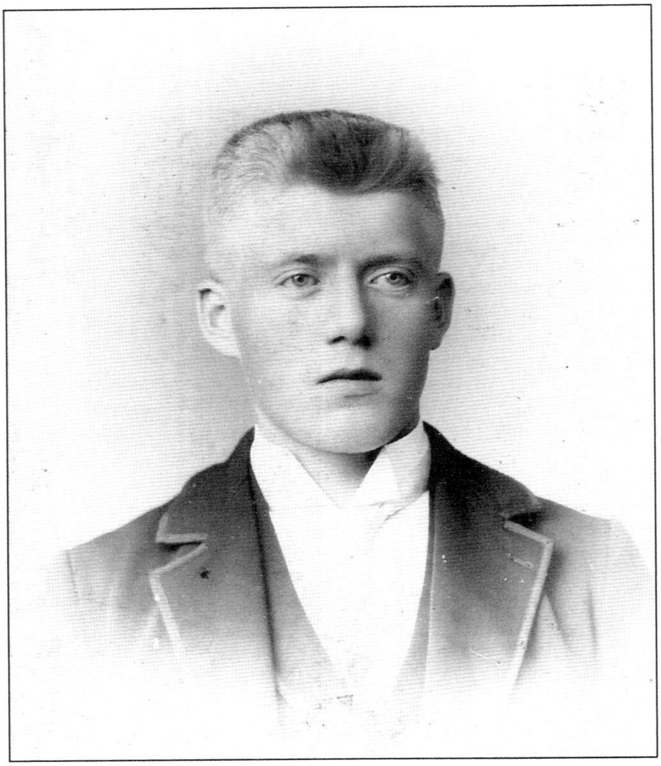

Stephen Augustus Keidel was born on Christmas Day 1873 in Wustensacher, Germany. He came to America when he was about 20 years old. He settled in South Foster on Breezy Hill. The following verse is from "Christmas Day" by Helen O. Larson: "And in the evening, as I kneeled to pray/ I thanked God above, for this Christmas day." (Courtesy of Michele Harris.)

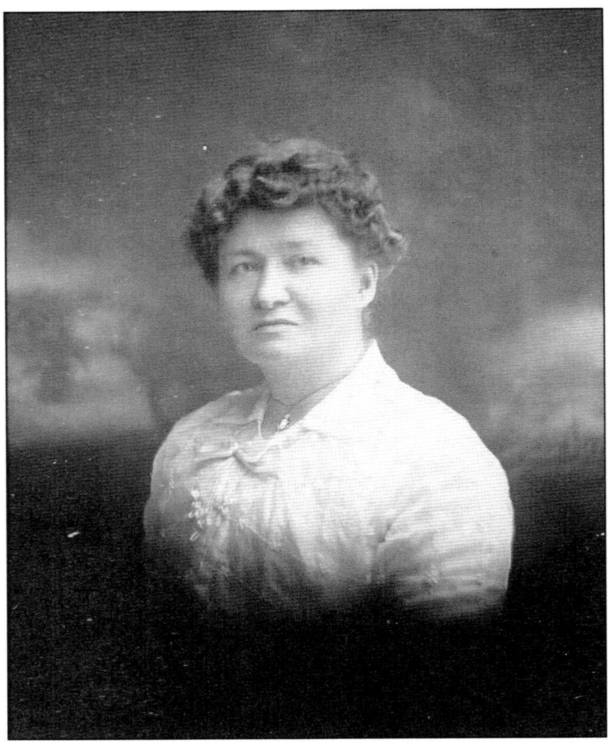

Mary Monica Enders-Keidel is pictured in the early 1900s. When she was three, her parents came to America from Germany. She later met and married Steven Keidel. One of their children, Ruth Monica Keidel, married John Edgar Hopkins, and together they raised their seven children. (Courtesy of Michele Harris.)

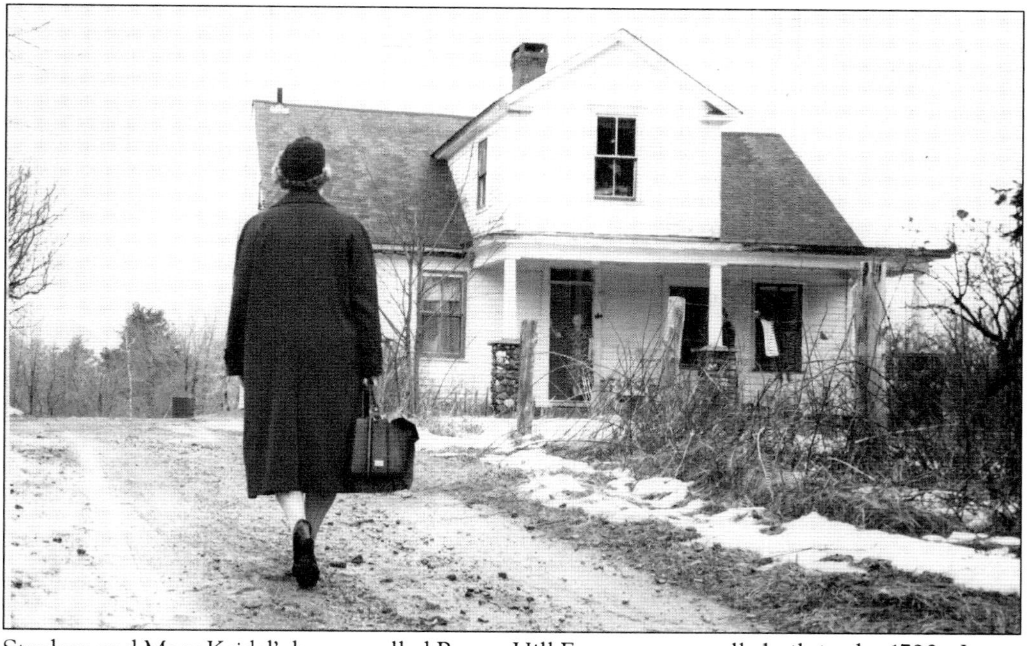

Stephen and Mary Keidel's house, called Breezy Hill Farm, was actually built in the 1700s. It was located on Danielson Pike (Route 6). Here, they would raise their children and spend the rest of their lives together. Mary Enders-Keidel is standing in the doorway as nurse Helen Henshal approaches for her routine visit. (Courtesy of Michele Harris.)

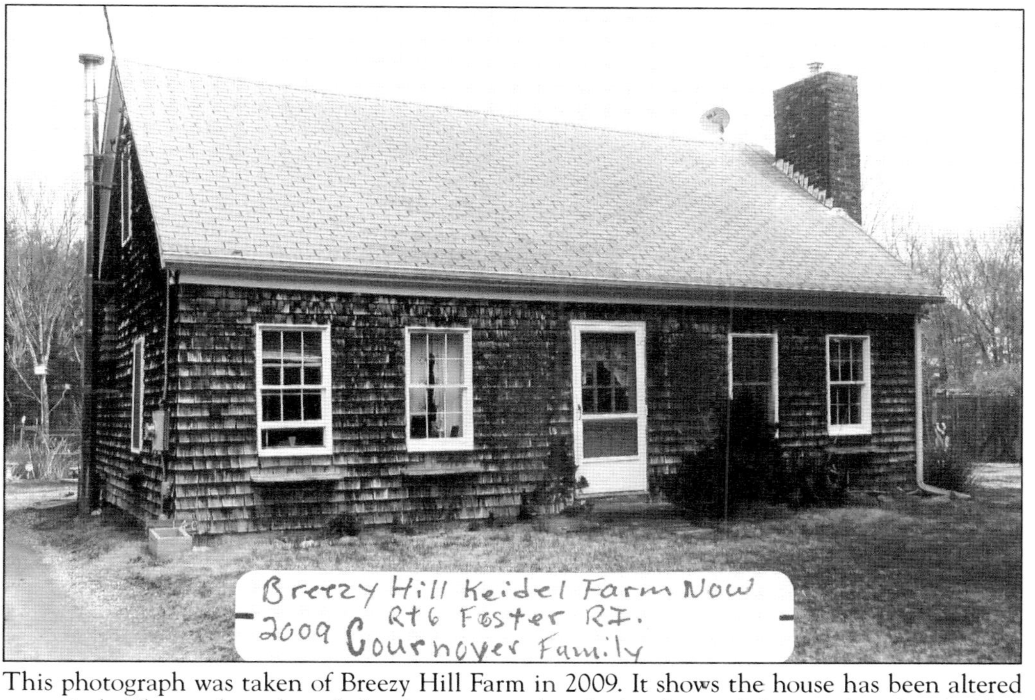

This photograph was taken of Breezy Hill Farm in 2009. It shows the house has been altered extensively. The porch on the right has been removed, and a fireplace and chimney have been added. The room above the porch in the front has also been removed. (Courtesy of Michele Harris.)

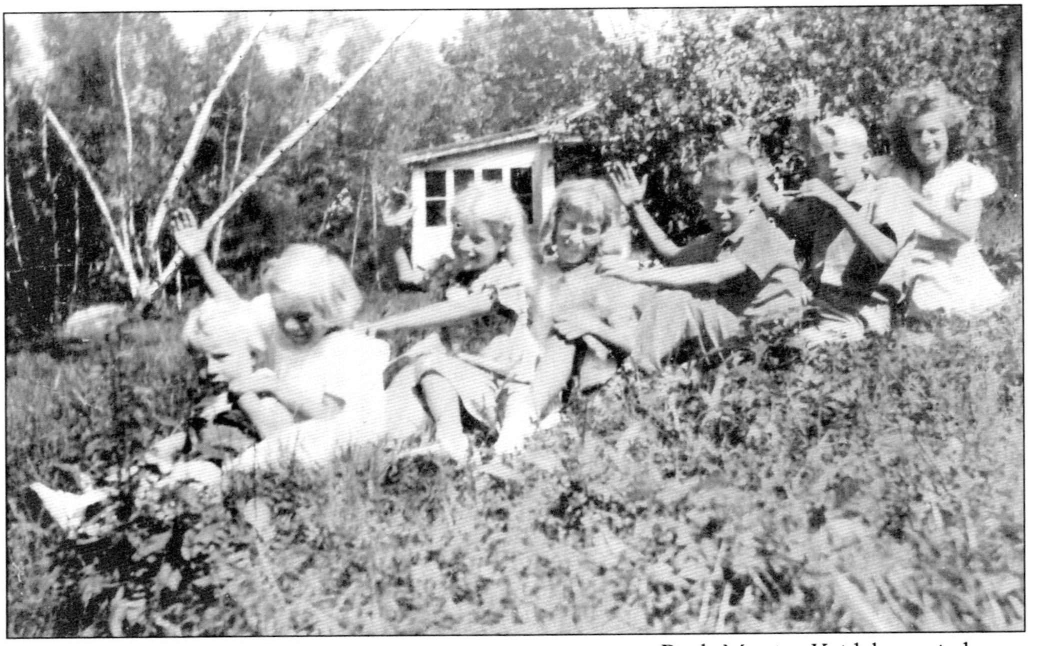

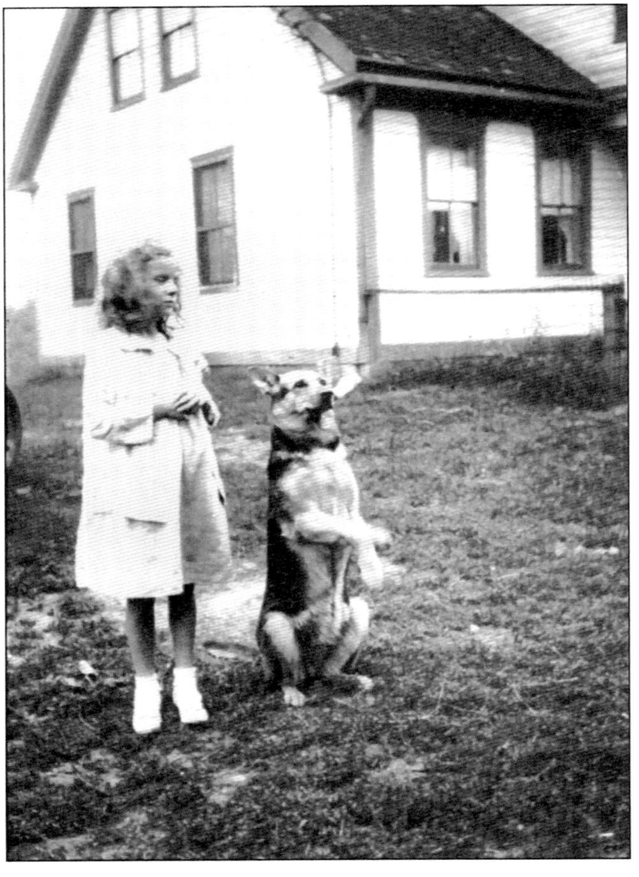

Ruth Monica Keidel married John Edgar Hopkins, son of John Fenner and Josephine Hopkins. Pictured in 1940 are Ruth and John's seven children. They are, from left to right, Richard, Carol Louise, Alberta, Mary Jo, Stephen, John, and Eileen. Recently, Alberta remembered, "I went to the same school that my father went to. It had all eight grades in one room and you would pick up something out of every class every day. All you had to do was listen." (Courtesy of Michele Harris.)

This photograph of Eileen Ruth Hopkins was taken in July 1935 when she was 10 years old. She used to walk the three miles along Danielson Pike on Saturdays from her home in Hopkins Mills to visit Gramma Keidel at Breezy Hill. Lady, her faithful German Shepherd, always accompanied her. (Courtesy of Michele Harris.)

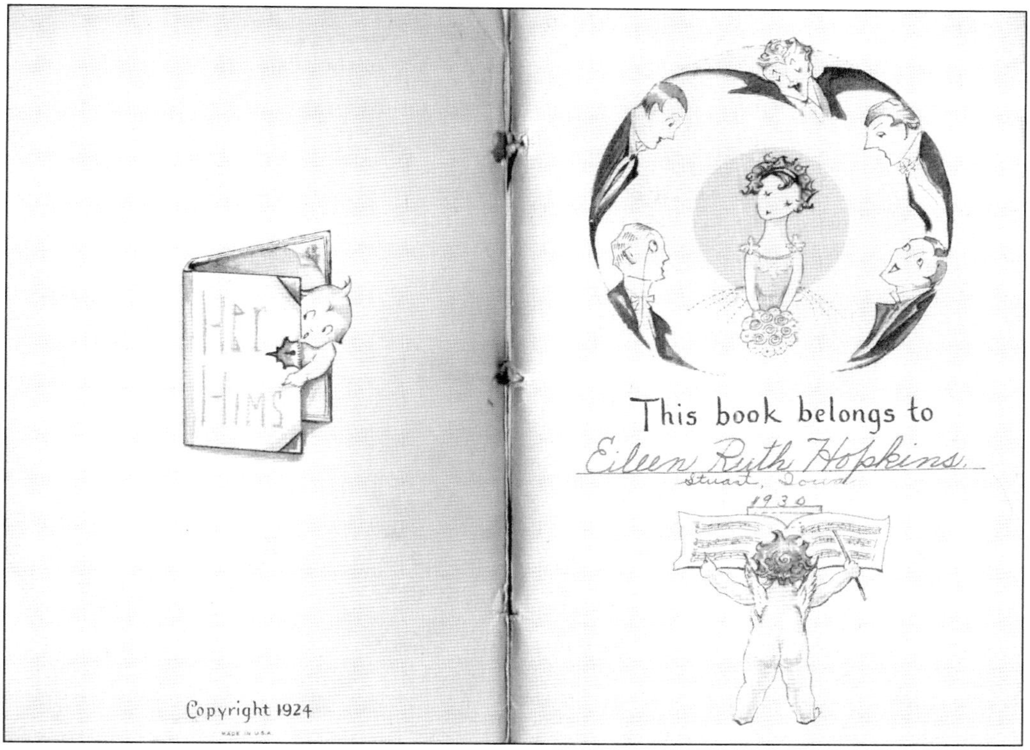

This is Eileen Ruth Hopkins's "My Him Book" from 1930. It recorded the following: First Hims, Childhood Hims, Puppy Love Hims, High School Hims, College Hims, Jazz Hims, Sad Hims, Movie Hims, Accidental Hims, Love Hims, Matinee Hims, National Hims, Popular Hims, Home Hims, and Wedding HIM. (Courtesy of Michele Harris.)

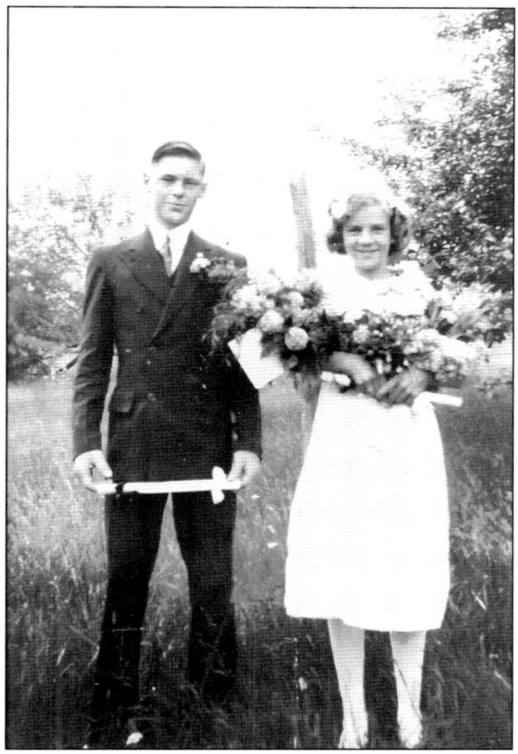

Eileen is standing beside George Brayton on their eighth-grade graduation day in 1941. George is recorded twice in Eileen's "Him Book" (above); however, it will remain Eileen's secret under which categories he is listed. (Courtesy of Michele Harris.)

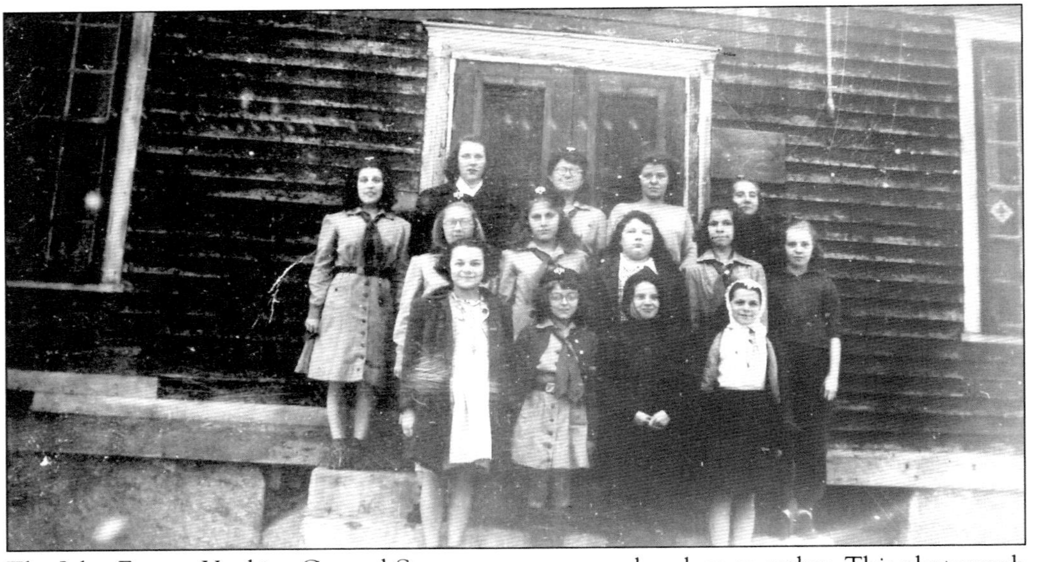

The John Fenner Hopkins General Store was a very popular place to gather. This photograph shows the Girl Scouts posing for the camera. From left to right are (first row) Alice Hallene, Joyce Corriveau, Carol Hopkins, and Marilyn Hopkins; (second row) Lee Pray, Nancy Bartlett, Norma Dutch, Glennis Hopkins, and Alberta Hopkins; (third row) Joyce Hopkins, Hope Tucker, Patricia Pray, Eleanor Perkins, and Mary J. Hopkins. (Courtesy of Michele Harris.)

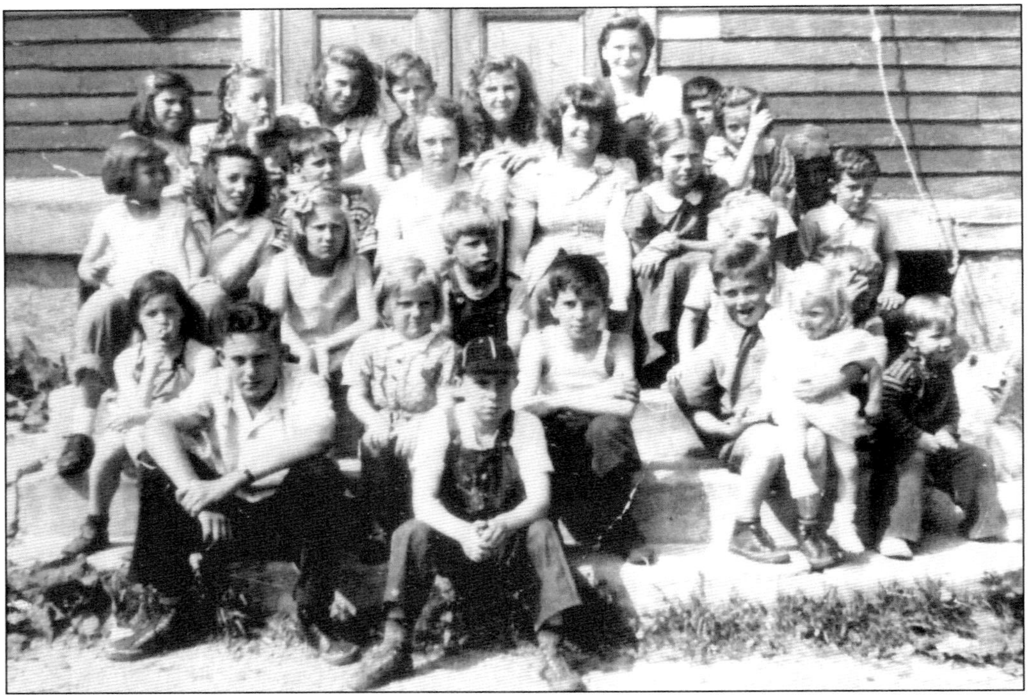

This photograph, taken in 1941, is another example of kids gathering in front of J.F. Hopkins's store. Nancy Bartlett is in the fifth row (fifth from left). Judith Bartlett is in the third row (third from left). Beside her is her brother William Bartlett. (Courtesy of George Newman.)

Four

Moosup Valley Area

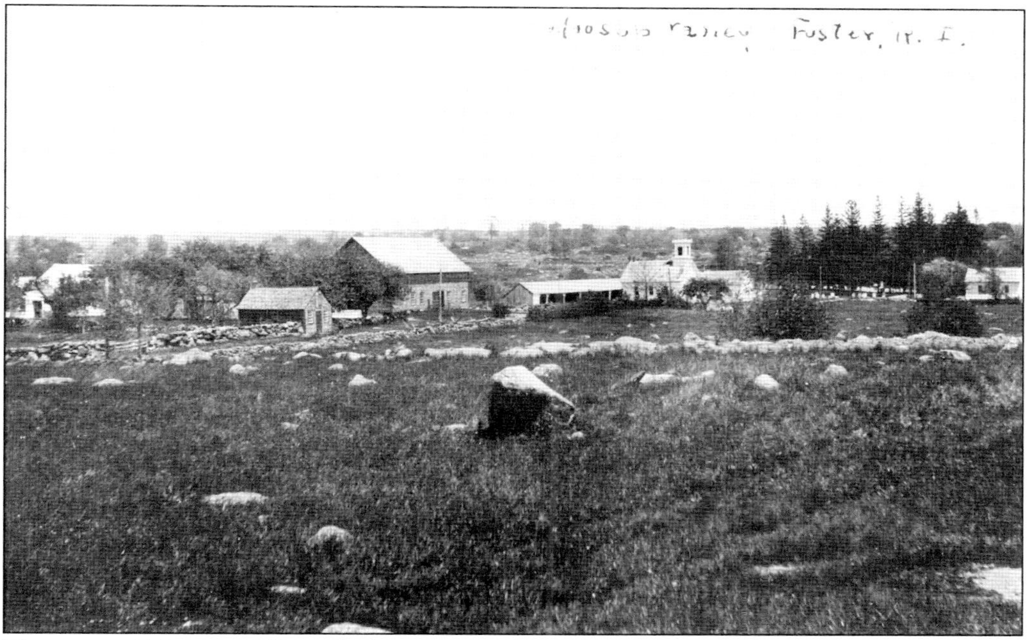

This view of Moosup Valley is looking eastward. Moosup Valley Road travels between the two stone walls to the left as it leads to the Moosup Valley Church. The carriage barn can be seen behind and to the left of the church, while the cemetery can barely be seen to the right of the church. The little building opposite the church is the one-room school (also seen on page 93).

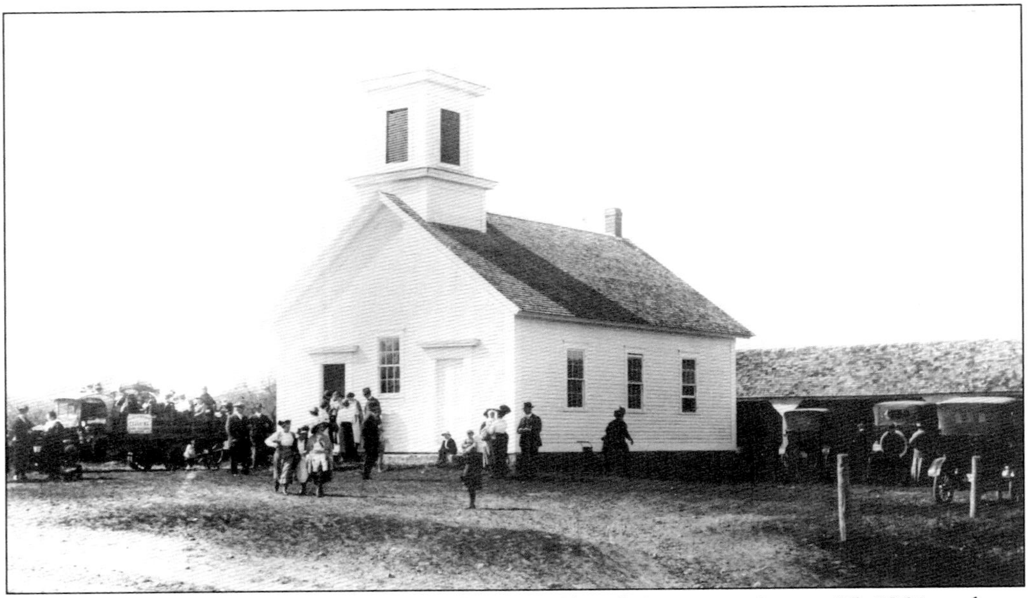

The construction of the Moosup Valley Christian Church began on August 25, 1864, and was completed in 1865. Elder George W. Kennedy served as the first pastor from 1868 to 1898. This postcard from 1919 shows a typical Sunday gathering. The following verse is from "Chapel in the Sky" by Helen O. Larson, written in 1988 at the age of 78: "I wonder if the stars are candles, burning every night / I wonder if angels are dancing, in the candle light."

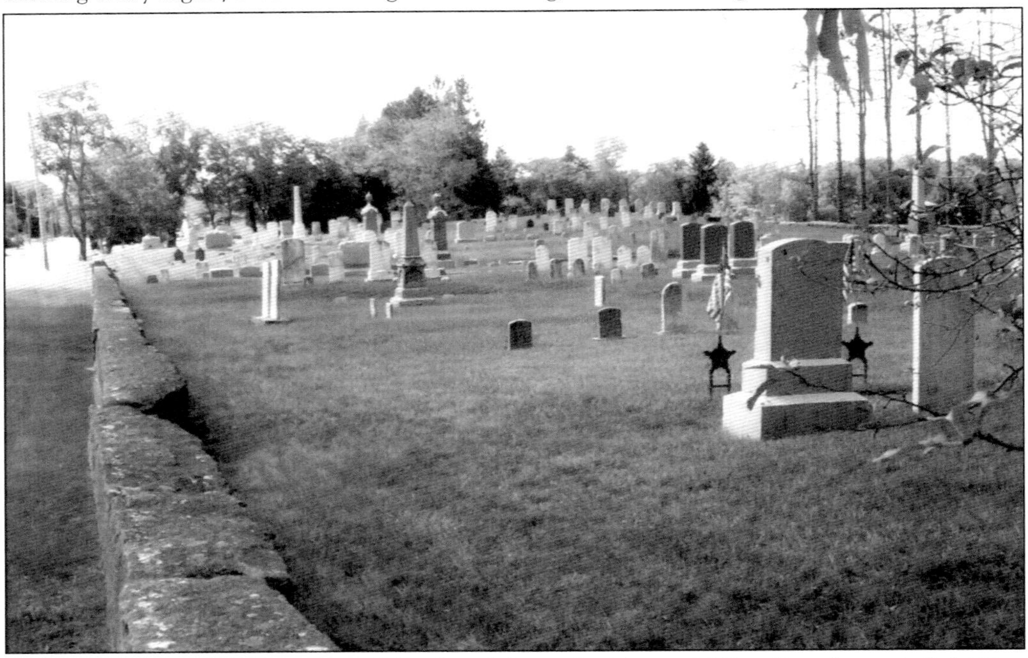

This view westward along Moosup Valley Road shows the Moosup Valley Church, partially hidden by the trees, and its cemetery. An interesting point of this graveyard is that all of the headstones are facing east except the two by the wall, which face north. They read: "Peleg Place, died February 26, 1840" and "Hannah Place, Wife of Peleg, died July 22, 1862." (Author's collection.)

The Union Free Will Baptist Church was also known as the Line Church. It was built on South Killingly Road in 1851 and was near the Rhode Island–Connecticut state line. Daniel Greene was the first pastor and served from 1868 to 1878. The Line Baptist Church was not officially named until it was rechartered in 1973.

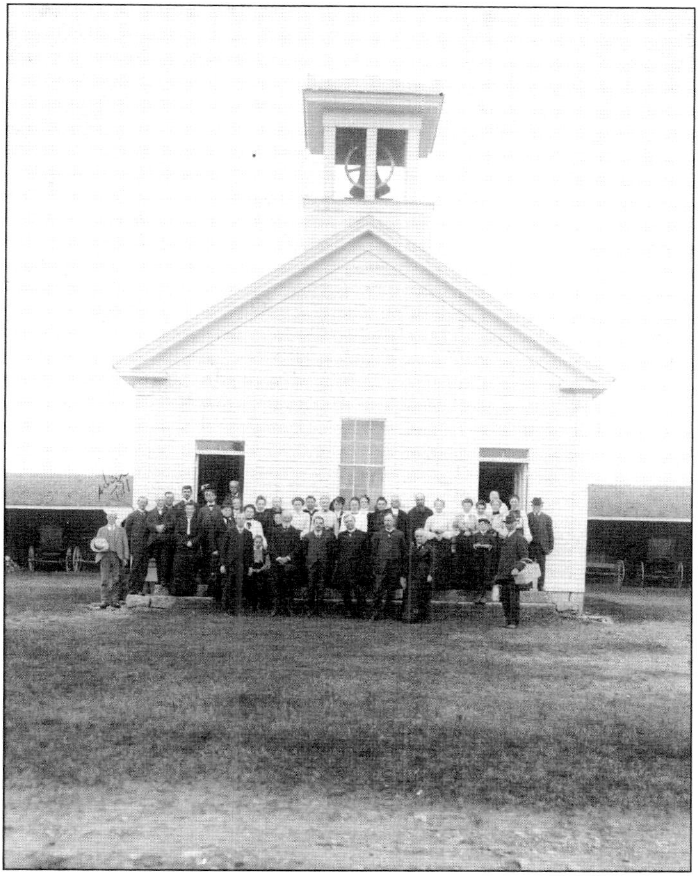

Elder Fred Buker, shown on this postcard, was the pastor of the Line Church in Moosup Valley and the Rice City Christian Church in Coventry from 1905 to 1912. Elder Buker was also the school superintendent and an accomplished carpenter. (Courtesy of Richard Siembab.)

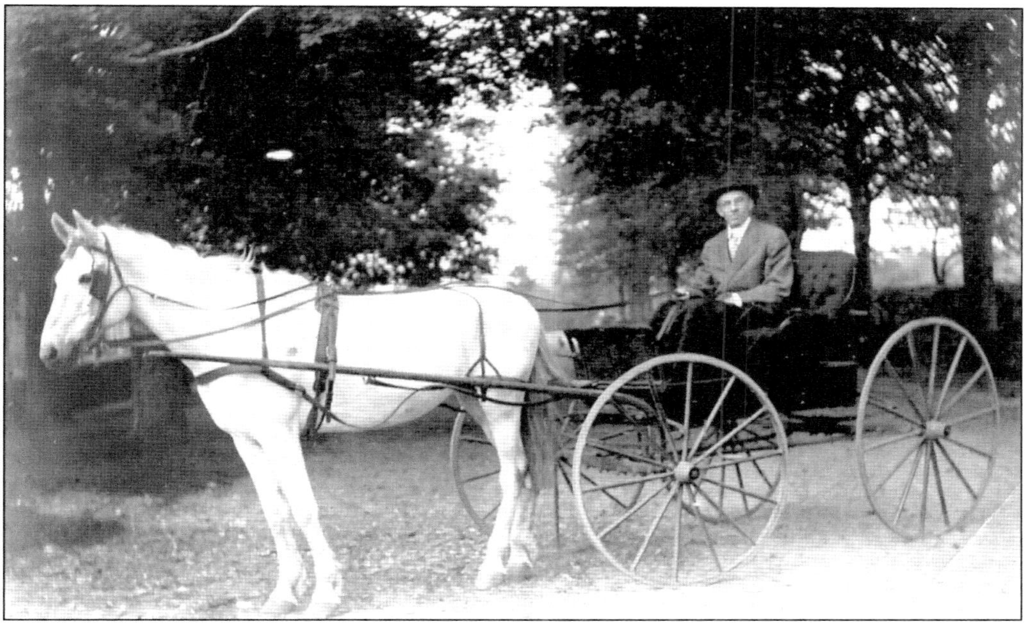

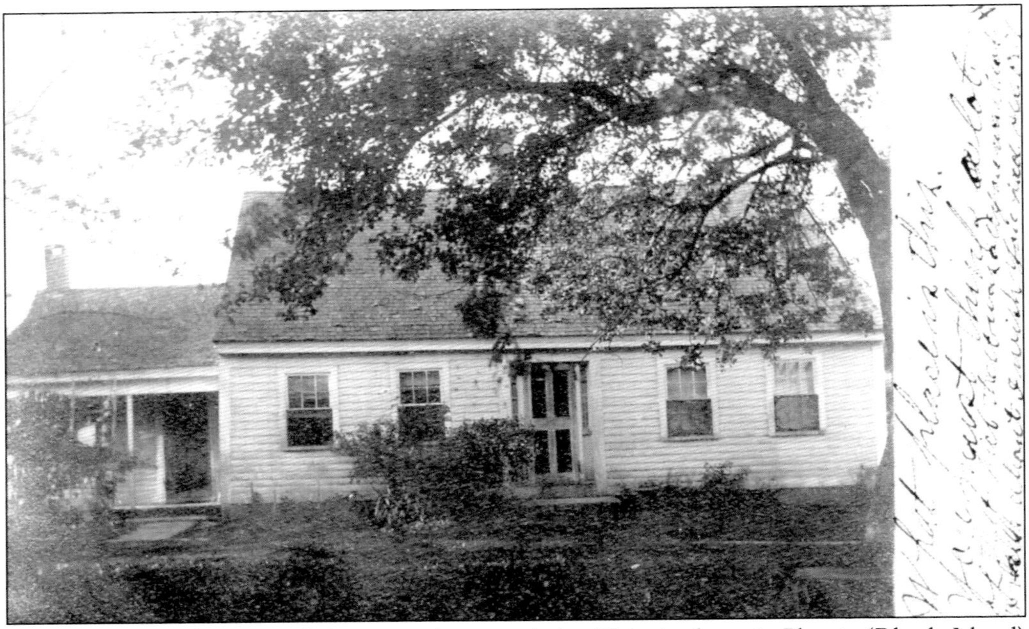

This postcard of the Kennedy homestead was mailed to Elsie Andrews in Phenix (Rhode Island) on October 24, 1905. The note to the right is interesting and reads: "What place is this? You must think a lot of that pick; that was all you wanted to talk about. I wish you had sex or ? Ha Ha." It is believed the name and address on the reverse is the handwriting of a female. (Courtesy of Richard Siembab.)

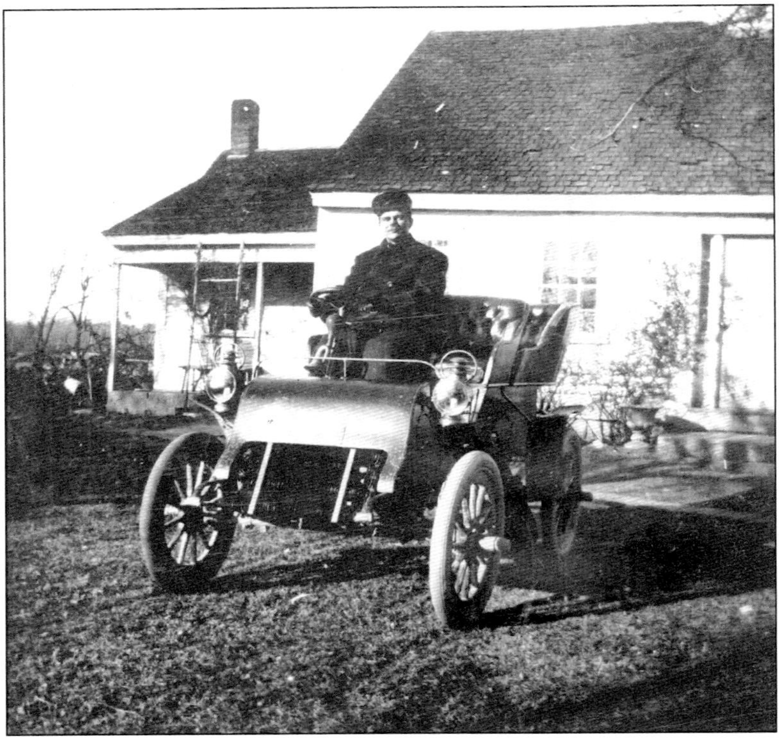

This postcard shows ? Kennedy sitting proudly at the wheel of his automobile. The steering wheel is on the right, lanterns are headlights, and there is no enclosure to protect riders from the elements. But it does look like a very luxurious padded-leather bench seat. Oh, and the driver had to crank it to get it started before going anywhere. (Courtesy of Richard Siembab.)

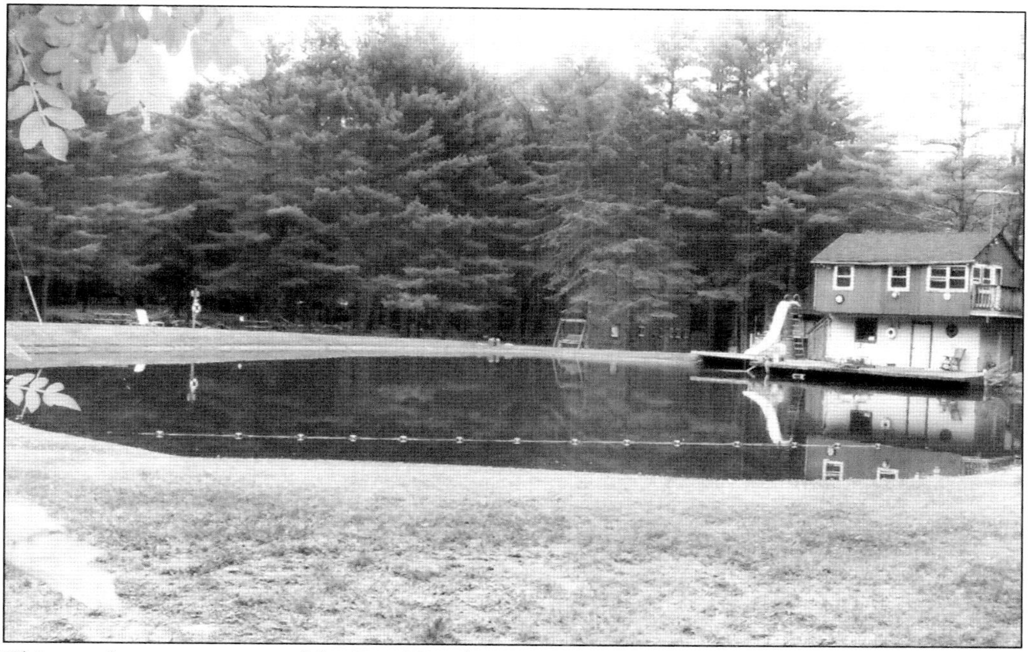

This was the serene setting of the Dyer Woods Campground in June 2011. It shows the lawn around the pond and the slide where older kids had fun. All of the campsites are to be found snuggled in the pines on this 200-acre paradise. A portion of the pond is roped off for the toddlers, as seen below, as the lifeguard keeps watch from his lofty perch close by. In the center, there is a play area, including a slide. As seen in the splattered surface of the pond, it had begun to rain hard by the time of the photograph below. The following verse is from "Whispering Pines" by Helen O. Larson: "Oh! How beautiful and quiet it was, no noise, no one around / So in this crazy world, a peaceful place I found." (Both, author's collection.)

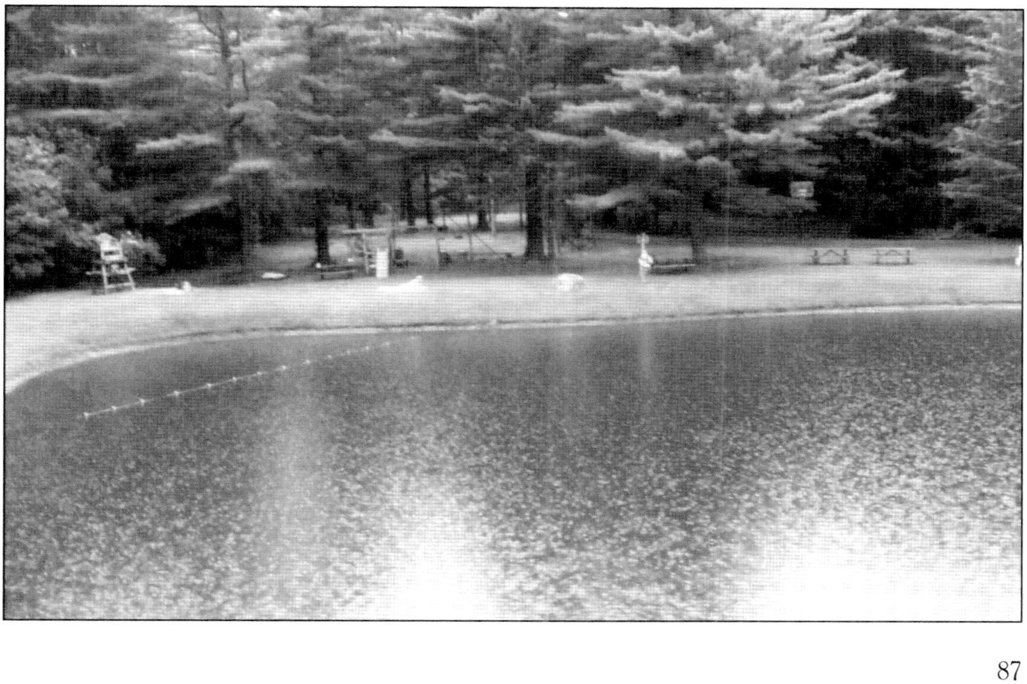

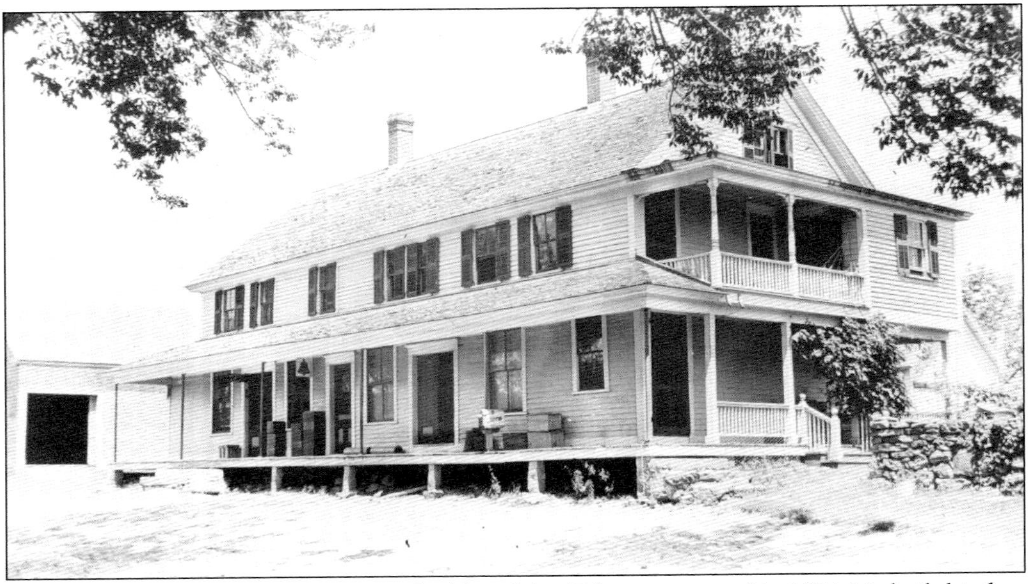

This postcard is of the large two-story building John Tyler constructed in 1834. He built his first store in 1812 and sold it in 1830. The post office was located in John's place, known as Tyler's General Store. In the early days, the postmaster would name the village; thus, the area was named Tylerville. Later, it would become known as Moosup Valley. (Courtesy of Richard Siembab.)

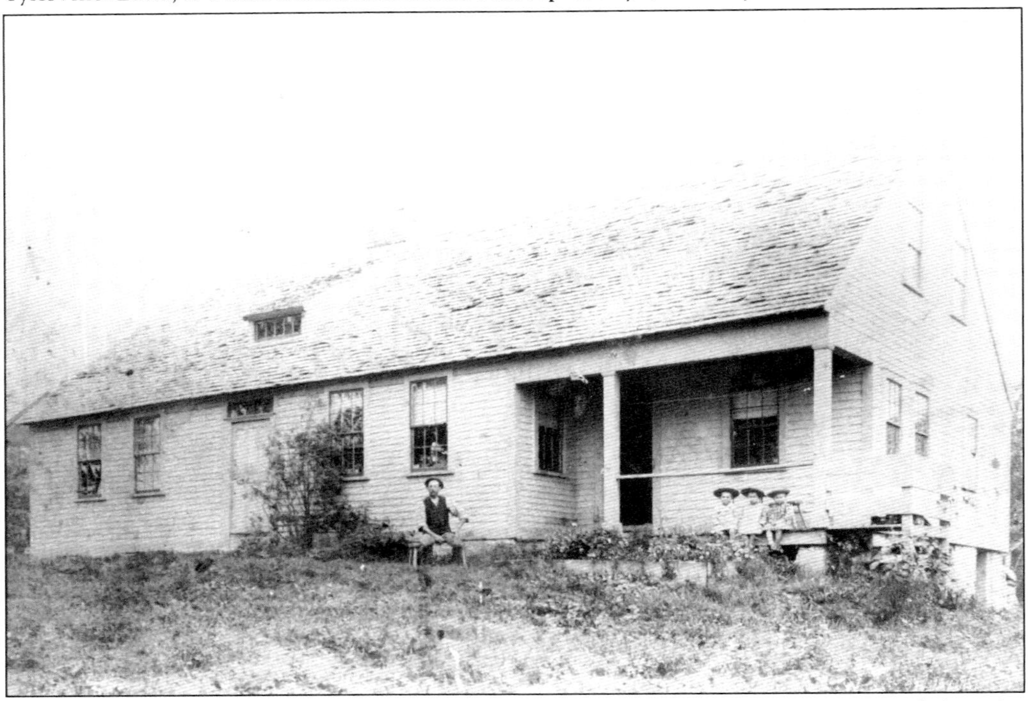

Capt. James Tyler built this large house in 1794, and made an addition in 1830. His father, the first John Tyler, and his uncle William Tyler had built a house on this site in 1728. It was torn down in 1790. John and William Tyler were very early settlers in southwestern Foster when they moved from Voluntown, Connecticut. (Courtesy of Maurice Dunbar.)

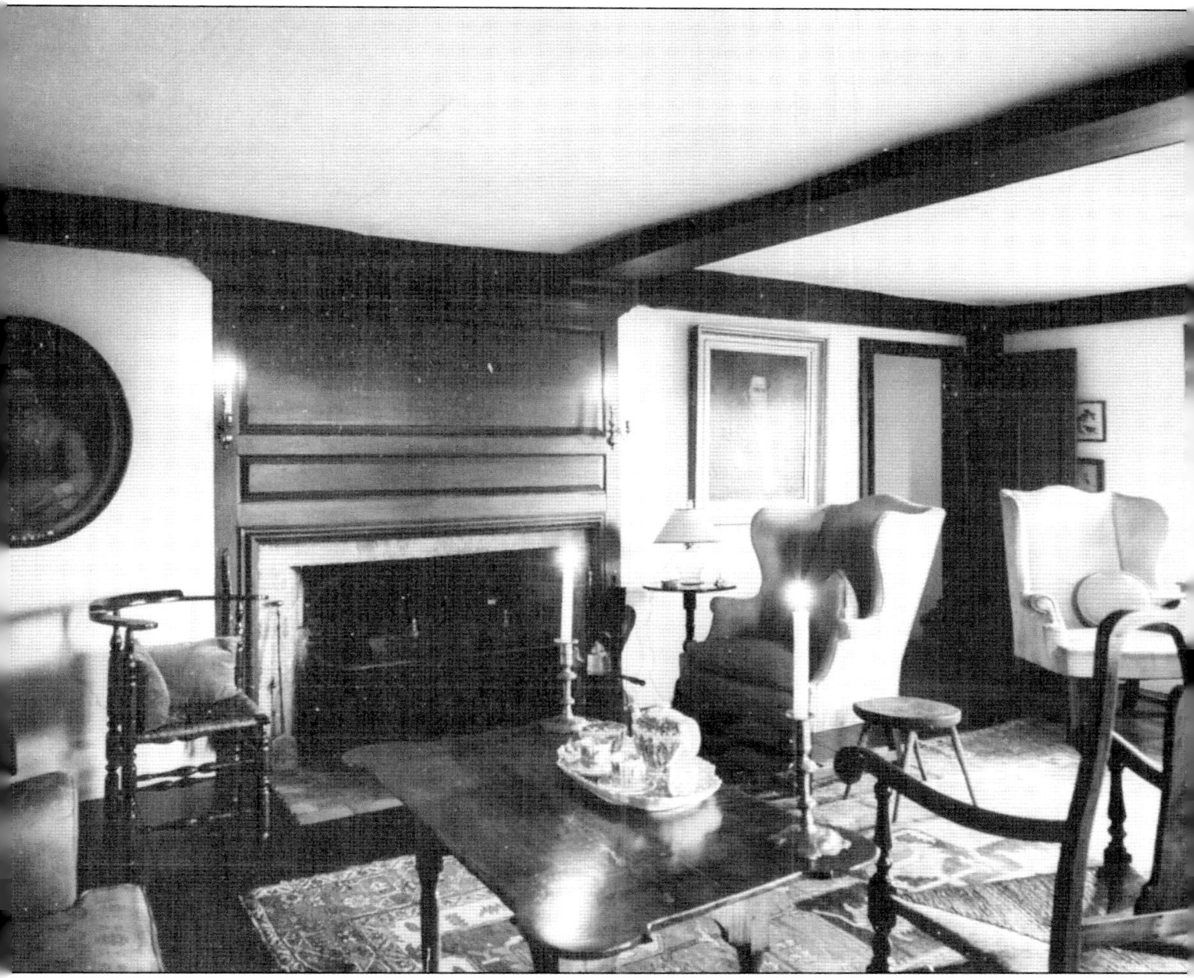

The Dorrance House was built in 1720 by George Dorrance. This view shows how homey and comfortable the parlor was. Samuel Dorrance was the first minister in Voluntown, Connecticut, and was given and also bought a large amount of land, part of which was in the area later to be Foster, Rhode Island. He gave part of the land to his brothers, George and John, who established a sawmill and a gristmill on the Quandoc River. The house, as shown in this photograph, was authentically restored in the 1950s and 1960s. The following verse is from "A Place Called Home" by Helen O. Larson: "Just to sit by the old fireplace, and see the flames rise high / It's the most restful place, beneath the blue and white sky. Just to rest in bed at night with a homemade quilt on the bed / It's so peaceful and homey, she wouldn't trade for a mansion instead."

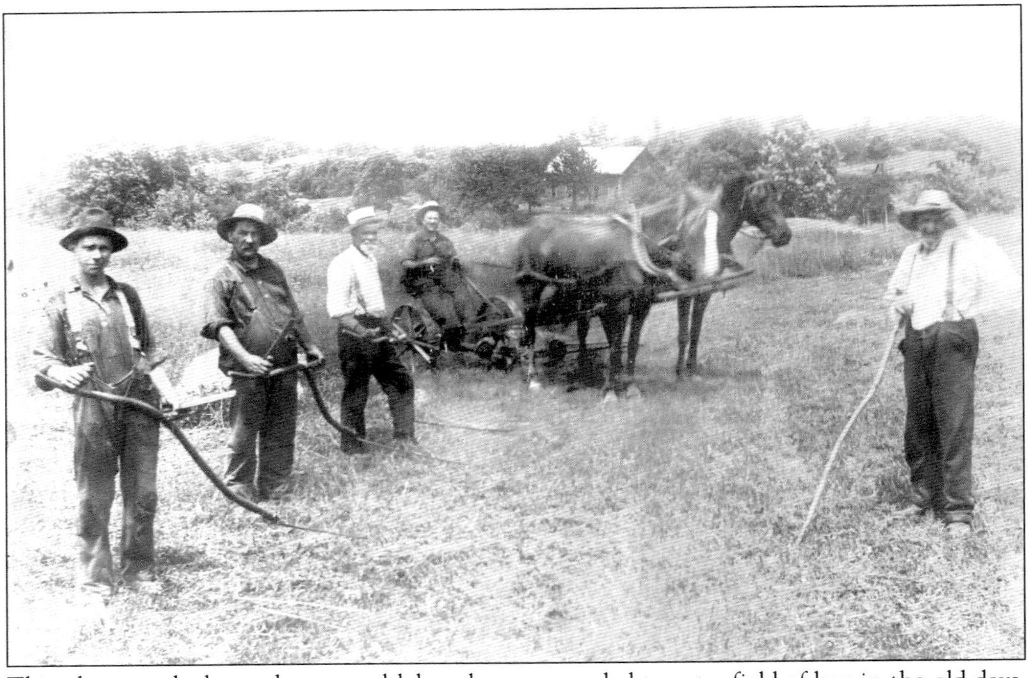

This photograph shows the manual labor that was needed to cut a field of hay in the old days. Neighbors pitched in to help each other with the task and got the job done. (Courtesy of Cathy Walls.)

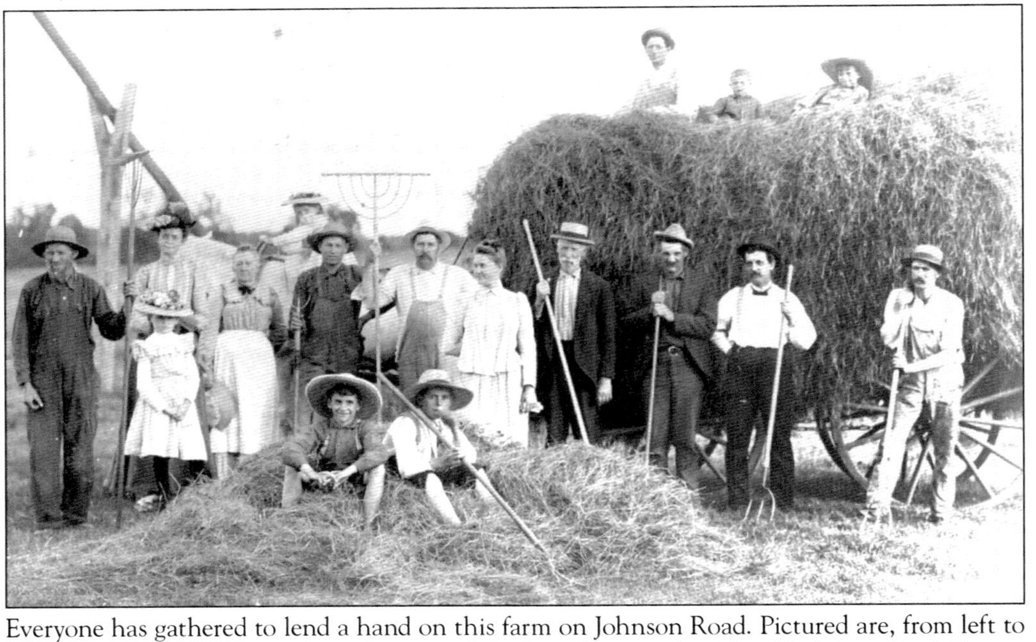

Everyone has gathered to lend a hand on this farm on Johnson Road. Pictured are, from left to right, (sitting on the haystack on the ground) Arthur Henry and unidentified; (standing) Harvey Lamphere, Susie Bassett, unidentified girl, Waity Bennett, unidentified girl, Almond Howard, Dr. James S. Phillips, Cora Phillips, Olney Cole, Charles Bassett, Frank Randall, and Louis Cole; (sitting on top of hay wagon) unidentified, George Tillinghast, and unidentified.

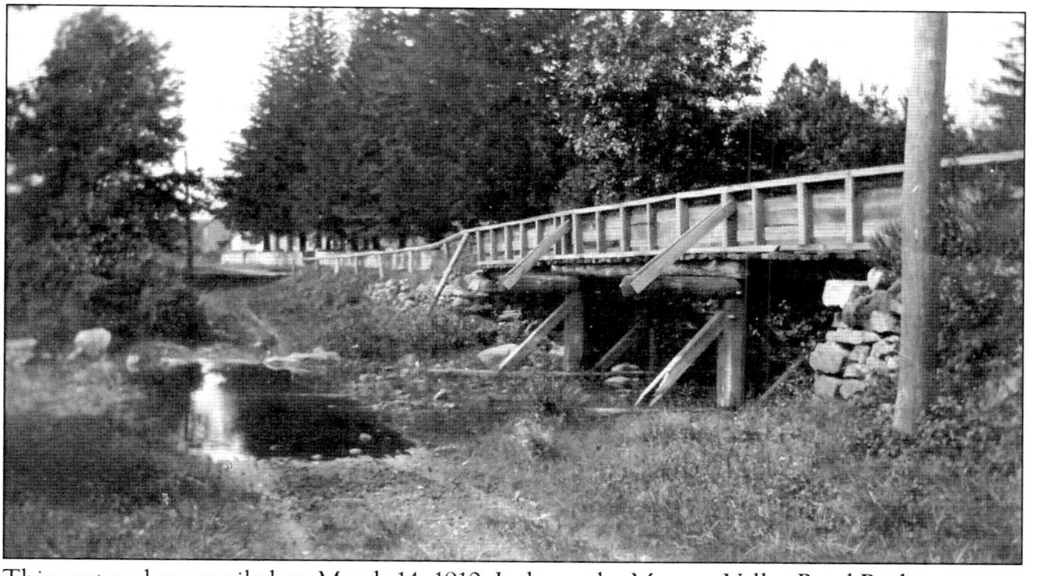

This postcard was mailed on March 14, 1910. It shows the Moosup Valley Road Bridge crossing the Moosup River as one enters the village heading west. (Courtesy of Richard Siembab.)

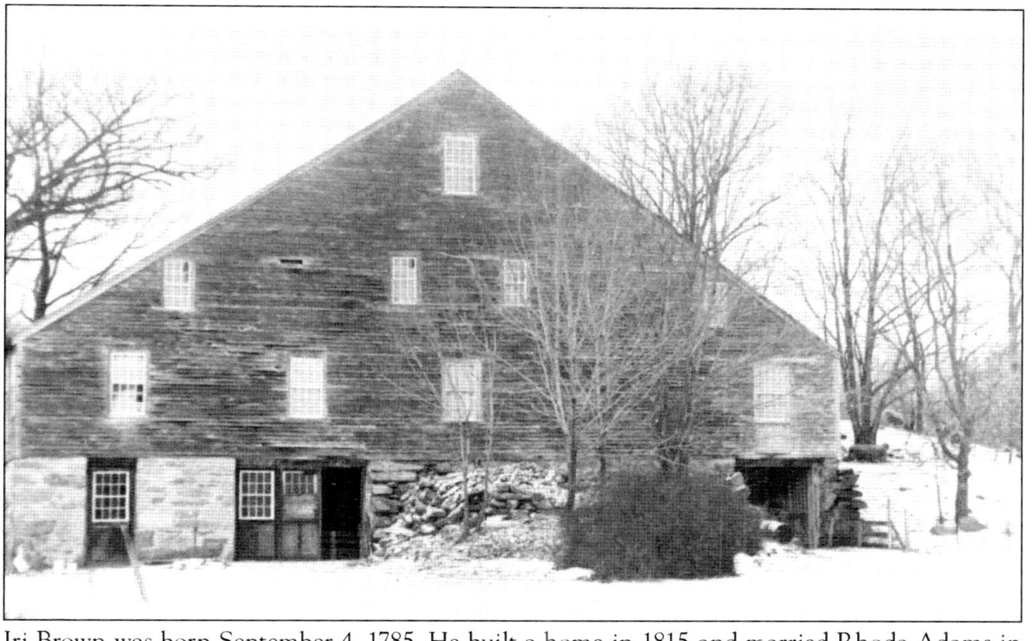

Iri Brown was born September 4, 1785. He built a home in 1815 and married Rhoda Adams in 1820. They had one daughter, Ann Eliza. Iri wanted to keep his grandson, Ann's son Curtis Foster, on the farm, so in 1885, he devised a plan to have Curtis help him build this barn. This huge four-story structure is built into a hill and is accessible on all four levels. According to the dates, Iri was 100 years old at the time.

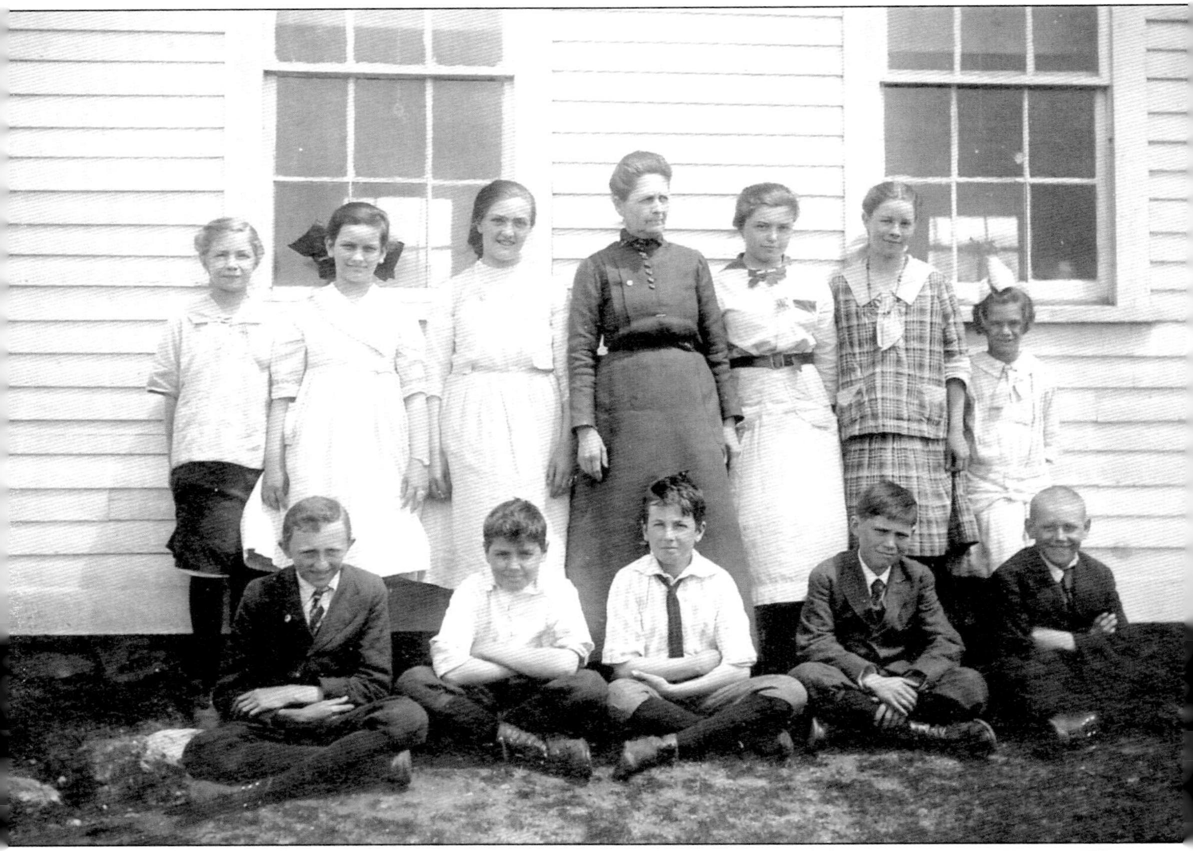

This photograph of a Dorrance School class was taken in front of the Foster Town House. The girls outnumber the boys, 6 to 5. Pictured are, from left to right, (sitting) Edward Schuman, Byron Burchard, Walter Burchard, unidentified, and ? Budlong; (standing) Berta Griffiths, Dorothy Crompton, Helen Johnson, Mrs. White (teacher), Ruth Johnson, Ruth Griffiths, and ? Budlong. The following verse is from "My School" by Helen O. Larson, written in 1999 at the age of 88: "Oh! That dear old school house, that I went to each day / We used to whisper and the teacher got mad, and after school we had to stay. I loved the children that went there, they were all friends of mine / And the memories will stay with me, for all time."

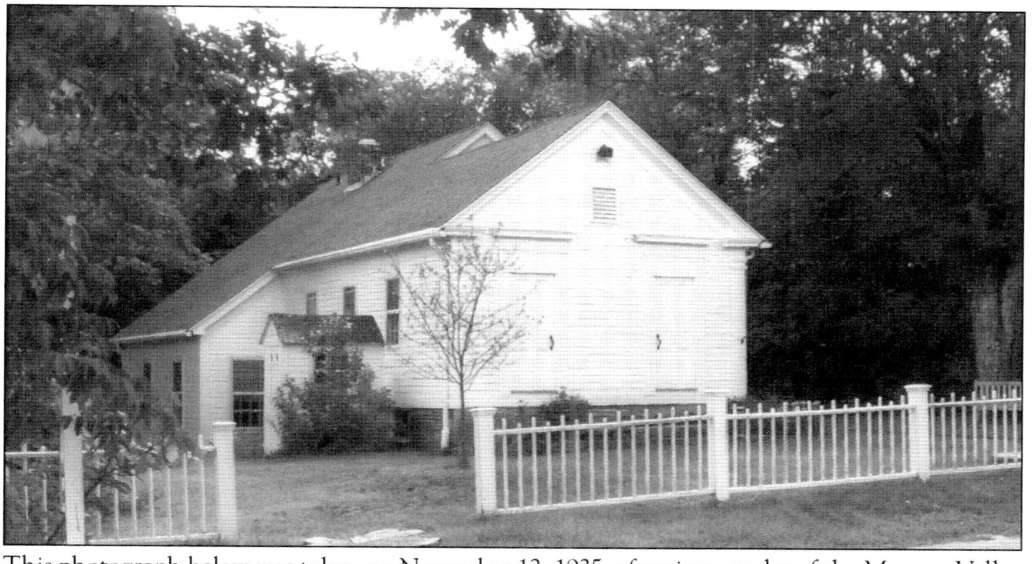

This photograph below was taken on November 12, 1935, of various grades of the Moosup Valley one-room school, pictured above. It is now the Tyler Free Library. From left to right are (first row) Raymond Sullivan, Eileen Sullivan, William Sullivan, and Lilly O. Taylor; (second row) Evelyn Sayball, Edgar MacDonald, William J. Harrington, William Henry Luther, Arnold Taylor, Ruth Dunbar, Martha E. Krvisto, and Mason A. Bennis; (third row) Margery Harrington, Doris Sayball, William Repak, Walter Carlson, Albert Dunbar, and Mary Hope Luther; (fourth row) Maurice A. Dunbar, Dorothy Nicholson, and Edwin Luther. Eleanor Carlson and Donald Sullivan were absent, and Howard Nicholson had gone home. (Above, author's collection; below, courtesy of Maurice Dunbar.)

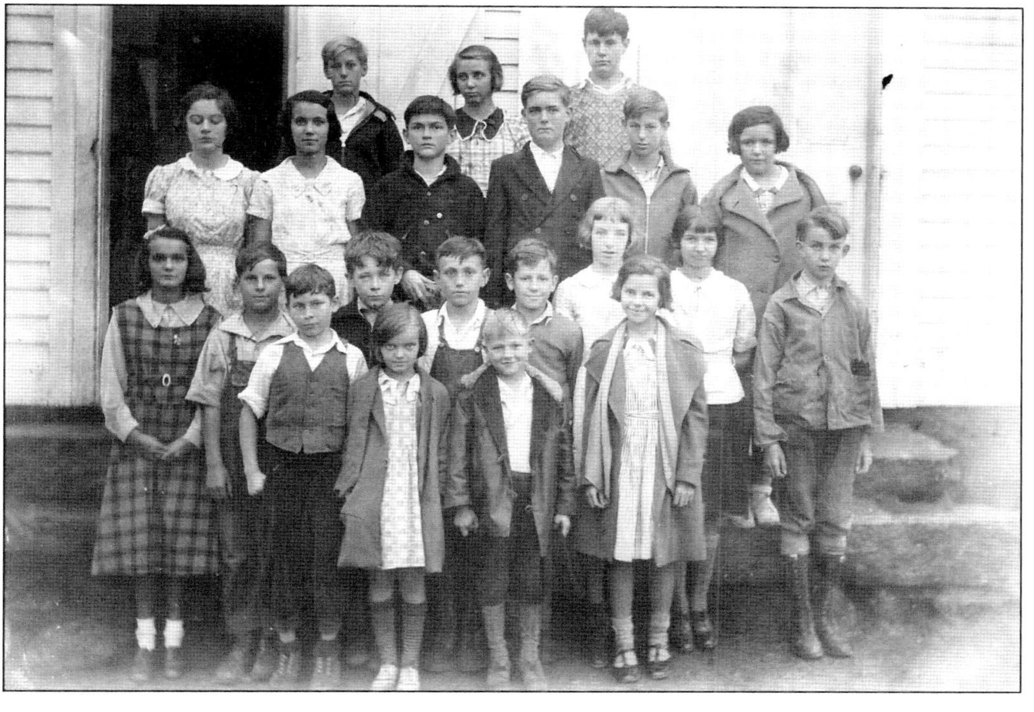

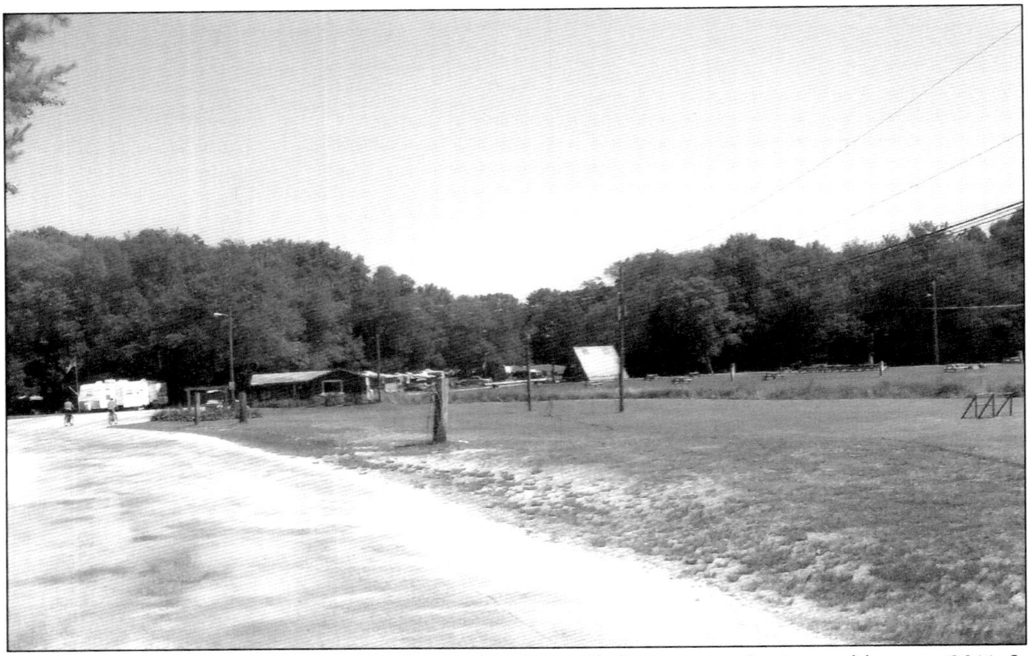

In 1966, the Bassett Farm was turned into the Ginny-B Campground, pictured here in 2011. It has grown to include 270 campsites on its 90 acres. The campground is located on Harrington Road and adjacent to the Foster Country Club. (Author's collection.)

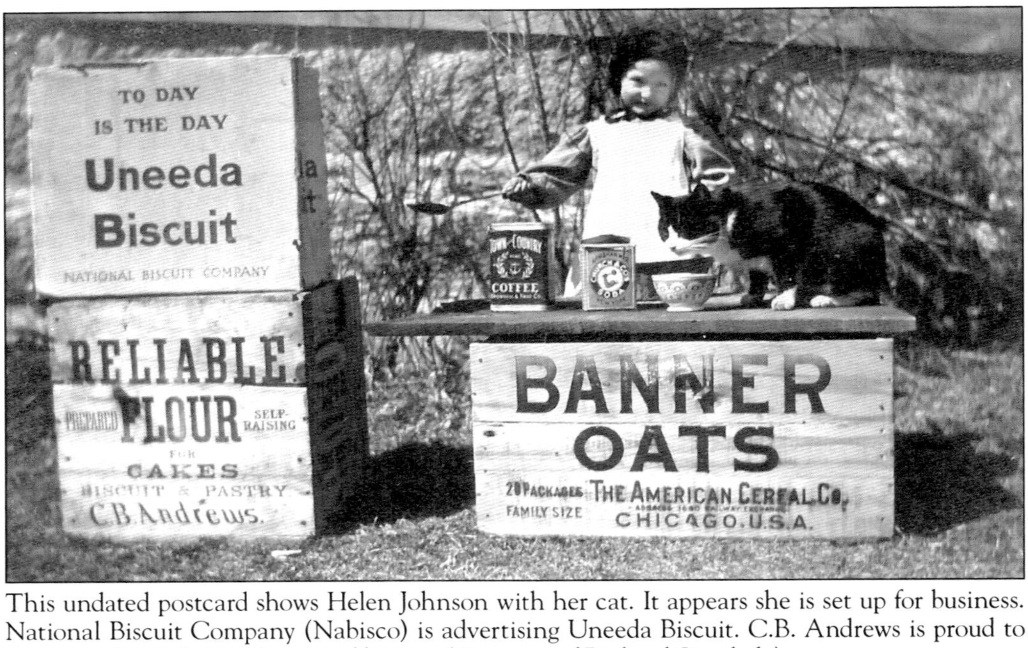

This undated postcard shows Helen Johnson with her cat. It appears she is set up for business. National Biscuit Company (Nabisco) is advertising Uneeda Biscuit. C.B. Andrews is proud to state that his Reliable Flour is self rising. (Courtesy of Richard Siembab.)

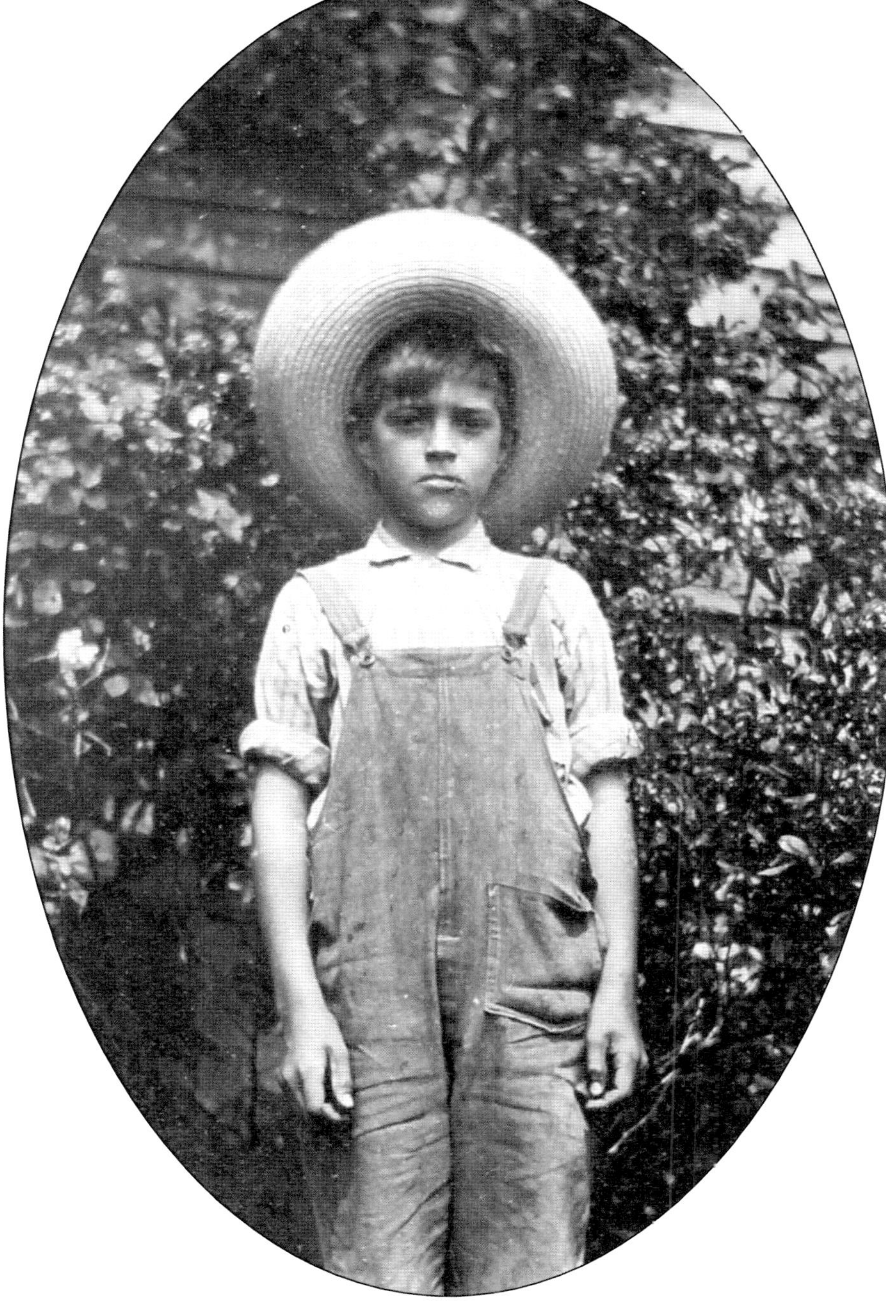

This postcard shows Earl C. Johnson posing for the camera. He and his sister Helen (on page 94) lived on the farm their father, Arthur D. Johnson, built on Barbs Hill Road. The following verse is from "The Road of Life" by Helen O. Larson: "The years come and go, as I walk the road of life each day / Hoping to meet a kind person, that will take the loneliness away. I will walk this road only once, I'll leave foot prints along the way / I know they will be seen, as others walk this road each day." (Courtesy of Richard Siembab.)

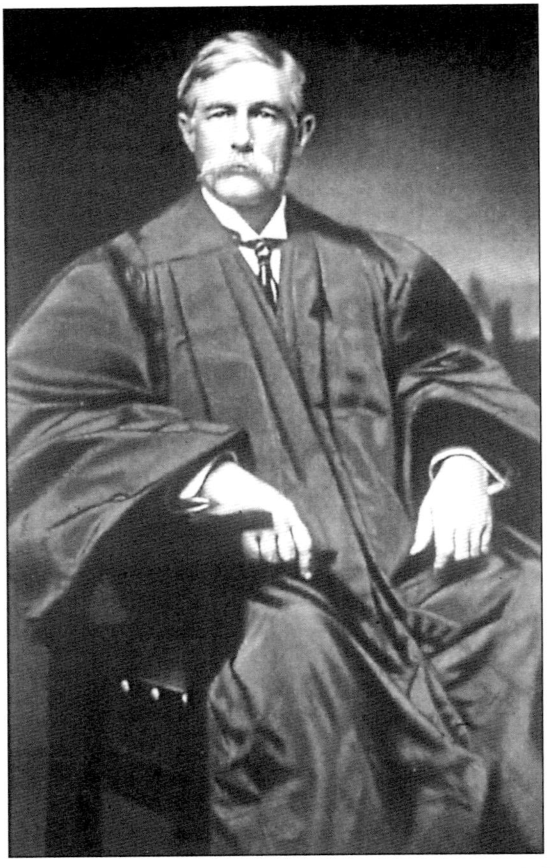

Clarke Howard Johnson was born November 18, 1851. He graduated from Brown University in 1877 and was admitted to the bar in 1879. On December 21, 1889, he married Ida Susan Harrington. Among his many titles, Johnson became Rhode Island's chief justice on January 27, 1913.

Below is a memo from attorney Clarke H. Johnson on December 30, 1901. He was located in Room 409 of the Industrial Trust Company Building in Providence. The memo is addressed to F.R. Young, mentions an enclosed deed of minerals from Samuel Bennett to Walter M. Bennett, and states Samuel will need to sign it in front of a notary public. (Courtesy of Cathy Walls.)

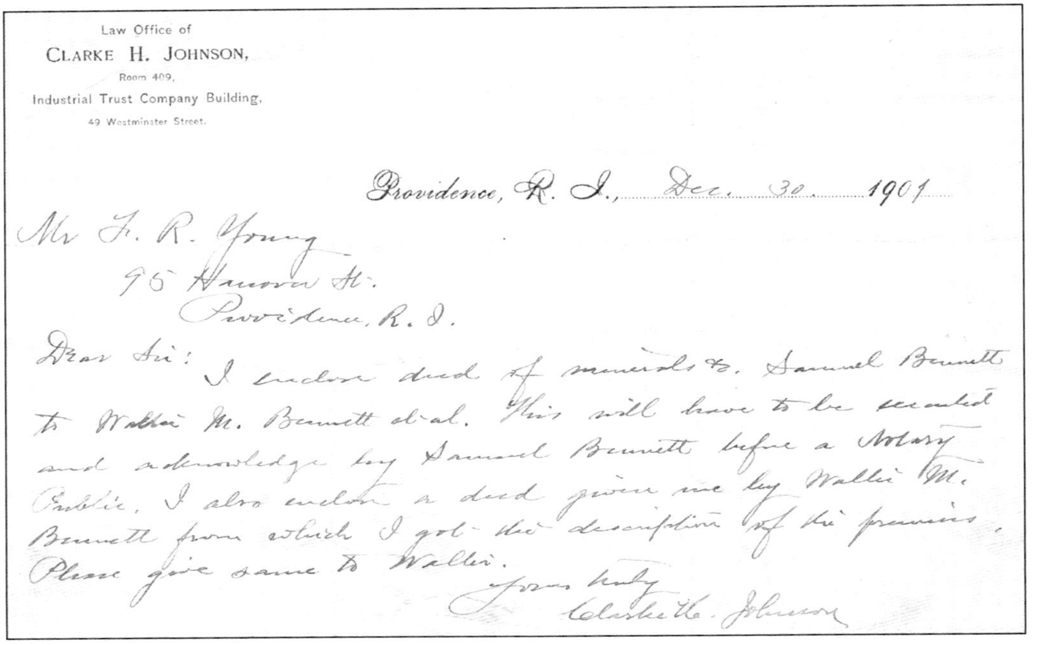

Law Office of
CLARKE H. JOHNSON,
Room 409,
Industrial Trust Company Building,
49 Westminster Street.

Providence, R. I., Dec. 30. 1901

Mr F. R. Young
95 Hanover St.
Providence, R. I.

Dear Sir: I enclose deed of minerals &c. Samuel Bennett to Walter M. Bennett et al. This will have to be executed and acknowledge by Samuel Bennett before a Notary Public. I also enclose a deed given me by Walter M. Bennett from which I got the description of the premises. Please give same to Walter.

Yours truly
Clarke H. Johnson

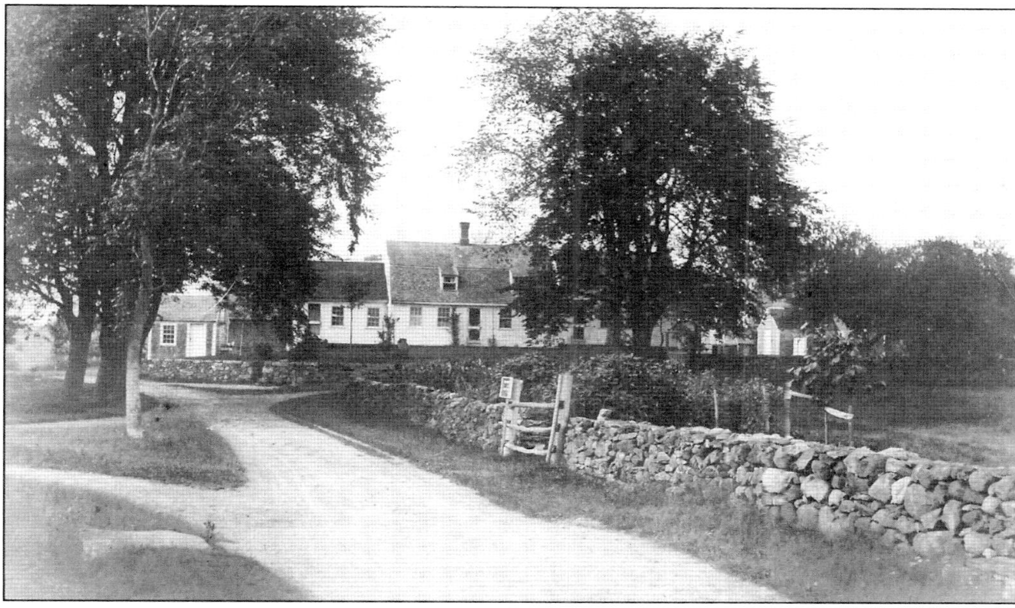

This postcard shows the beautiful house that Judge Johnson and his wife, Ida, resided in on Johnson Road. Harrington Road is shown bearing to the left. The complex is now the Foster Country Club, pictured below. The main house is now the clubhouse and a pro shop. A large banquet hall has been added to the rear. (Courtesy of Richard Siembab.)

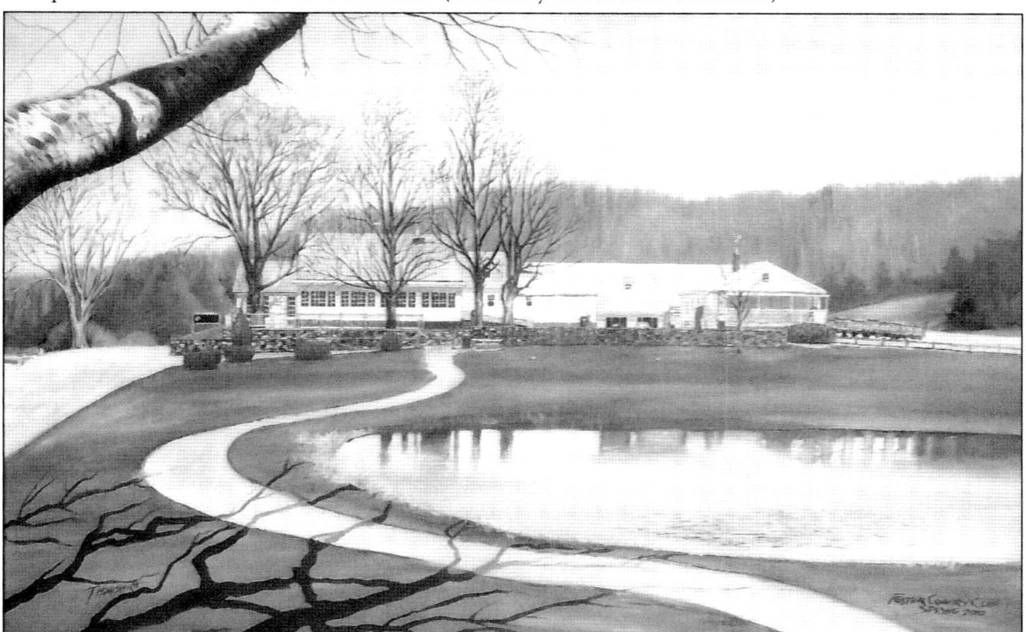

This painting of the Foster Country Club was done in the spring of 2010. It shows the wall in front of the former Johnson homestead is still present; however, the wall along Johnson Road to the left has been eliminated. Construction began in 1959, and the club opened nine holes in 1961. In 1962, it completed an 18-hole course on its 150 acres. (Courtesy of Foster Country Club.)

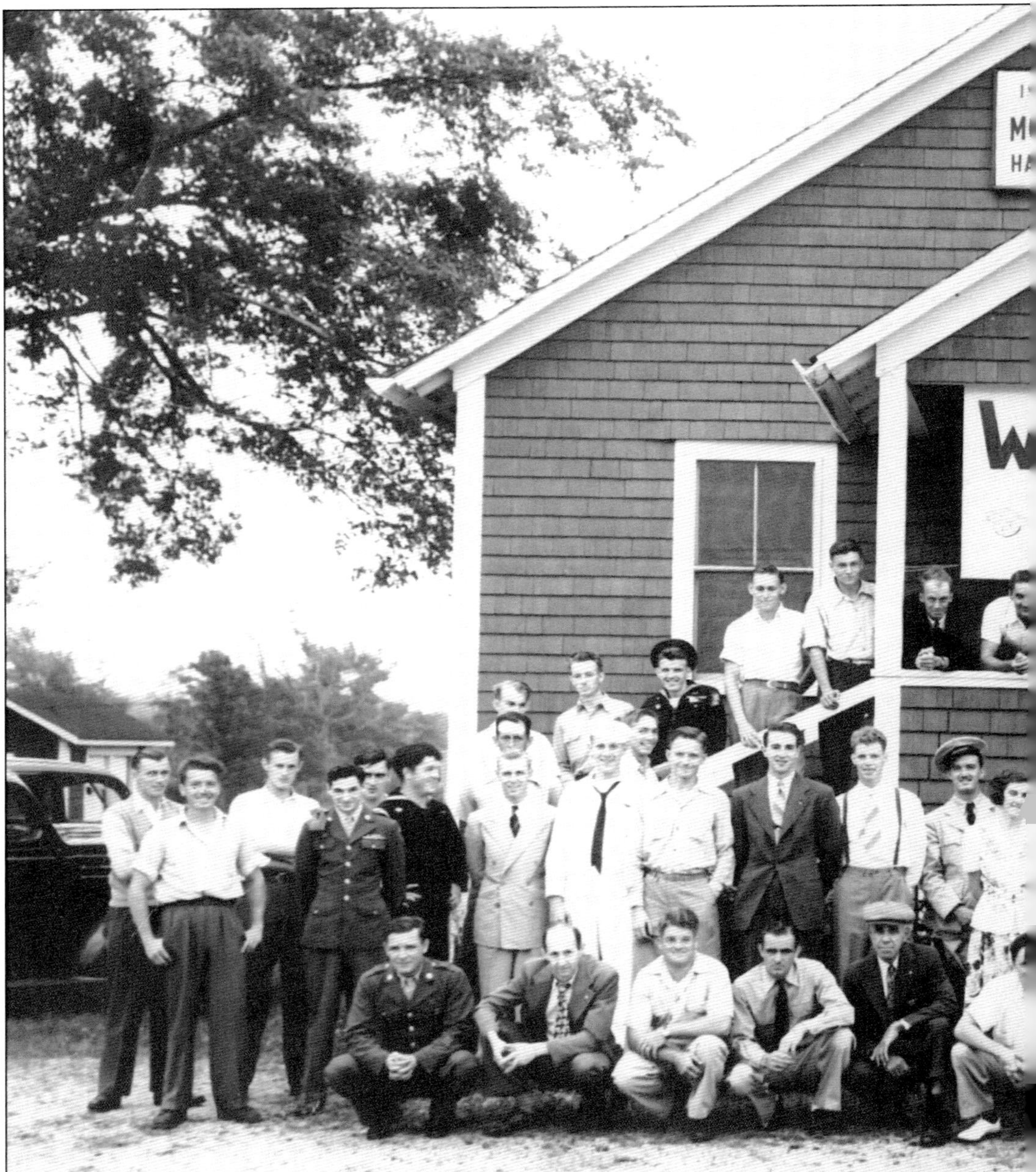

The Moosup Valley Grange held a "welcome home" celebration for Foster World War II veterans in August 1946. From left to right are (kneeling) Joseph Brooks, ? Gill, Charles Dexter, Clifford Farrell, Russell Wells, Albert Tacey, Tommy Chatterton, Albert Hendrick, Leon Shippee, Maurice Dunbar, Fred Kettle, Raino Tikkanen, Monroe Knight (rear), Jim Rounds, William McCormick (rear), Howard Blackmar, Sidney, Kennedy, Walter Jehu (rear), Arnold Kennedy, George Newman, and Norman Tucker; (standing) Robert Rickard, Walter Law, Walter Bartlett, Bruno Becarrie, Walter Brayton Jr. (rear), Charles Cole, Granville Ryder, ? Shippee (rear), John Keidel Hopkins (sailor), Walter Grass (rear), Walter Shippee, Charles Holher, Russell Borders, Frank Law, Helen Bodge, Leslie Law (rear), Virginia Springler, unidentified (rear), Dot Huse Rounds, Gorton

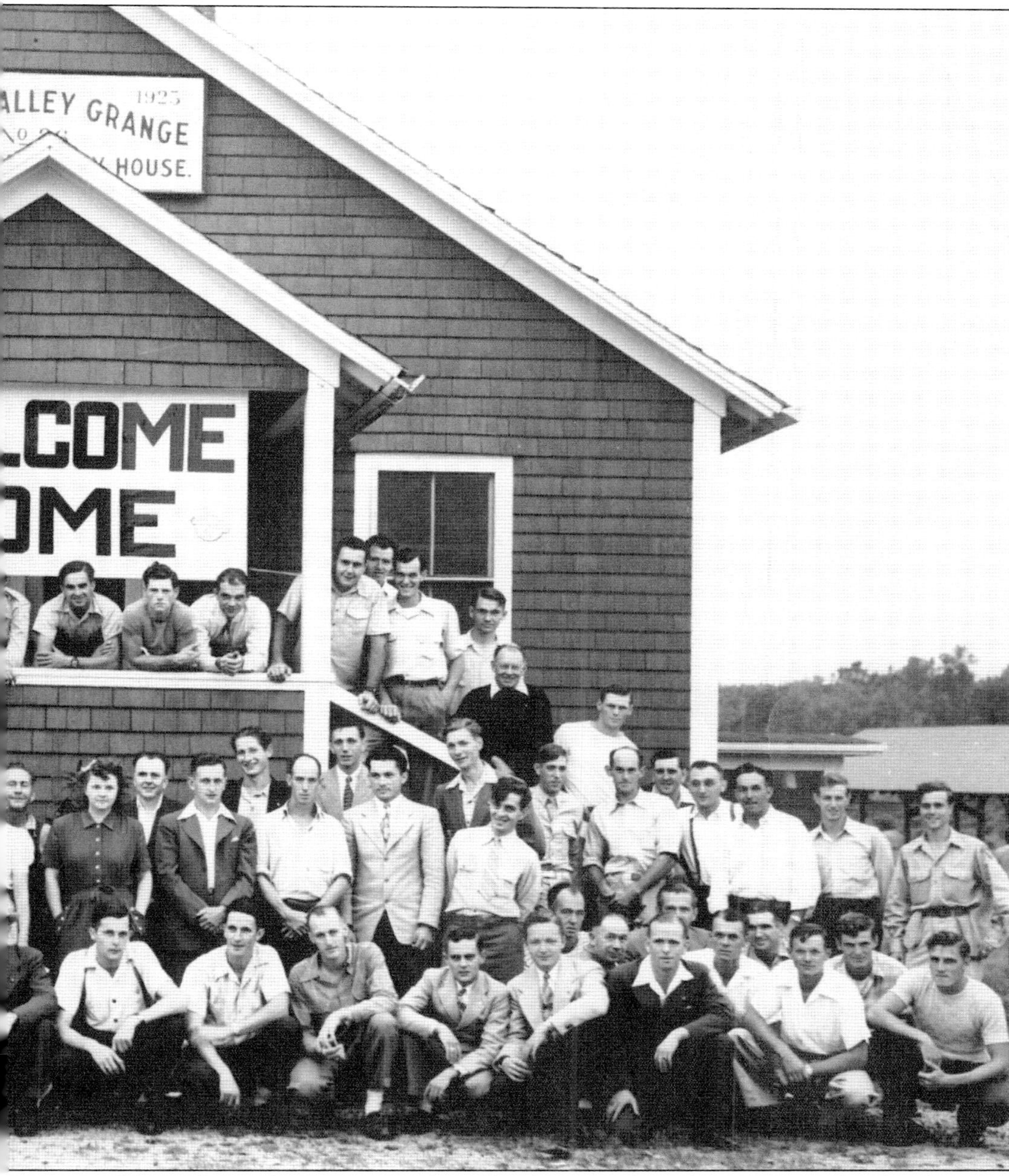

Truesdale, William Thoman, Kenneth Walker (rear), Paul Dunbar, Henry Luther (rear), Harold Vannasse, Richard Belanger (rear), unidentified, William Bellows, Harold Sweet, John Jehu (rear), Kenneth Farolie, Charles Sweet Jr., Albert Dunbar, and Bob Salisbury; (on stairs) Mason Bennis, Jarvis Dunbar, Walter Grass, Mason Lenth, David Lenth, Norman Potter, Leonard Kivisto, Berrick Dewhirst, George Kivisto, Alcott Phillips, Roland Kennedy, Edwin Luther, unidentified (rear), Dick Henry, unidentified, and George Brayton. The following verses are from "Welcome Home" by Helen O. Larson: "They're boarding the plane, they're flying back home today / They're tired but happy soldiers, soon they'll land in the U.S.A. All of the troops are heroes now, the war has been won / God bless all of you, thanks for a job well done." (Courtesy of George Newman.)

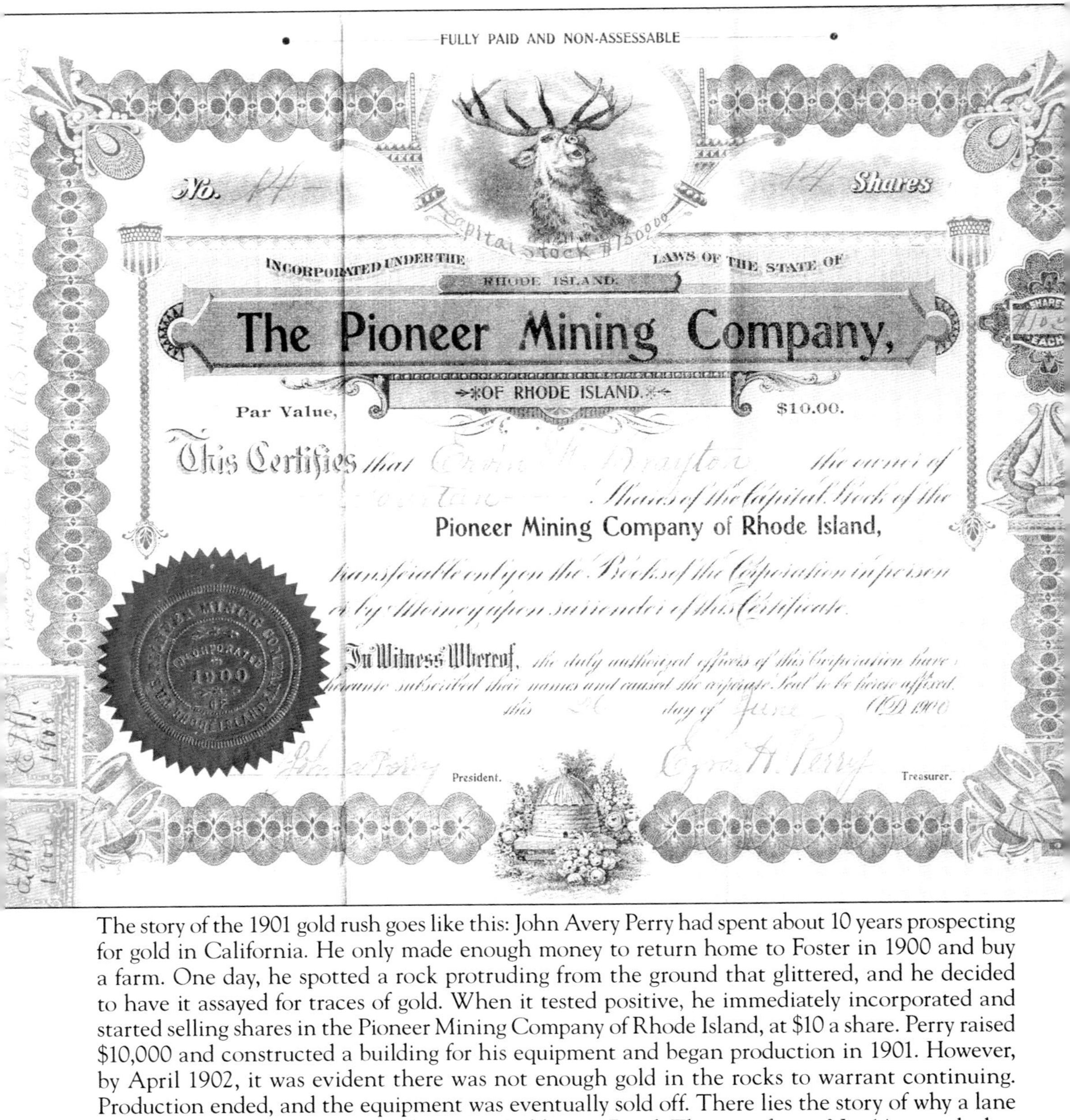

The story of the 1901 gold rush goes like this: John Avery Perry had spent about 10 years prospecting for gold in California. He only made enough money to return home to Foster in 1900 and buy a farm. One day, he spotted a rock protruding from the ground that glittered, and he decided to have it assayed for traces of gold. When it tested positive, he immediately incorporated and started selling shares in the Pioneer Mining Company of Rhode Island, at $10 a share. Perry raised $10,000 and constructed a building for his equipment and began production in 1901. However, by April 1902, it was evident there was not enough gold in the rocks to warrant continuing. Production ended, and the equipment was eventually sold off. There lies the story of why a lane off Cucumber Hill Road carries the name Gold Mine Road. This certificate, No. 14, records that Ervin F. Brayton bought 14 shares on June 26, 1900. It is signed by John A. Perry, president, and Ezar H. Perry, treasurer. The official gold seal of the corporation is affixed. (Courtesy of Dorothy Pierce-Brayton.)

Five

Mount Vernon Area

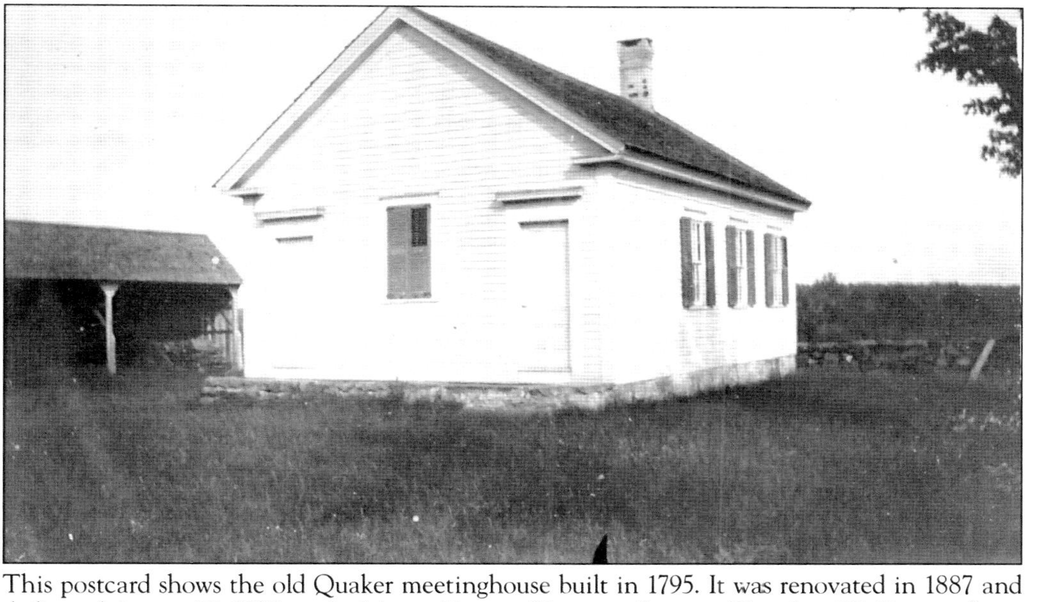

This postcard shows the old Quaker meetinghouse built in 1795. It was renovated in 1887 and dedicated August 29, 1889, as the Mount Vernon Christian Society. Theodore W. Sheppard was the first pastor, serving from 1889 to 1892. In 1895, it became Mount Vernon Baptist Church. The church is located between Moosup Valley and Mount Vernon on Moosup Valley Road. One could park his or her carriage in the building to the left while at the service. (Courtesy of Richard Siembab.)

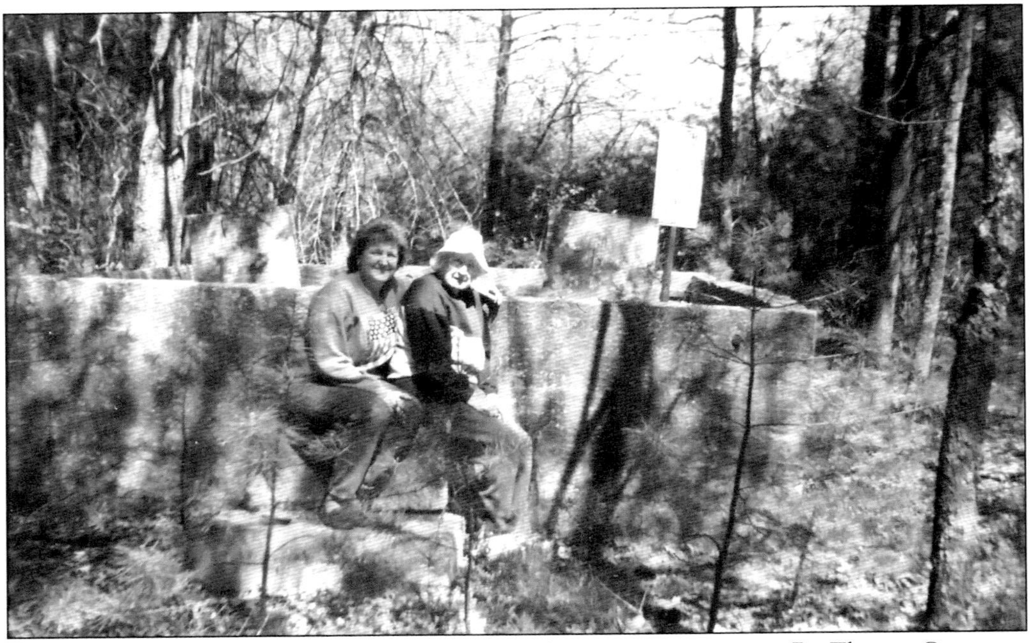

Arline Bucci (left) and Viola Ulm are sitting beside the Carpenter cemetery. Dr. Thomas Carpenter was married three times; however, only one of his wives stayed with him. Therefore, he wanted four stones measuring 12 feet long by 4 feet high placed around him and his favorite wife, Henrietta. The other two wives are buried outside of the enclosed area. (Courtesy of Viola Ulm.)

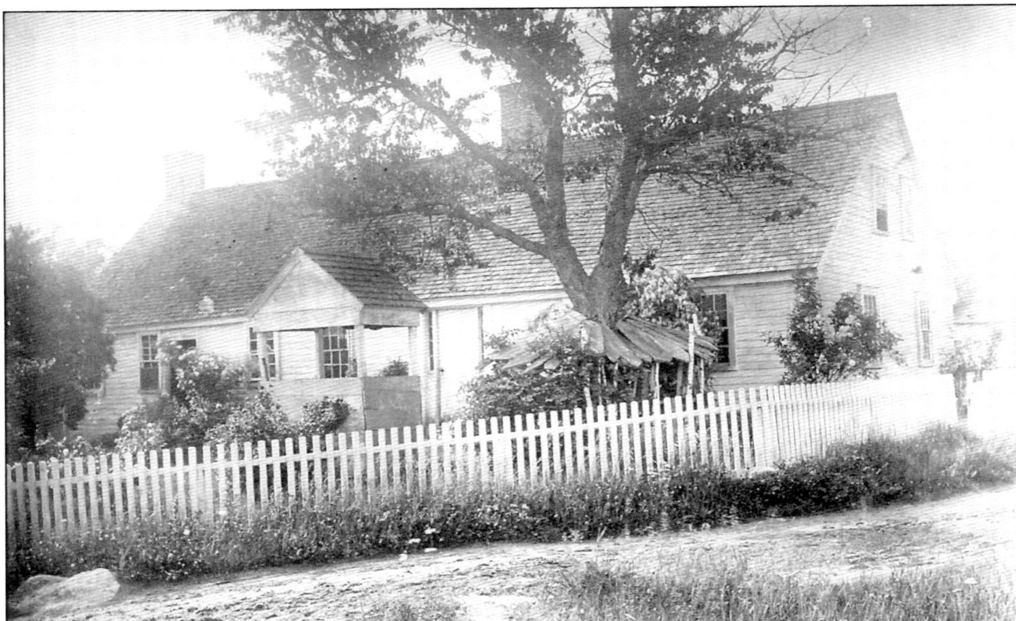

This postcard shows Gardner Howard's homestead, built in 1831 and located on Howard Hill Road. To make room for his home, he razed the house that Isaac Howard built in 1755. In May 1880, Samuel and Sara Goldsmith bought the house and lived here for 25 years. (Courtesy of Richard Siembab.)

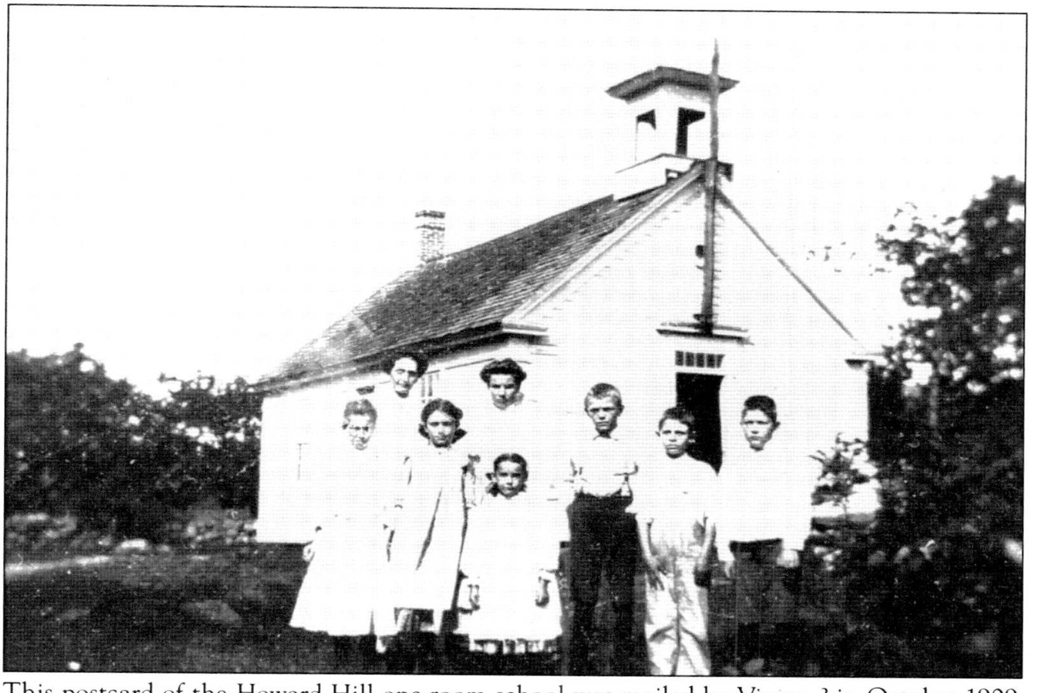

This postcard of the Howard Hill one-room school was mailed by Vivian ? in October 1909. Teacher Ida O. Howard (second row, left) is lined up with her entire class—three boys and four girls, of various ages. Vivian states she is in the first row, second from the left. It is unusual to see the school was built with only one entrance. (Courtesy of Richard Siembab.)

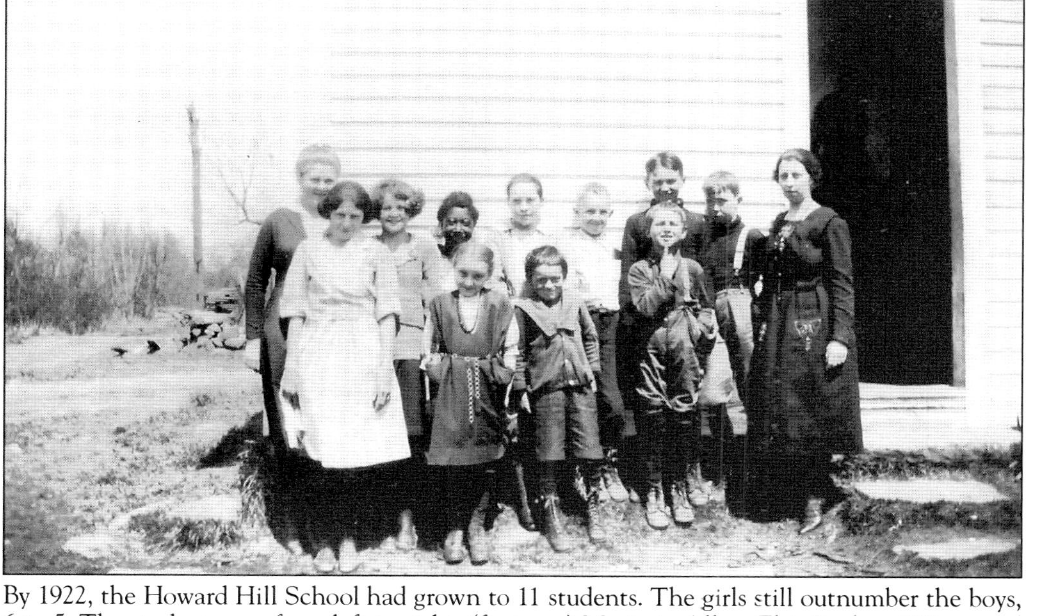

By 1922, the Howard Hill School had grown to 11 students. The girls still outnumber the boys, 6 to 5. The students are, from left to right, (first row) Marjorie Allen, Elsie Luther, ? King, and Joseph Wood; (second row) Evelyn Wilson, Clara Nye, Hattie Bennett, Roswell Collins, Otto Knight, Leo Stewart, Monroe Knight, and teacher A.M. Fry. (Courtesy of Richard Siembab.)

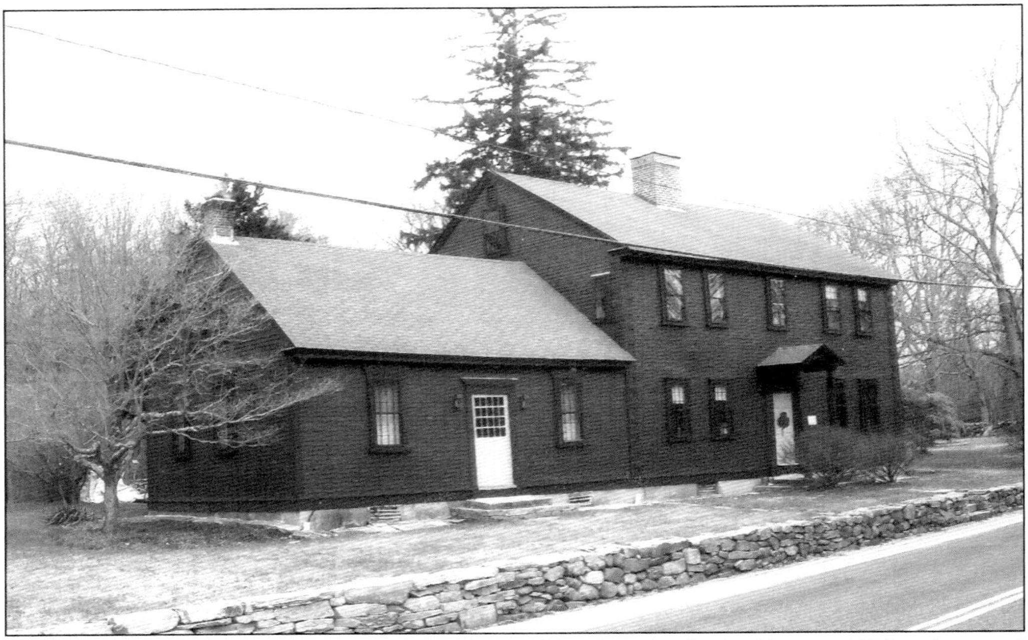

This building was constructed in 1760. Pardon Holden bought the building in 1814 and opened the Mount Vernon Tavern in 1815. The addition to the left housed a store and, after 1828, the post office. Mount Vernon has the honor of having the only bank ever to be chartered in Foster, when in 1823 the Mount Vernon bank opened in the front west chamber over the tavern. It is now restored and a private residence. Below is a photograph of the beautifully restored Mount Vernon Baptist Church, also seen on page 101. Both photographs were taken in March 2011. (Both, author's collection.)

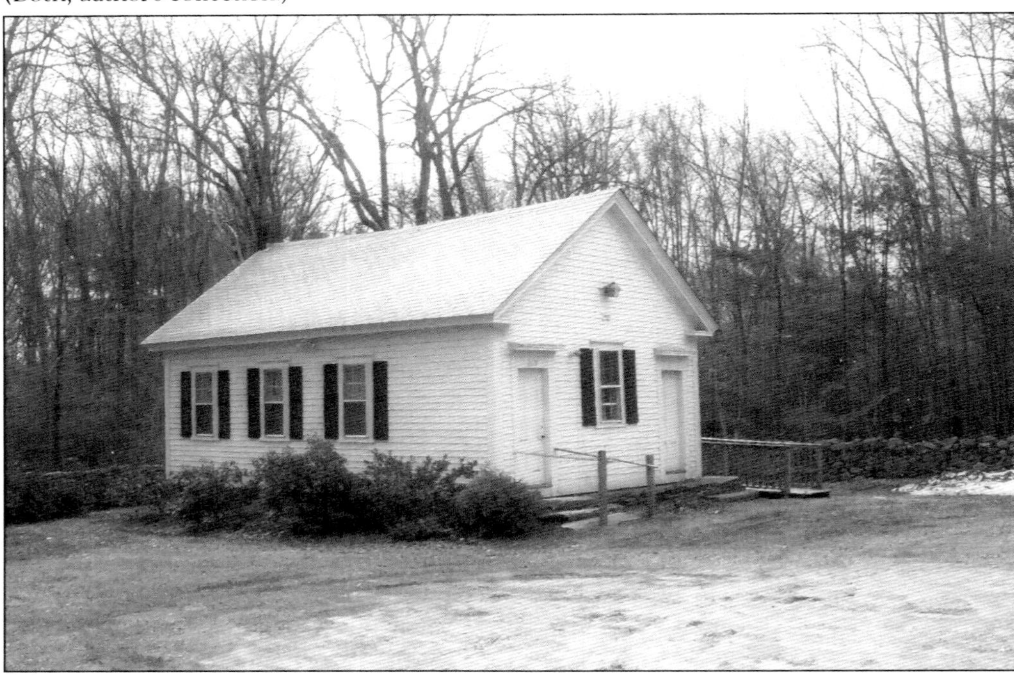

Six

North Foster Area

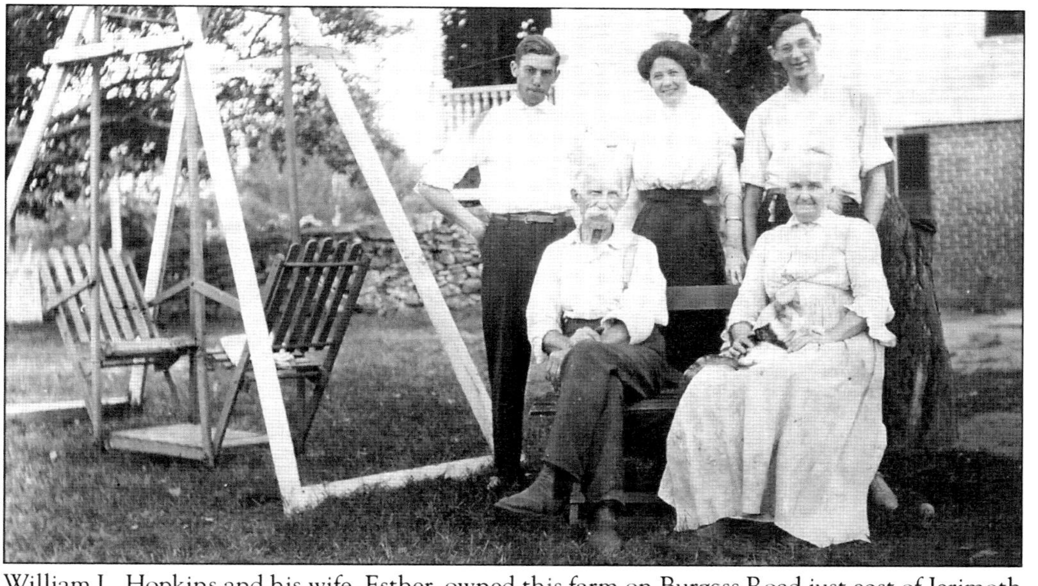

William L. Hopkins and his wife, Esther, owned this farm on Burgess Road just east of Jerimoth Hill. Their children are, from left to right, Stephen, Esther, and unidentified. The town of Foster holds the designation of having the highest elevation in the state. It is 812 feet above sea level on Jerimoth Hill. Even though there is a sign announcing Jerimoth Hill is on Hartford Pike, the actual location is off the highway and a short walk through the woods.

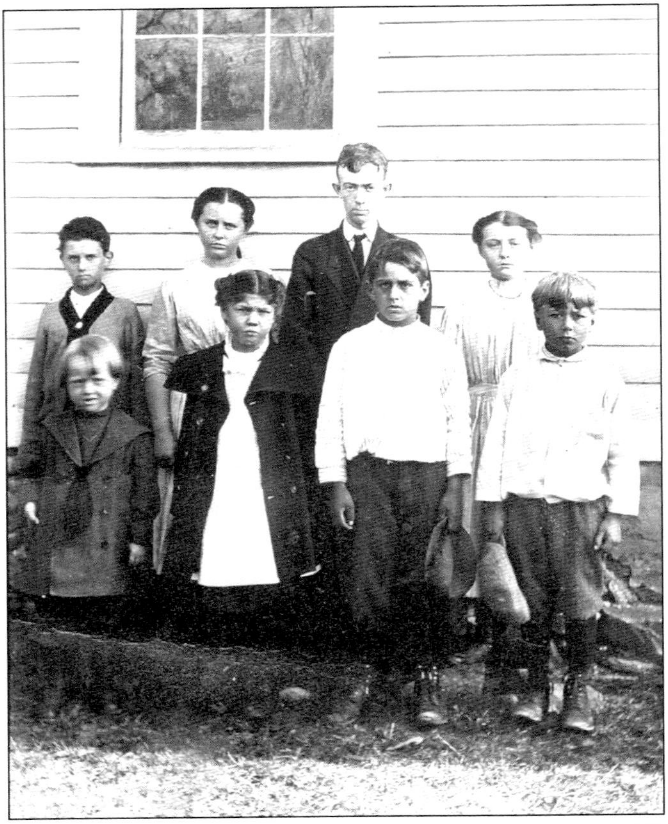

This postcard shows a teacher and his class in front of Mount Hygeia School. No one is identified. Foster maintained a one-room school system until 1952.

In 1755, a deed for a schoolhouse lot in the Mount Hygeia area is the earliest reference to any school in Foster. It was built in 1840 and has survived the test of time. Mount Hygeia School was still in use in 1952, when Foster combined all the one-room schools into the new Capt. Isaac Paine School. This beautiful school of old still sits beside Route 101 today. (Author's collection.)

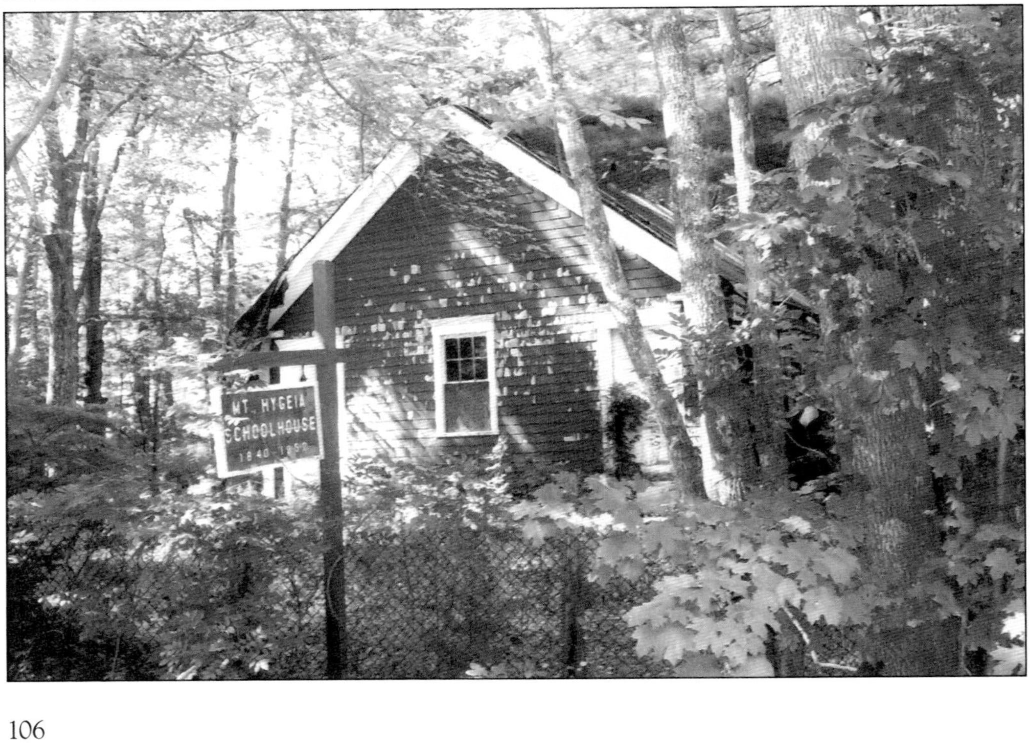

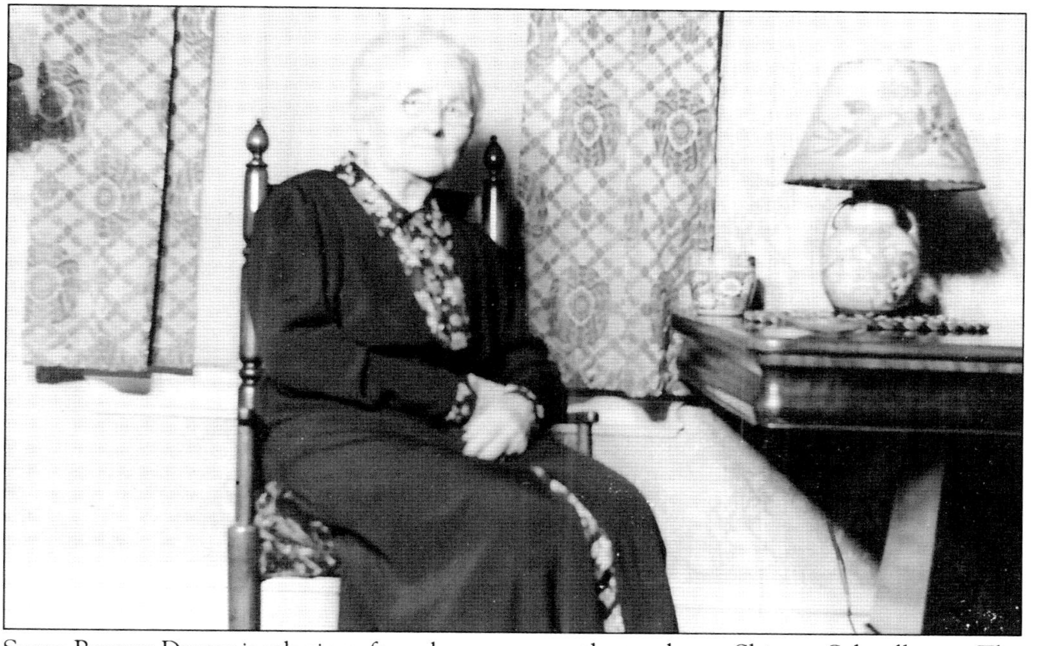

Susan Burgess-Dexter is relaxing after a long career as the teacher at Shippee Schoolhouse. The following verse is from "She Sits by the Fireside" by Helen O. Larsen written in 2000 at the age of 89: "She sits alone by the fireside, she bows her head to pray / She wonders if she will see you, on this Mother's Day." (Courtesy of Susan Boucher.)

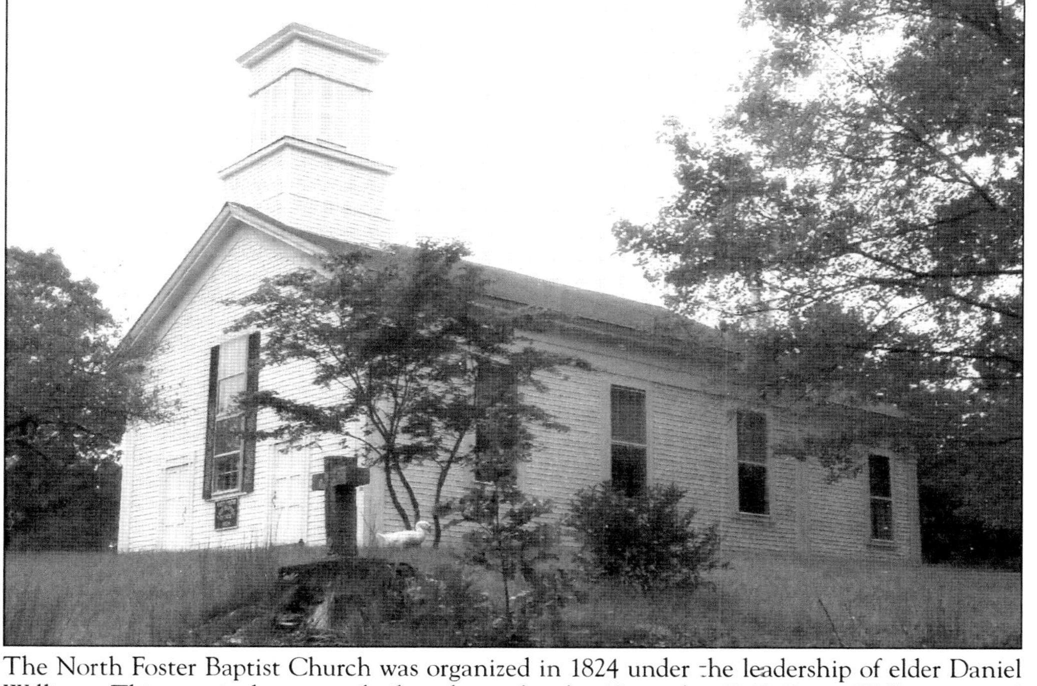

The North Foster Baptist Church was organized in 1824 under the leadership of elder Daniel Williams. This meetinghouse was built and completed in November 1843. Pastor Williams served from 1824 until he passed away on July 16, 1873. (Author's collection.)

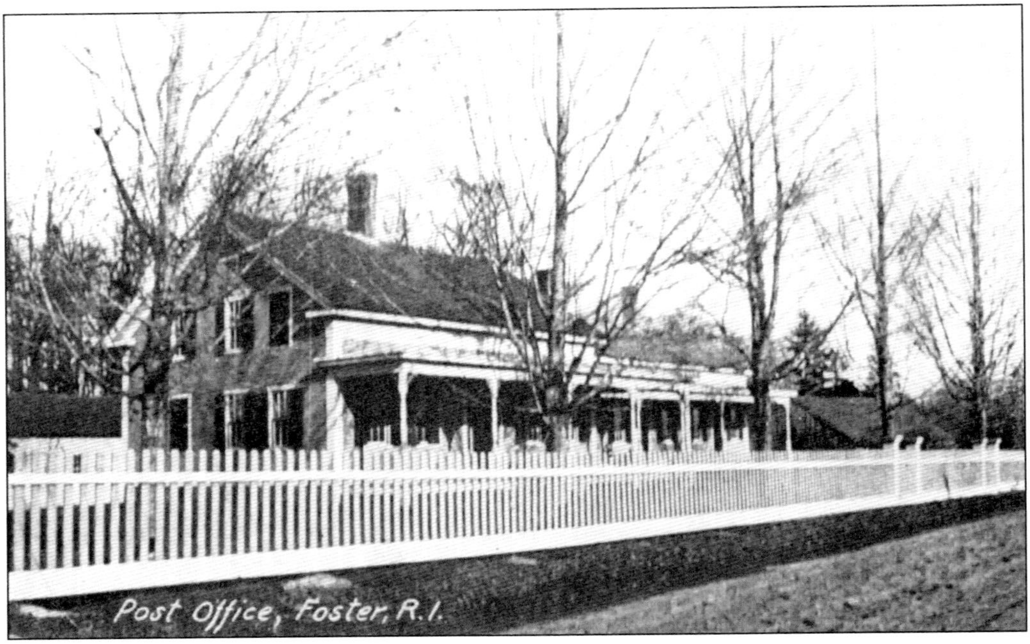

This postcard of Hon. H.J. Paine's house, built in 1855, was mailed in August 1910. This house was also the original post office for North Foster. The post office building to the right can also be seen below and on the facing page. The road passing in front of the white picket fence is Hartford Pike (Route 101). Mount Hygeia School, built in 1840, was located next door. Below, Mount Hygeia Road (Route 94) is intersecting Hartford Pike in front of the post office and James Cook's store, built in 1920. It appears a man is leaving the post office with his son and his dog as another man is walking down the pike approaching him. (Both, courtesy of Richard Siembab.)

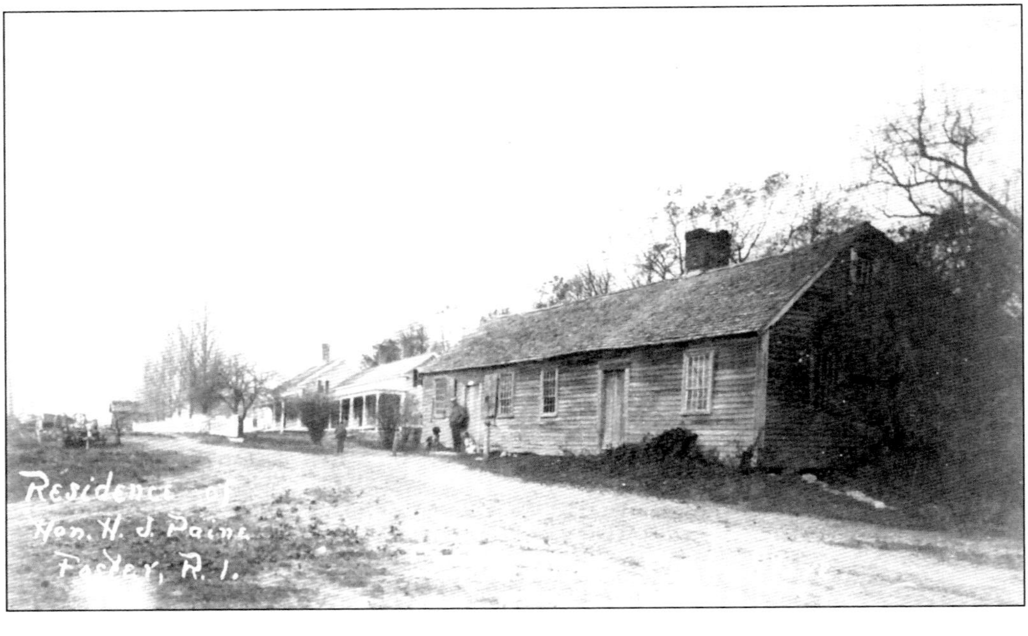

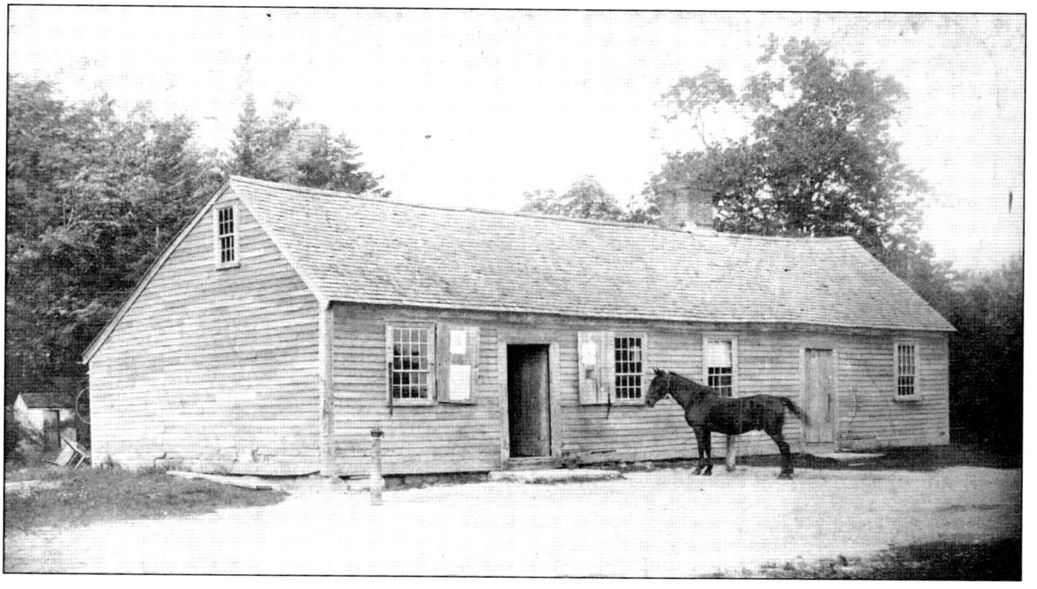

James Cook ran a store on the right portion of this building in 1900 when this photograph was taken. Ada Paine ran the post office on the left. The security shutter on the left displayed wanted posters, and the one on the right contained notices. It was located on the corner of Routes 94 and 101. The outhouse can be seen in the rear. Nathan Hopkins owned this house (below) on the corner of East Killingly and Paine Roads. This postcard was mailed on September 24, 1912, from North Scituate and shows a good example of a well sweep. (Both, courtesy of Ernest Ross.)

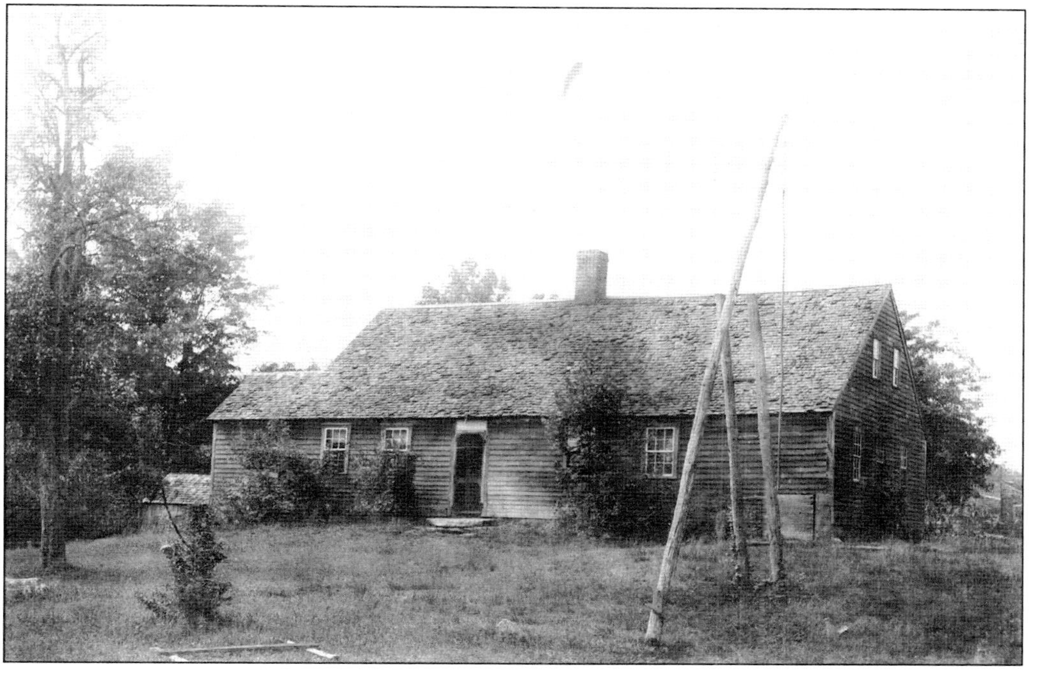

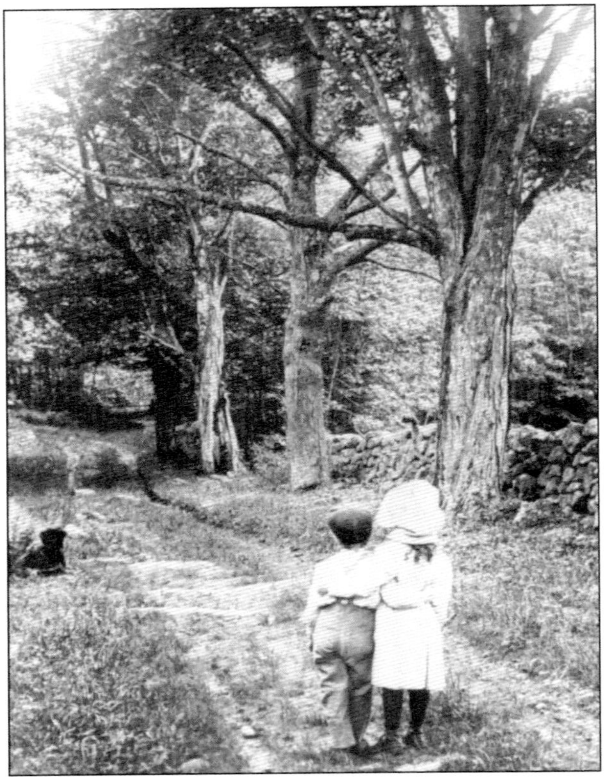

Donald Ross and his sister Esther are strolling down the lane to reach the gate and the entrance to the Drowne homestead. The following verses are from "Walking Down a Lane" by Helen O. Larson: "We were walking down a lane, it was a nice summer day / And we could smell the scent of the flowers, as we walked along the way. We were holding hands, and laughing all the time / That day so long ago, with that brother of mine.

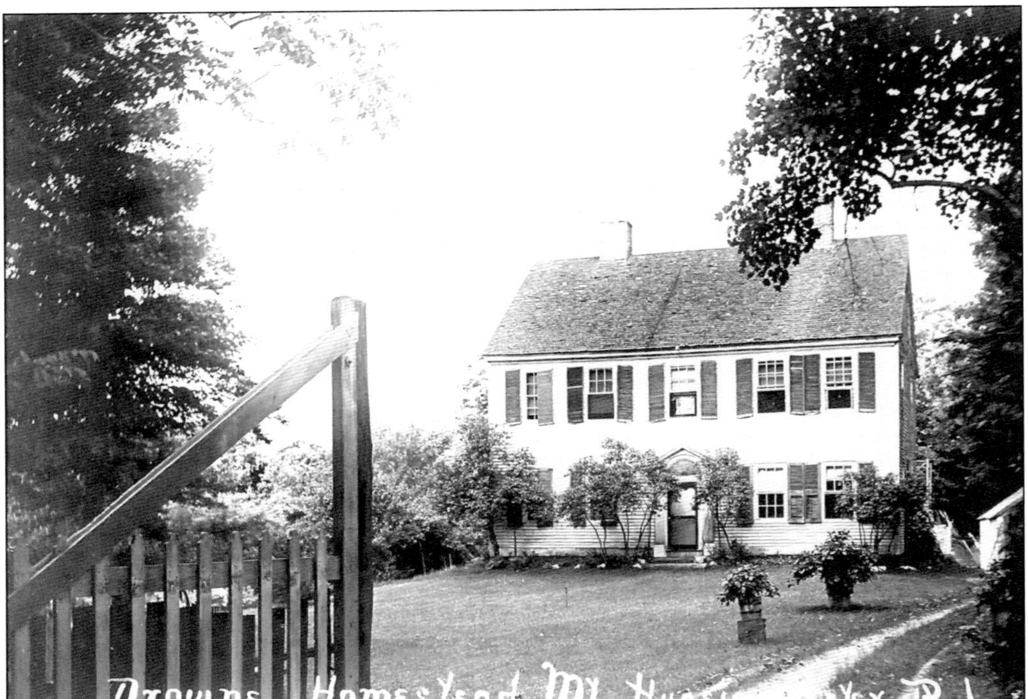

Dr. Soloman Drowne had this house built in 1807 at the end of a long lane leading from Mount Hygeia Road. After he passed away in 1834, it was opened as a private museum. However, when the last direct descendant died in 1941, the house began to fall into deterioration. By 1963, it was in bad condition. Fortunately, it was completely restored in 1975. (Courtesy of Mary Thoman.)

This postcard shows Clara McKenzie-Drowne entering the Drowne homestead. Soloman had named his new house Mount Hygeia after the Greek goddess of health. (Courtesy of Richard Siembab.)

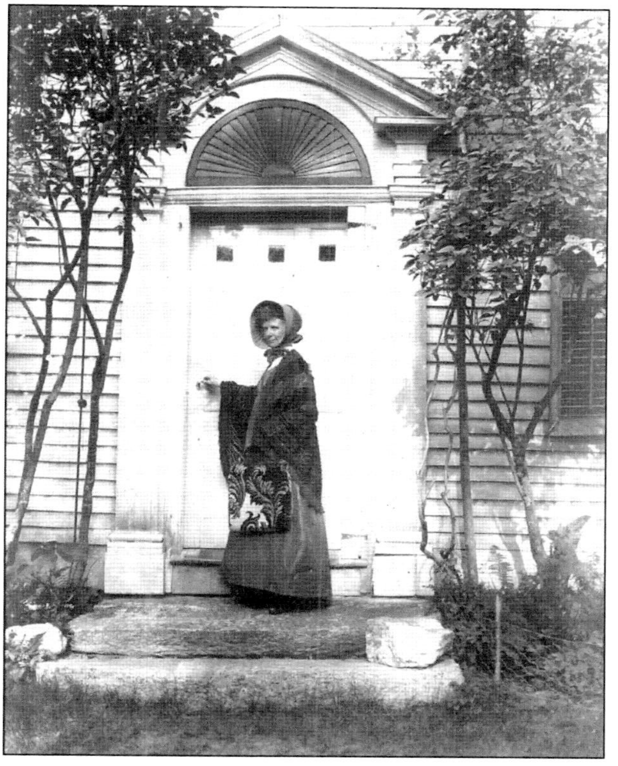

This is the interior of the Drowne homestead. This may be a daughter using the spinning wheel. The following verse is from "A Place Called Home" by Helen O. Larson: "She is cooking a kettle of soup in the fireplace, and smells the rich flavor it gives / She wouldn't trade it for a mansion, the home where this women lives. (Courtesy of Richard Siembab.)

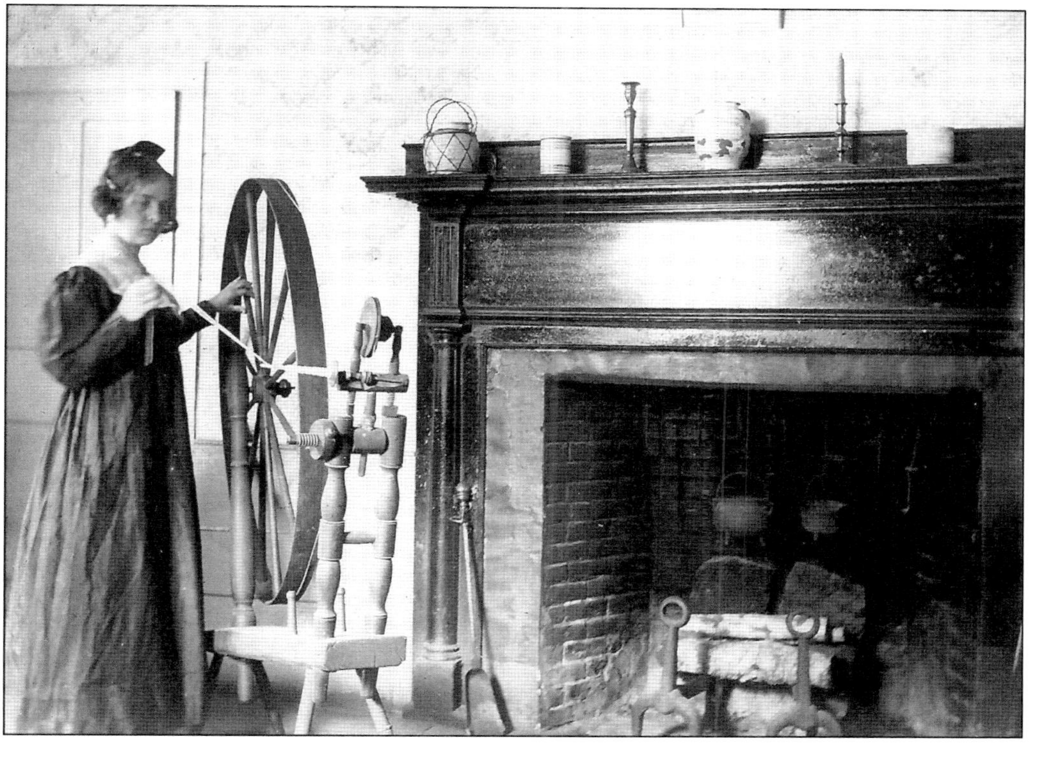

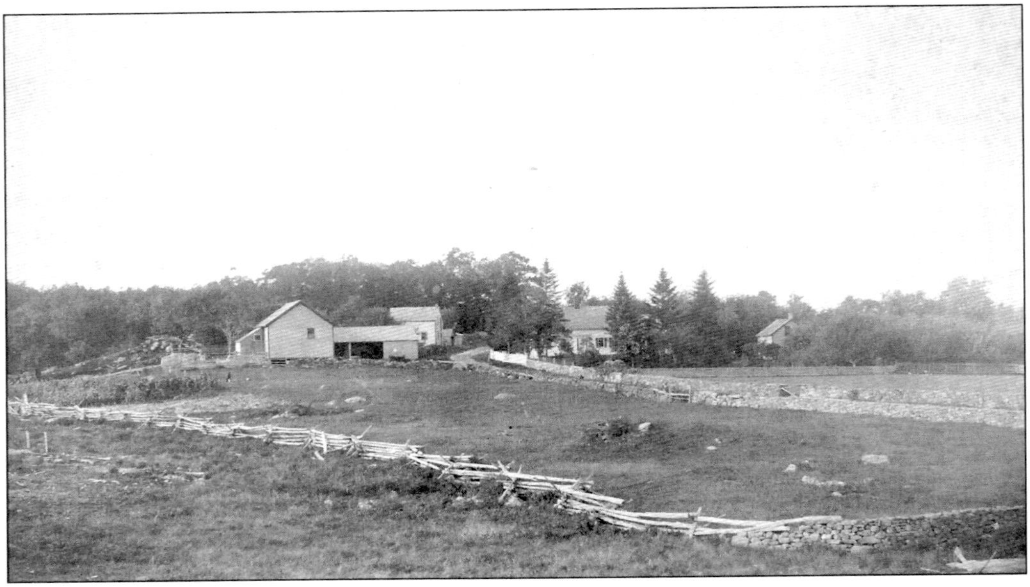

This photograph of the Paine Farm was taken around 1890. Zuriel Paine built the first part of the house in 1785; his son Andrew built the main part. The outbuildings were constructed in the early 1800s. The magnificent stone walls on the property were built by Andrew's son Isaac, the great grandson of Capt. Isaac Paine. Andrew's daughter Hannah married a Ross, and the property remains in the Ross family. The photograph below of the Paine cemetery was taken about 1902. The Paines, Rosses, and other families have been buried here since as early as 1822. (Both, courtesy of Ernest Ross.)

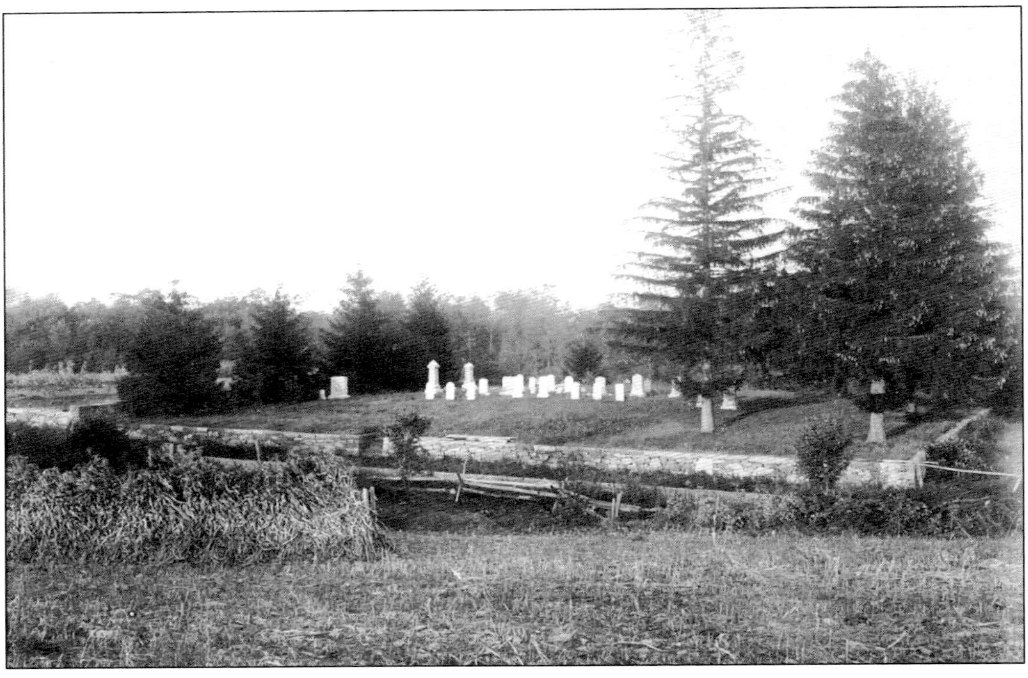

Seven

SOUTH FOSTER AREA

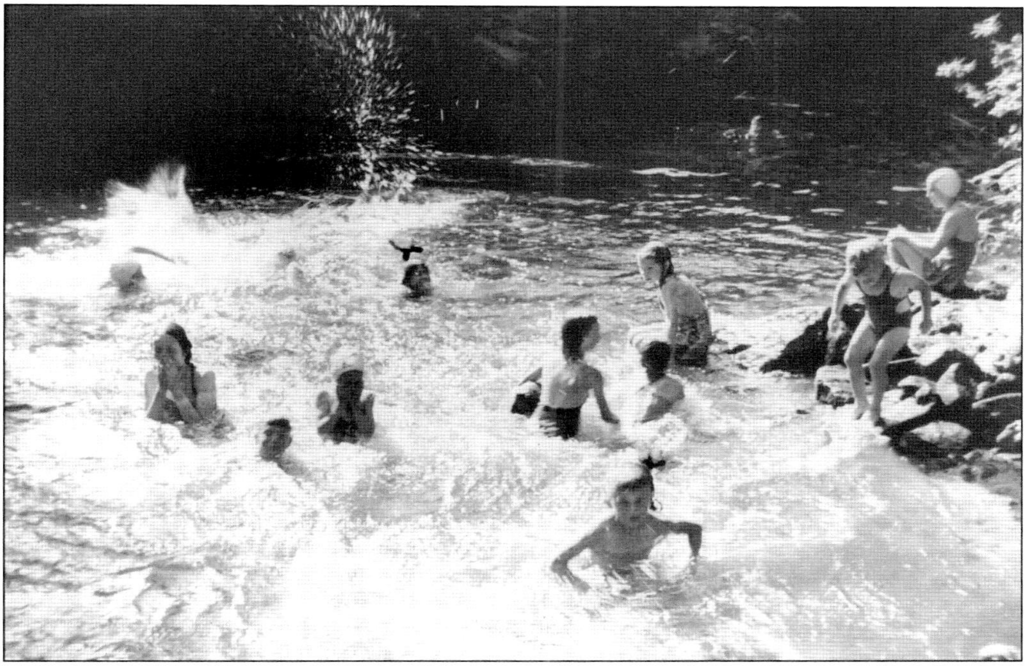

This photograph was taken in the summer of 1943. The kids are out of school and are enjoying the swimming hole on Rams Tail Road. Their parents know where they are and that they are having nothing but good clean fun and staying out of the heat. (Courtesy of George Newman.)

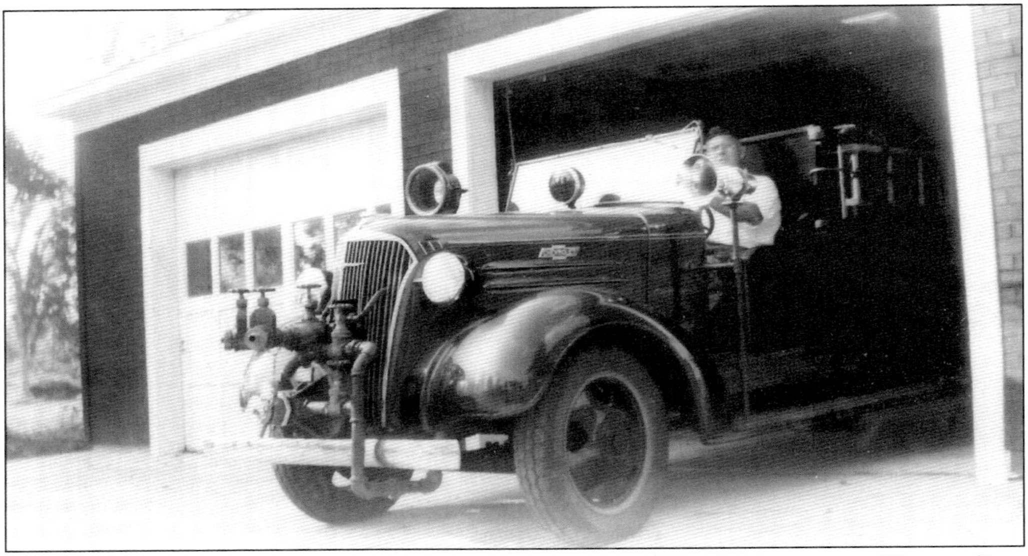

Chief Charles McGinty is behind the wheel of this 1936 Chevrolet fire engine. He is pulling out of the South Foster Fire Company station. This fire engine was made from a used chassis, with horsehair seats from an old Reo fire engine. A water pump was attached to the front, and a water tank was added in the rear. A wooden spool used for cable was used to reel in the hose. (Courtesy of George Newman.)

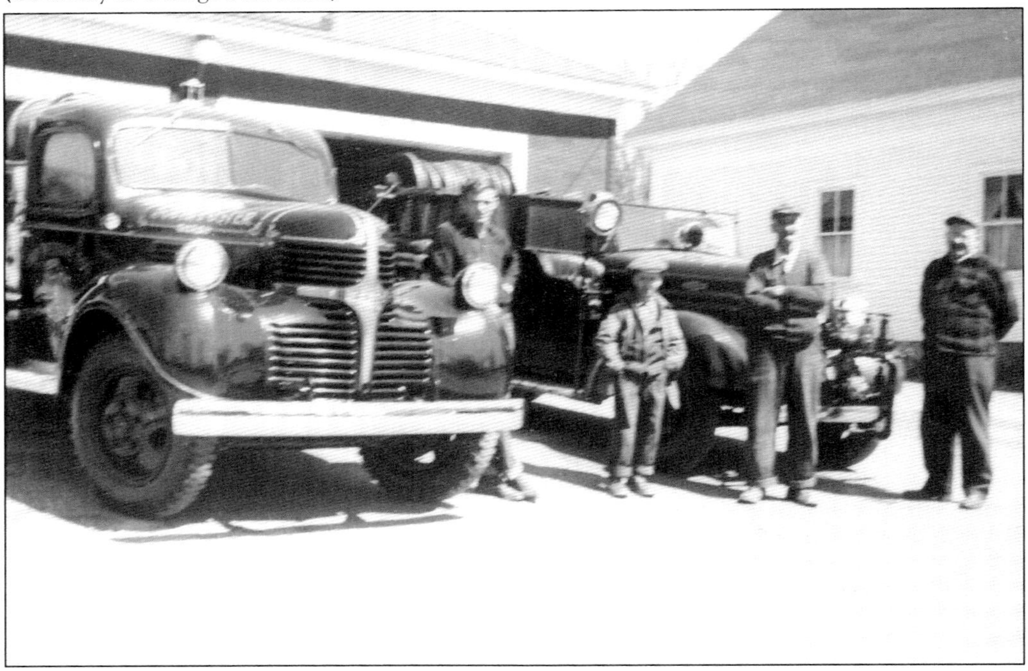

From left to right, George Newman, Raymond Cooke, Andrew Shippee, and Earl Pray are displaying all their fire apparatus. The following verses are from "Dedicated to Firemen" by Helen O. Larson: "These men are right on the job, whenever there's a fire / Though it's icy cold, the firemen are right there. So when the weather is nice, let's honor all these men / Because all kinds of weather, so dedicated they've been." (Courtesy of George Newman.)

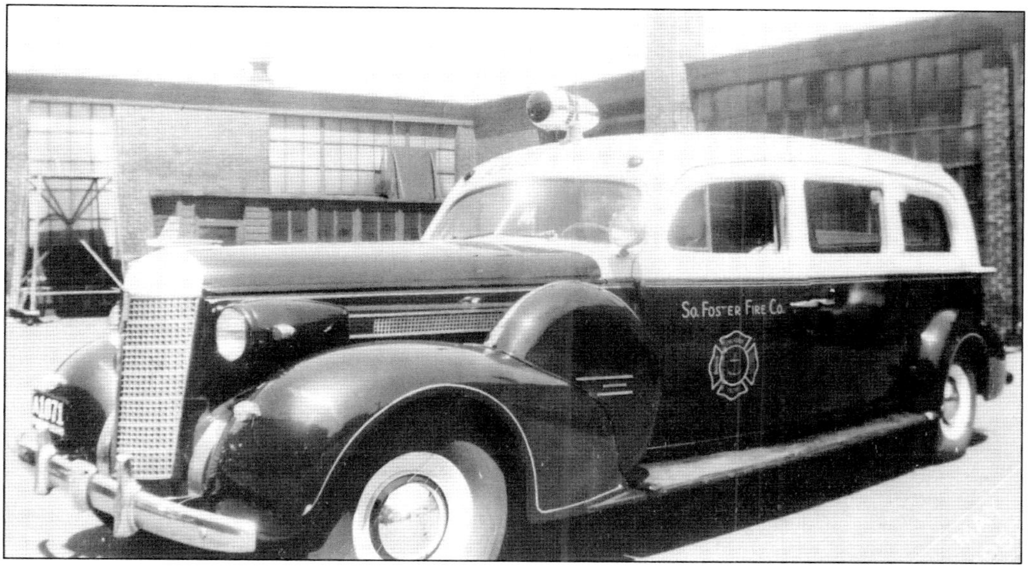

Before the South Foster Fire Company bought this vehicle, it was a hearse. This photograph was taken in May 1952, after it had been transformed into a beautiful ambulance. The photograph below, taken in 1955, gives a good view of all the equipment inside. It has a nice reclining bed and a fan overhead to keep the patient comfortable on the way to the hospital. The sign to the left of the fan reads, "Watch for Sudden Stops." Out the window by the bed, the Plymouth car dealer is announcing the new 1955 DeSotos. (Both, courtesy of George Newman.)

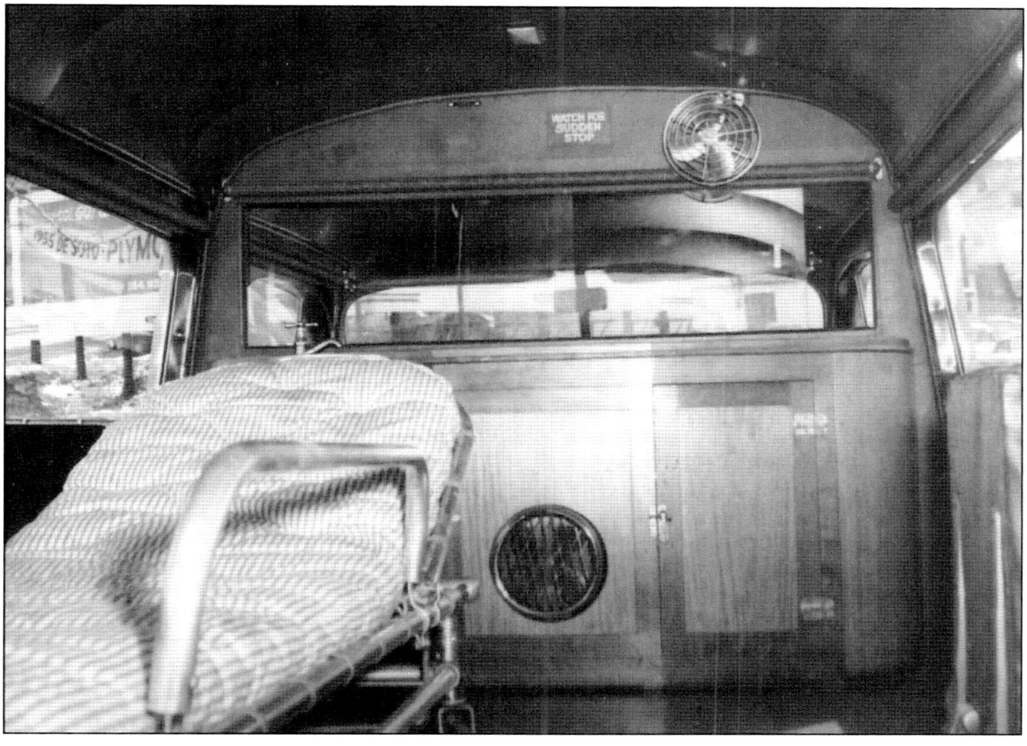

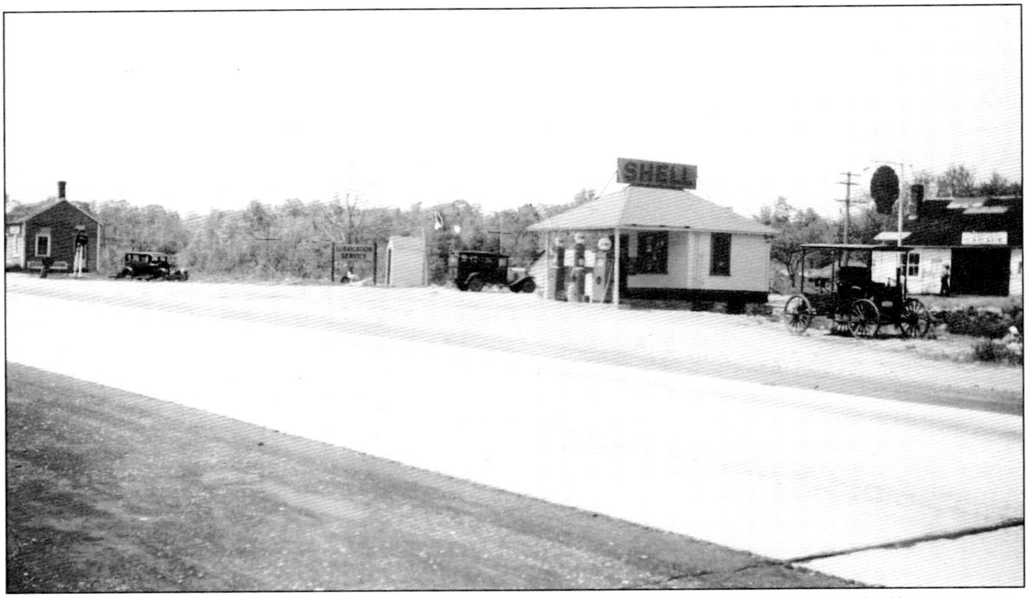

In 1939, when Danielson Pike was a main highway, Claude Pierce operated a Shell gas station with three pumps and a repair garage behind it. Pierce went to an auction in 1930, and before he knew it, his $9.50 bid had bought a 1909 Sears Roebuck Coupe (shown parked in front). It did not run; however, being a good mechanic, Pierce was able to locate the parts to make it drivable. (Courtesy of Dorothy Pierce-Brayton.)

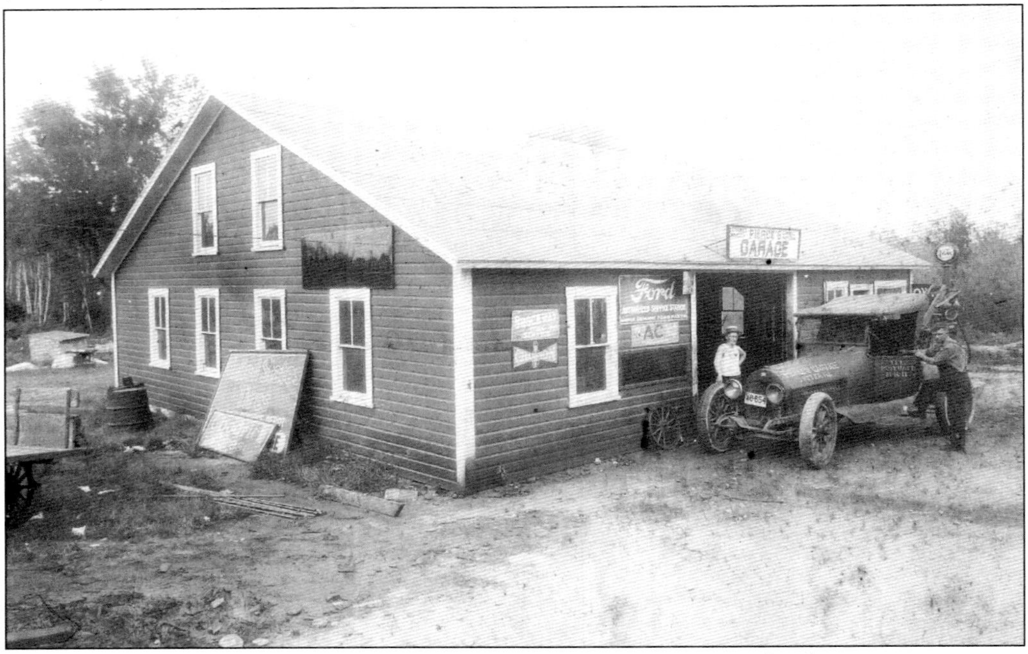

This is Claude Pierce's garage behind the Shell station. A sign over the door announces it is a Ford Authorized Service Station. Clarence Cook is about to open the door of his tow truck. A message painted on the truck door tells potential customers to telephone "Scituate 31-R-11." Timmy Lyons is looking on. (Courtesy of Dorothy Pierce-Brayton.)

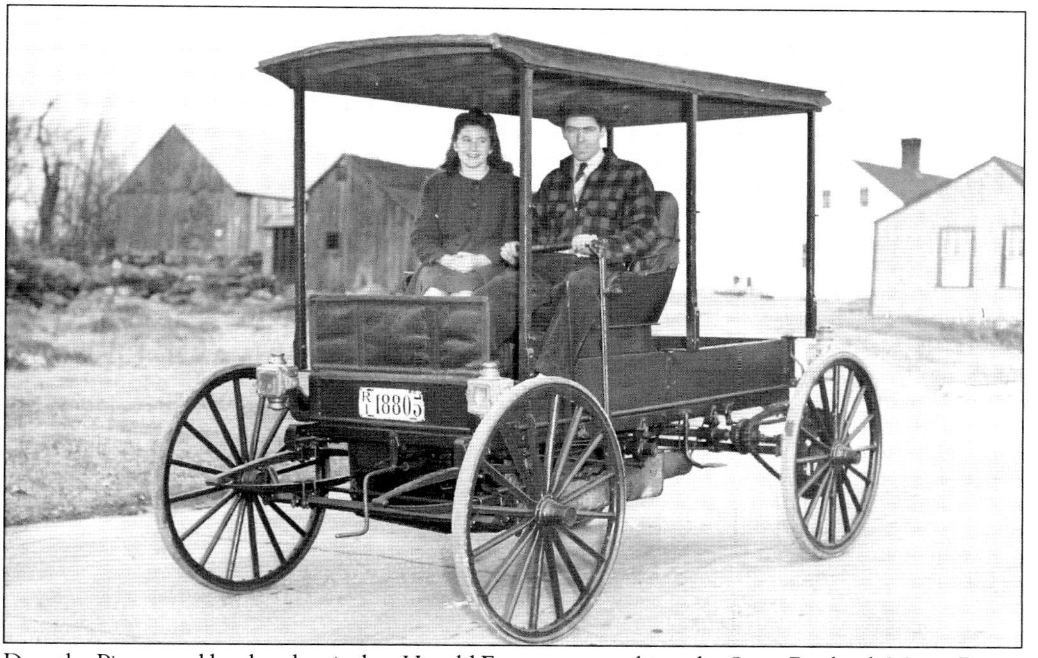

Dorothy Pierce and her brother-in-law Harold Eastman are taking the Sears Roebuck Motor Buggy for a spin. Dorothy's sister Ina "Stubby" used it to go to her job as a spotter at the Air Observation Post on Mount Hygeia during World War II. She could not drive it on main roads; it only had one brake and gas headlights and therefore could not be registered. She said that, occasionally, she would open her up to the top speed of 12 miles per hour when alone. Ina received the Foster Gold-Headed Cane January 1, 1985. (Courtesy of Dorothy Pierce-Brayton.)

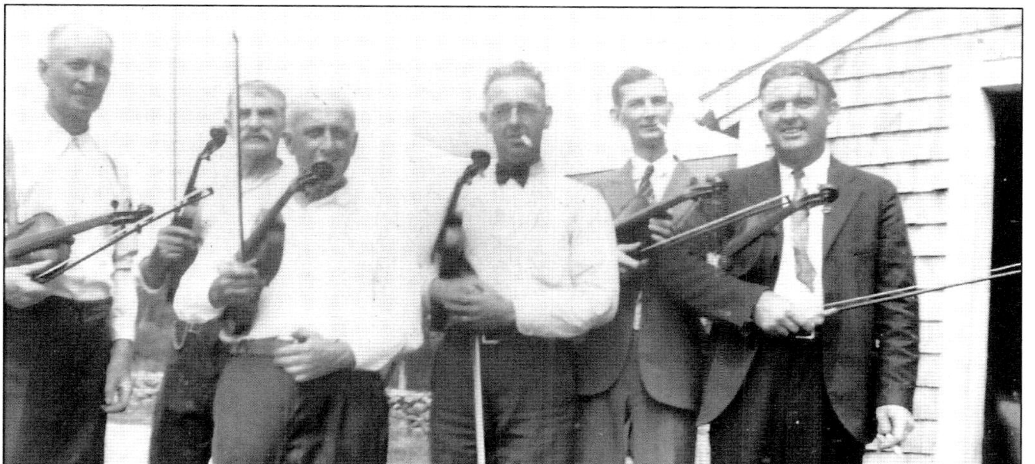

The members of the Old Fiddlers Club are, from left to right, Phil Harris, three unidentified men, Phil Paul, and Claude Pierce, the club's first president. The following poem, "Fiddleishness" is by an unidentified author: "If you have never heard him fiddle, you have missed a rare treat / For he has the personality, and a smile that can't be beat. He can reel them off and peal them off, and draws a mean bow / He can stand them up and sit them down, and keep them on the go. Claude is our Past President, Pierce is his last name / And to say he is a hot sketch, is putting it rather tame." (Courtesy of Dorothy Pierce-Brayton.)

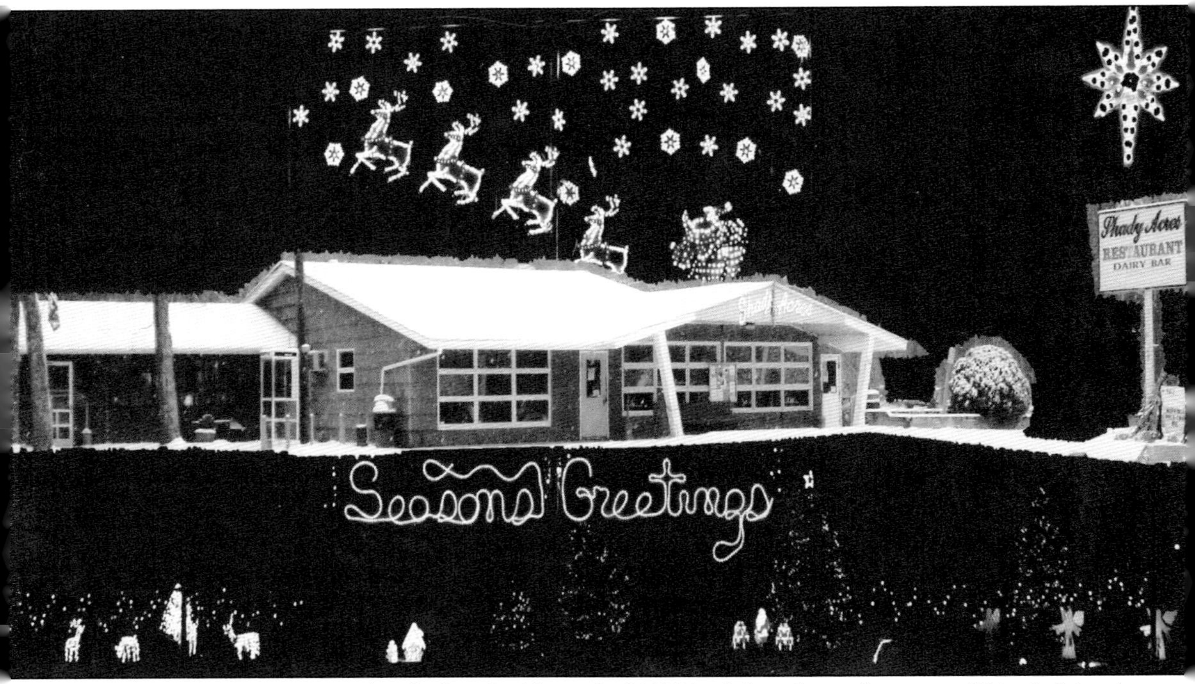

This painting was completed after the blizzard of 1978 had shut down the state of Rhode Island. Pictured is Shady Acres Restaurant and Dairy Bar snowed in along Route 6. The restaurant opened on July 1, 1962, and is still in business today. The following verses are from "The Blizzard of '78" by Helen O. Larson, written February 1978 when she was 67: "The blizzard came on February 6th, in every county and town / It didn't seem so bad, when the snow first came down. Then it snowed faster, and the wind blew / We had a state of disaster, to us it was something new. And I have also heard, some old timers say / They never saw anything like, the blizzard that came that day. Several people lost their lives, it was an act of fate / So we will never forget, the blizzard of '78." (Courtesy of Janet Brayton.)

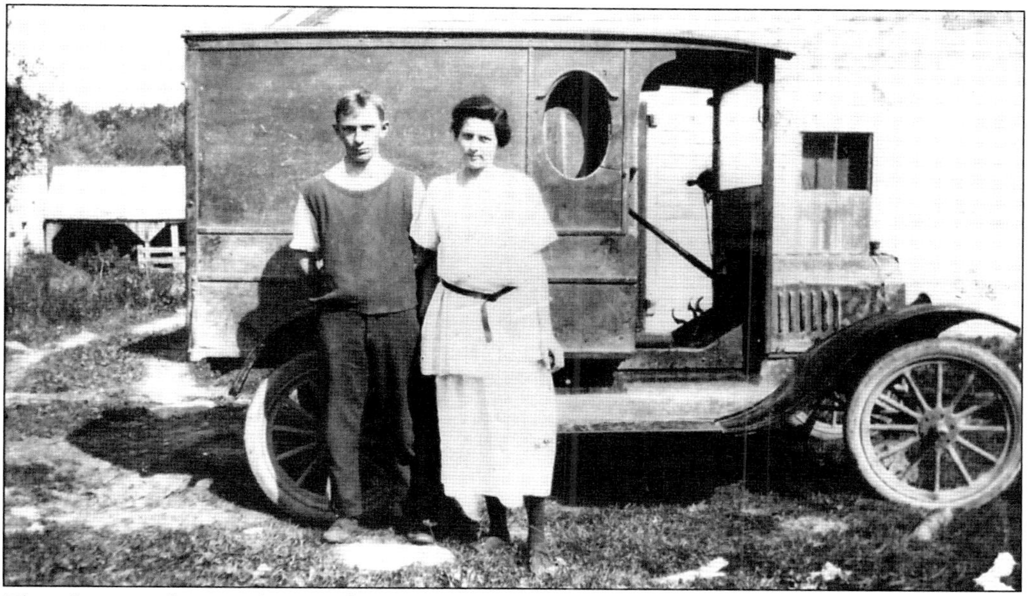

This photograph was taken in the 1920s. It shows Emery and Mildred Sweet on their farm on Balcom Road. The young couple is standing in front of the truck Emery used to deliver meat and fish to neighbors throughout Foster. (Courtesy of Mildred Arline Corey.)

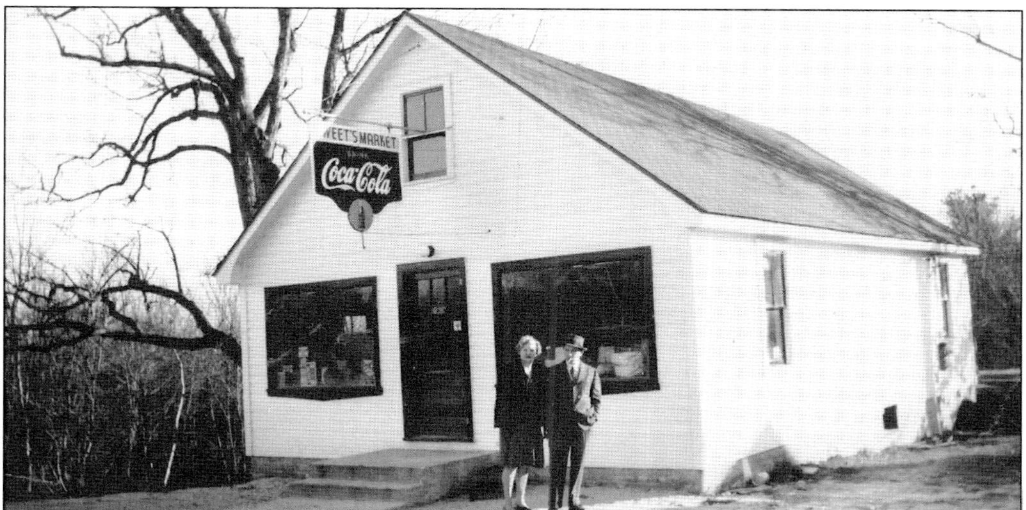

This photograph was taken about 1942, just after Emery and Mildred Sweet had opened their store on Danielson Pike. Of course, they named it Sweet's Market. The Sweets dispersed groceries and sundries to residents in the area for many years from this building. An addition has been added onto the back, and the structure is now used as a tattoo parlor. (Courtesy of Mildred Arline Corey.)

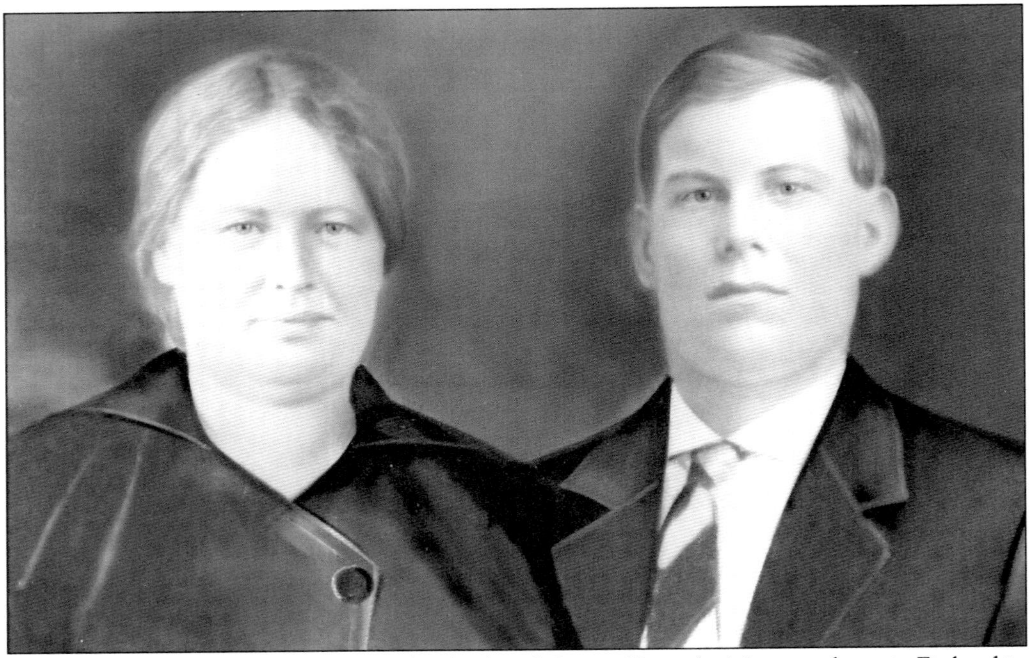

This is a portrait of Mary Seppala and her husband, Simon Kerttula. Mary was born in Finland in 1884 and came to America by way of Canada when she was 18. She met Simon, married, and had three children. In 1937, they bought 35 acres in Foster. They first built a small two-room dwelling, later a chicken coop, and, per the Finnish tradition, finished the sauna before the permanent house. Simon then built two more houses and a large chicken coop, seen below, which held as many as 5,000 chickens. Mary was the recipient of the Boston Post Cane in 1979. Simon passed away in 1956, and Mary joined him in 1980. Below are, from left to right, John Tyvela, Jean Jackson (rear), Carol Ann Kerttula (now Sholly and current owner of the farm), John Jackson, and Carole Tyvela. (Both, courtesy of Carol Lyons Sholly.)

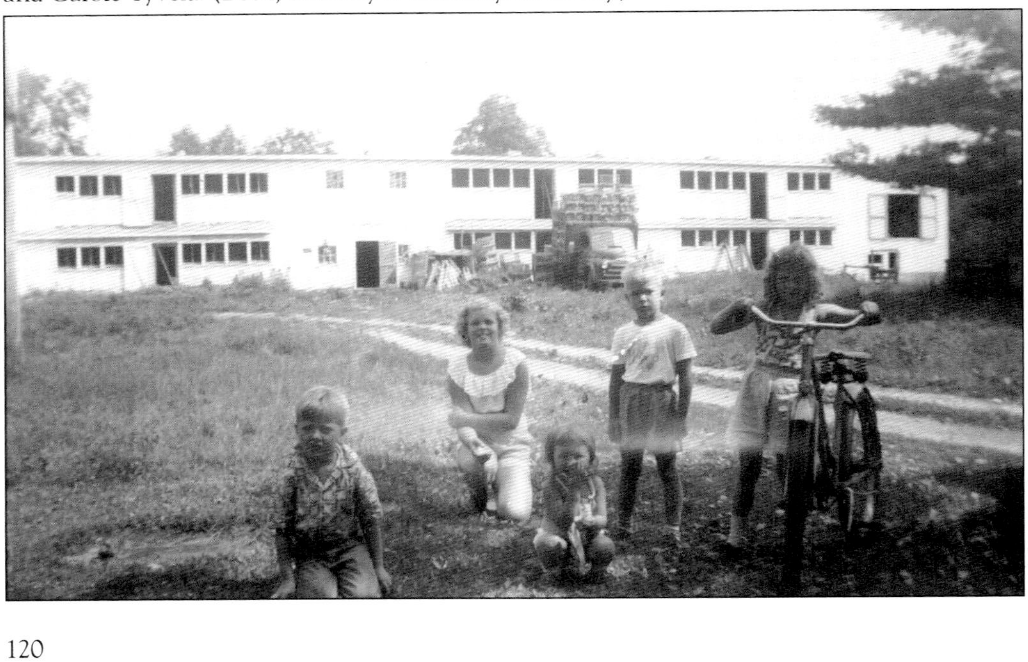

Eight

THE BOSTON POST CANE

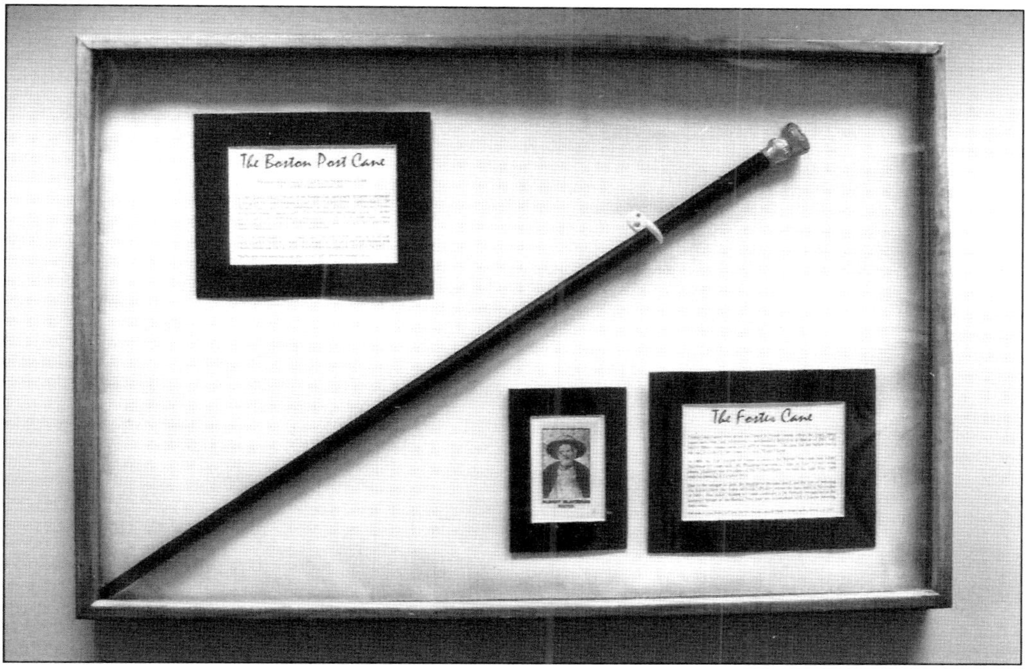

In 1909, Edwin Atkins Grozier of the *Boston Post* newspaper initiated a campaign to recognize the oldest resident in each New England town. Approximately 700 Boston Post canes were distributed to the selectmen of these communities. The canes were to be awarded to the oldest resident and then, upon their passing, transferred to the next oldest resident. J.F. Fradley and Company of New York made the canes out of African ebony imported from the Congo. The wood was lacquered and finished with French varnish with an ornate engraved golden head affixed to the top. The *Boston Post* ceased publication in 1956. (Courtesy of John Lewis.)

Albert Blackmar................ August 28, 1909 – October 1913
Melissa Hopkins-Burchard......... November 1913 – May 1916
Samuel J. Goldsmith................ July 1916 – September 1917
Emily Ann Tegwood.............. November 1917 – May 1918
Sarah Marietta Arnold.............. February 1919 – June 1920
Searles Bradford Young.................... 1920 – August 1925
Esther Dorrance..................... December 1925 – May 1930
Henry Paine...................... October 1930 – November 1932
* No holder of the cane........ November 1932 – November 1935
Ray Howard.................... December 1935 – February 1942
Caroline Johnson Carroll................ April 1942 – May 1944
Nabbie Emogene Kennedy............ June 1944 – March 1945
Jennie Foster Bennis...................... April 1945 – May 1948
Eleanor E. A. Hopkins.............. October 1948 – March 1952
* No Holder of the cane.................. March 1952 – May 1954
Wheaton Leroy Harrington.............. June 1954 – May 1956
Mary Druscilla Hill........................ June 1956 – July 1959
Mattie Ann Battey...................... August 1959 – June 1961
George Collins..................... October 1962 – October 1964
Manfred H. Bennett.................... January 1965 – May 1965
Edith Leona Weatherbee........... July 1965 – November 1969
Silas Spink... 1969 – May 1975
Walter DeLoss Collins.................. July 1975 – August 1979
Mary Ann Bailey.............. September 1979 – October 1979
Mary Kertulla....................... November 1979 – June 1980
Lola Watson.......................... August 1980 – March 1981
Joseph Cayer........................... July 1981 – October 1984
Ina Lenora Pierce.............. January 1985 – September 1986
Alice Wilcox......................... October 1986 – March 1988
Jeannette A. Guertin....................... April 1988 – left town
Elizabeth Blackmar................ August 1990 – January 1993
Lillian Stone.......................... February 1993 – May 2004
Fred G. Pierson......................... August 2004 – May 2005
* No holder of the cane.................. May 2005 – October 2007
Elsie Fasteson................ November 2007 – December 2007
Mildred Farrell..................... January 2008 – October 2008
Jeannie R. Pierson....................................... March 2009
Dorothy Packard Kilham................. August 2009 – present

The *Boston Post* gave 21 canes to Rhode Island towns in 1909. Today, it is believed there are only 12 Rhode Island canes that still exist. The Town of Foster officially retired its cane in November 2007, after having Vangel Jewelers totally restore it. The restored cane seen in the photograph on the previous page has been placed in a framed display case and hangs on a wall in the Foster Town Hall. The oldest resident of Foster continues to be formally recognized as the honorary holder of the cane and receives a plaque denoting his or her status. Over the past 100 years, from when Albert Blackmar received the cane in 1909 to when Dorothy Packard Kilham received her plaque in 2009, the cane has become affectionately known as the Foster Gold-Headed Cane. This plaque lists all of the recipients chronologically from 1909 to the present day. The asterisk denotes periods when some folks have refused the honor of accepting the cane.

Albert Blackmar lived on a lane off Anthony Road when he was the first recipient of the Gold-Headed Cane on August 28, 1909. He was 97 years old at the time. He passed it on in the fourth month after his 101st birthday. This milestone would not be reached again until 1993, when Elizabeth Blackmar would pass the cane on at 102 years old.

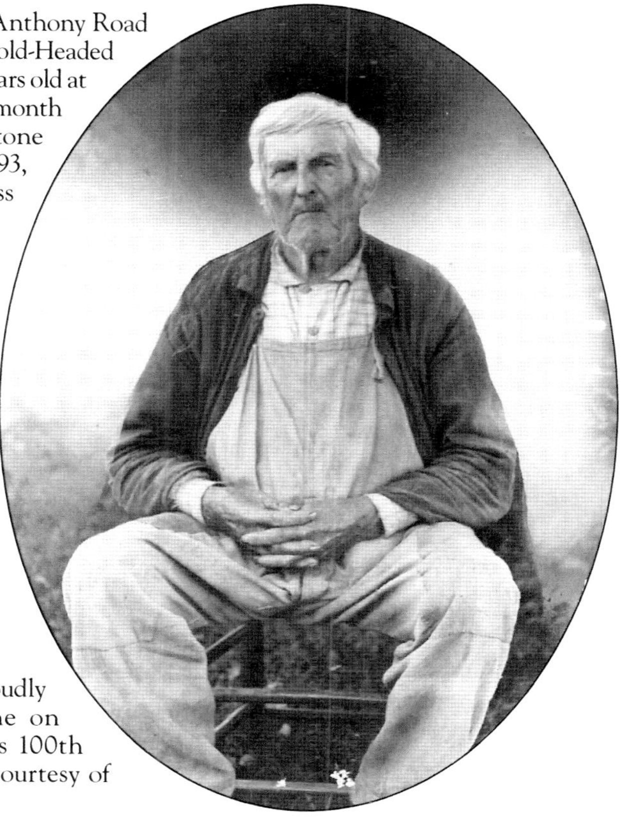

Albert Blackmar is pictured below proudly displaying the Gold-Headed Cane on June 13, 1912. He is celebrating his 100th birthday with friends and family. (Courtesy of George Newman.)

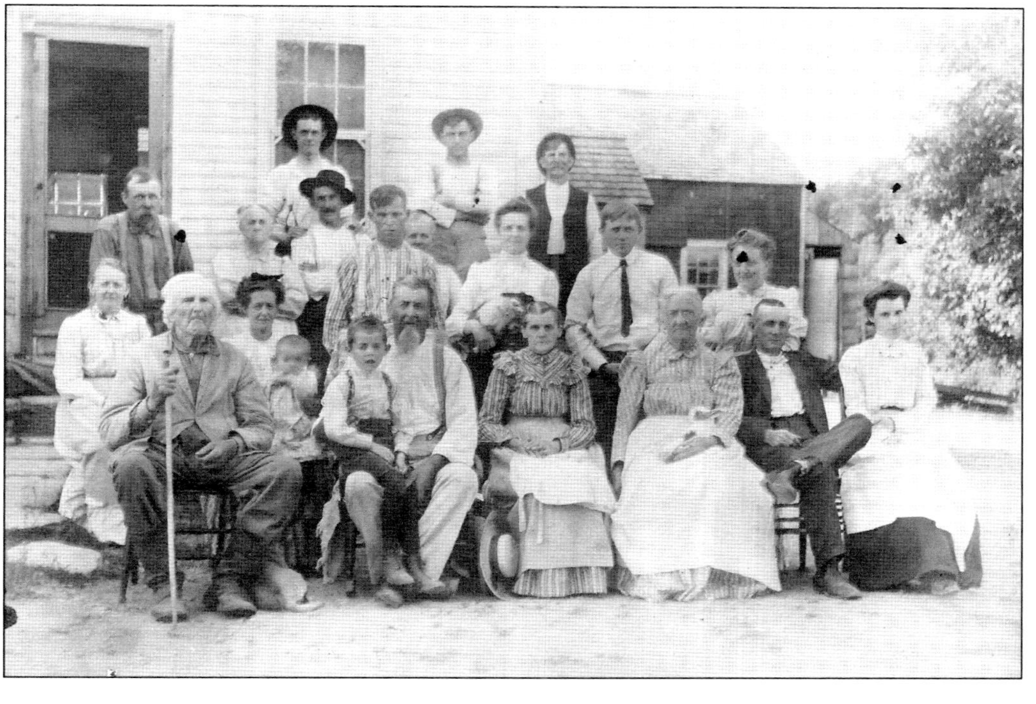

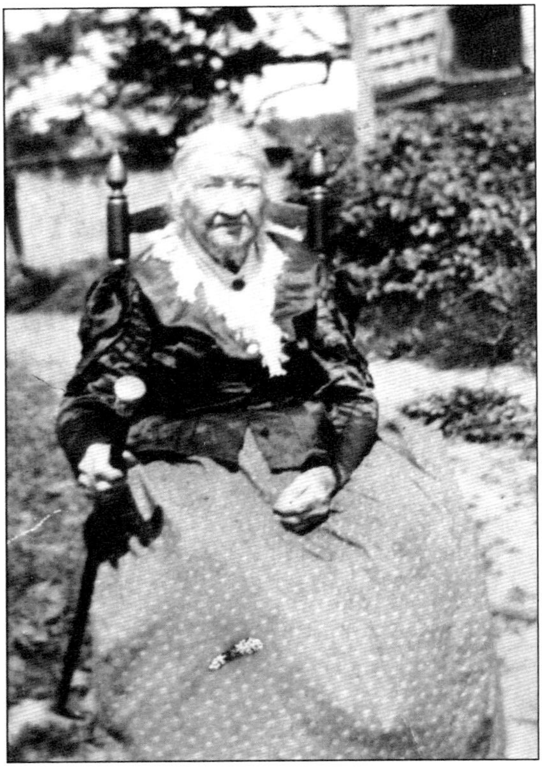

Melissa Ann Hopkins-Burchard is pictured here receiving the Gold-Headed Cane on November 1, 1913. She was the second recipient. She is also the great-great-great-grandmother of the author. Her father was born in 1787 into the Nipmuc tribe, located over the border in nearby Kentuck Woods, Connecticut. (Courtesy of Viola Ulm.)

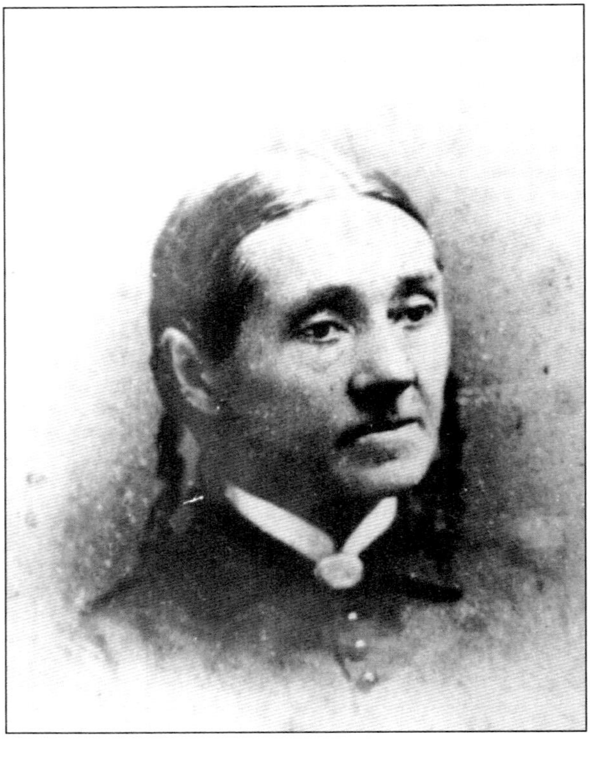

This is a photograph of a young Melissa Ann Hopkins. When he was a baby, Melissa's father was adopted by Jeptha and Anna Bucklin-Hopkins, who lived in Foster. They named their new baby Jeptha Jr. He grew up and married his unrelated cousin Olive Hopkins. They were blessed with Melissa in 1824. She married David Burchard, and in 1862, a grandson was named David E. Burchard. (Courtesy of Viola Ulm.)

On February 4, 1993, Lillian Stone, far right in this 1994 photograph with Lucinder Mellor-Neal, was the 30th person to receive the Gold-Headed Cane. She was also given the privilege of being the first person to cross over the new Swamp Meadows Covered Bridge. After Elizabeth Blackmar, Lillian was the next person to break the 100-year milestone, raising the bar and living to 108. (Courtesy of Heidi Colwell.)

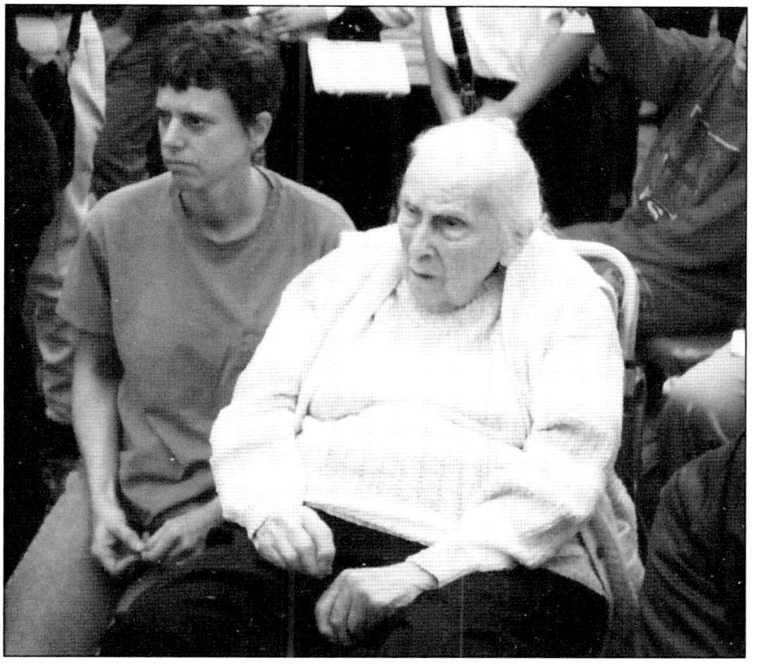

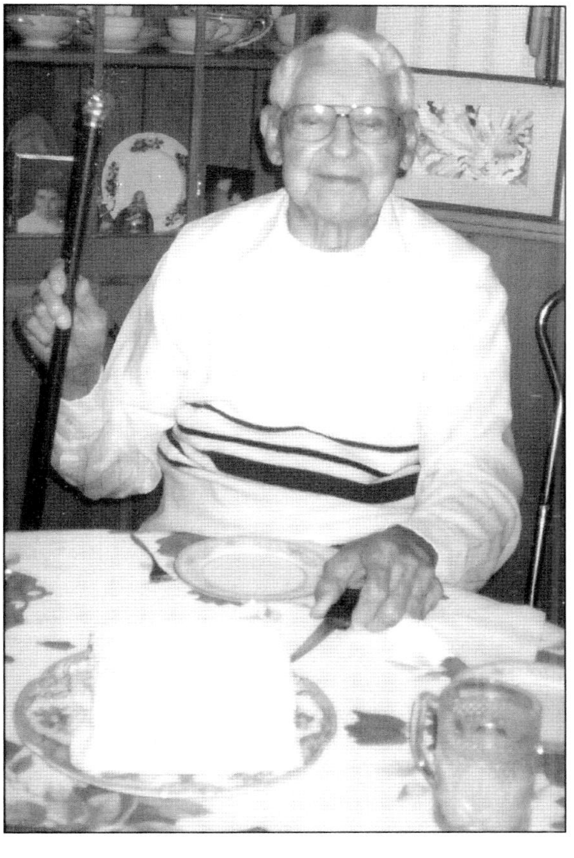

This photograph of Fred G. Pierson was taken on August 5, 2004, at his home. He did not realize it at the time, but he has the distinction of being the last recipient to actually receive the Gold-Headed Cane. It was retired in 2007. His wife Jeannie R. Pierson would receive a plaque four years later. (Courtesy of Frances Grass.)

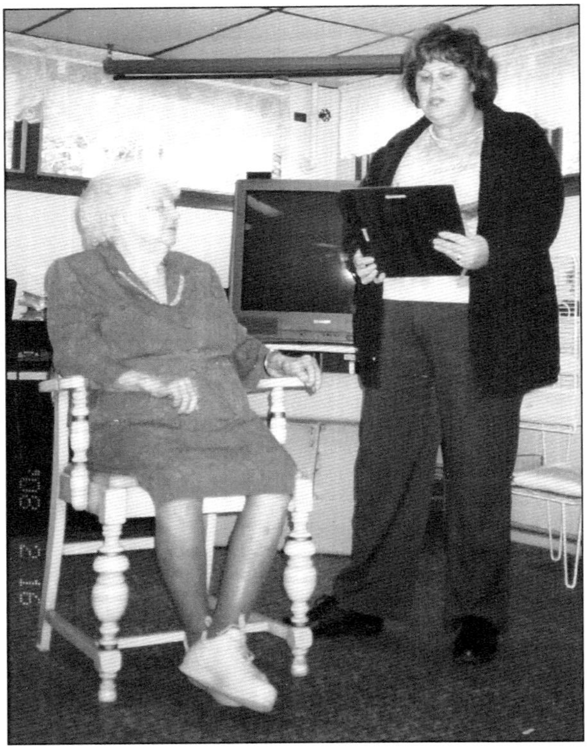

This photograph was taken February 14, 2008. It shows Mildred Farrell (left) as the 33rd recipient receiving the plaque and the title of Holder of the Boston Post Cane. It was presented to her by Colette J. Matarese, president of the Foster Town Council. (Courtesy of Brenda Moffat.)

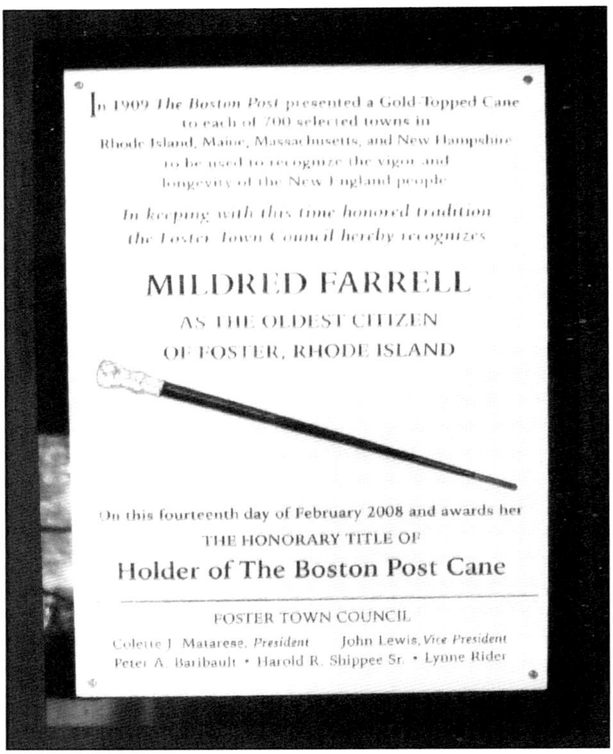

After the Boston Post Cane was restored in November 2007 and retired to a wall in the town hall, a plaque was created. It states: "In keeping with the time honored tradition the Foster Town Council hereby recognizes the Oldest Citizen of Foster, Rhode Island." Community members of Foster are to be applauded for keeping the tradition alive and well as they have entered a second century of recipients. (Courtesy of Brenda Moffat.)

Elsie Fasteson was the first recipient to receive a plaque stating she held the honorary title of Holder of the Boston Post Cane. It was awarded to her on November 8, 2007. She was the 32nd person to receive the honor.

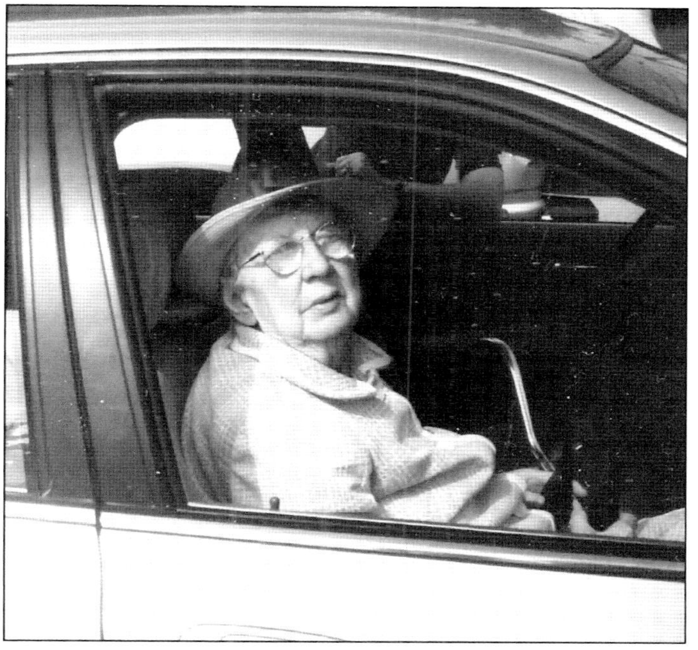

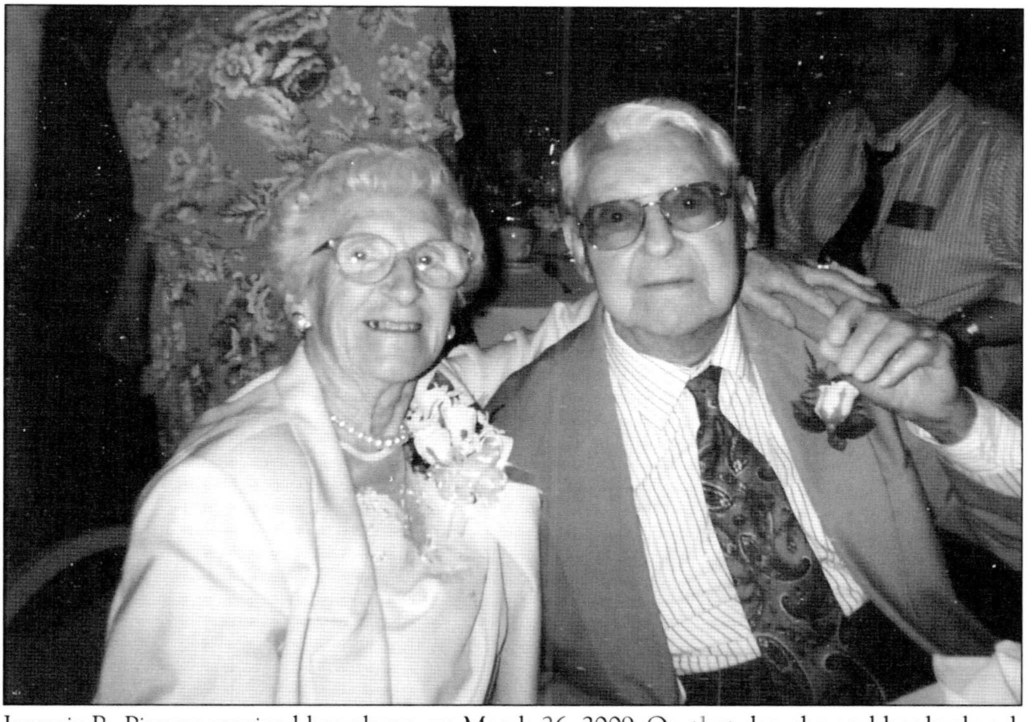

Jeannie R. Pierson received her plaque on March 26, 2009. On that day, she and her husband, Fred, acquired the title of being the only husband and wife team to be members of the exclusive Gold-Headed Cane Club. Jeannie was born in Aberdeen, Scotland, in 1912 and came to the United States in 1952. She and Fred were married, moved to Foster, and built their permanent home. (Courtesy of Frances Grass.)